Roundell P. Selbourne

A Defence of the Church of England Against Disestablishment

Roundell P. Selbourne

A Defence of the Church of England Against Disestablishment

ISBN/EAN: 9783337161675

Printed in Europe, USA, Canada, Australia, Japan

Cover: Foto ©Lupo / pixelio.de

More available books at **www.hansebooks.com**

A DEFENCE

OF THE

CHURCH OF ENGLAND

AGAINST

DISESTABLISHMENT

WITH AN INTRODUCTORY LETTER TO THE
RT. HON. W. E. GLADSTONE, M.P.

BY

ROUNDELL, EARL OF SELBORNE

London
MACMILLAN AND CO.
AND NEW YORK
1886

CONTENTS

INTRODUCTORY LETTER TO RIGHT HON. W. E. GLADSTONE, pages xi.-xxxv.

Midlothian Address, September 1885, xi. What is 'Consent of the Nation'? xii. Is Consent to be Subdivided? xiv. Equity and Liberality, xvi. 'Current' in the Civilised World, xix. United States and British Colonies, *ibid.* Southern and Central America, xxv. European Nations, *ibid.* Republican Nations, xxix. European Monarchies, xxxi. General Results, xxxiv.

PART I

THE CHURCH AND ITS ESTABLISHMENT

CHAPTER I

THE CHURCH OF ENGLAND BEFORE THE REFORMATION, pages 3-26

The Church not a creation of the State, 3. England and Rome, 4-9. Liberties, Law, and Jurisdiction, 9-13. Appeals, 13-17. Bishoprics and Benefices, 17-24. Bishops in Parliament, 24-26. Legislation concerning Matters of Faith, 26.

CHAPTER II

THE REFORMED CHURCH OF ENGLAND, pages 27-50

Continuity of the Church, 27-31. Royal Supremacy, 31-35. Liberties, Law, and Jurisdiction, 35-41. Appeals, 41-43. Bishoprics and Benefices, 43-45. Bishops in Parliament, 45. Doctrine, etc., 46-50.

CHAPTER III

THE BOOK OF COMMON PRAYER, pages 51-67

Part taken by Convocation, 51. Registers of Convocation, 52. King Edward's First Book, 53-56. King Edward's Second Book, 57-62. Queen Elizabeth's Book of 1559, 62-65. Changes in 1604, 65. Book of 1662, *ibid.* Recent Relaxations of Acts of Uniformity, 66.

CHAPTER IV

PRINCIPLES CONSIDERED, pages 68-91

Establishment, 68-71. Reasons for Establishment, 72-77. The 'Religious Argument,' 77-81. The Practical Question, 81-84. Corruption and Reform, 84-91.

PART II

CHURCH ENDOWMENTS

CHAPTER V

ORGANISATION AND PROPERTY, pages 95-110

Organisation, 95-97. Aggregate Church Income, 97-104. Extravagant Estimates, 104-106. Proportion of Means to Work, 107. What is meant by 'Church Property,' 108-110.

CHAPTER VI

FABRICS AND LANDS, ETC., pages 111-124

Different Kinds of Church Property, 111. Churches, 112-116. Parsonage-houses and Glebes, 116. Episcopal and Capitular Estates, 117-122. Patronage, 122-124.

CHAPTER VII

TITHES, GENERALLY, pages 125-137

Origin of Tithes, 125-127. Continental Customs, 128. Anglo-Saxon Canons and Laws, 129-132. Special Endowments with Tithe, 133-137.

CHAPTER VIII

PAROCHIAL TITHES, pages 138-159

The Parish System, 138-141. King Edgar's Laws, 142. Sub-Division of Parishes, 143. Later History of Tithes, 143-146. 'Tithes and the Poor,' 146-159.

CHAPTER IX

AUGMENTATION FUNDS AND MODERN GIFTS, pages 160-176

Queen Anne's Bounty, 160-163. Ecclesiastical Commissioners, 163-166. Parliamentary Grants, 166-170. Church Rates, 170. Recent Private Gifts, 171-174. New Bishoprics, 174-176.

CHAPTER X

THE 'NATIONAL PROPERTY' ARGUMENT, pages 177-192

What is 'National'? 177-179. What is 'Public,' 179-181. Test of Law and History, 181. Gifts by Private Persons, 182-184. Gifts by Kings, 184. Tithes, 185. Parliamentary Grants, 186. Public Regulation, 186-189. Redistribution of Surplus Funds, 189-192.

PART III

THE ADVERSARIES AND THEIR CASE

CHAPTER XI

NON-CONFORMITY, pages 195-208

Church Membership, 195-198. State Law as to Non-Conformists, 198. Royal Supremacy, 198-200. Principles of Judicature on religious Questions, 200-205. State Courts, 205-208.

CHAPTER XII

DISSENTERS' ENDOWMENTS, pages 209-227

Non-Conformist Places of Worship, 209, 210. State Grants to Non-Conformists, 211. Regium Donum in England, 212-214. Regium Donum in Ireland, 214-217. Irish Presbyterian Church Act, 1871, 217. Dissenters' Chapels Act, 1844, 218-224. Practical Conclusions, 224-227.

CHAPTER XIII

POWER AND JUSTICE—PRECEDENTS, pages 228-246

Power of the State, 228-231. Justice and Injustice, 231, 232. The Irish Precedent, 232-235. Contrast between English and Irish Church, 236-238. Irish Endowments, 239-241. Monasteries, etc., 241, 242. How Disendowment would work, 242-246.

CHAPTER XIV

CHURCH WORK, AND THE CHARGE OF FAILURE, pages 247-266

The Parochial System, 247-250. Admissions of the Adversary, 250. The Charge of Failure, 251-253. Comparative Numbers, 254. Local Ministrations, 255-258. Marriages, 258, 259. Elementary Education, 259-262. Liberality, 262-265. Increased organic activity of the Church, 265, 266.

CHAPTER XV

THE (SO-CALLED) RELIGIOUS CENSUS OF 1851, pages 267-282

Mr. Horace Mann's Report, 267. His Method of Inquiry, 268-272. Mr. Mann's Tables and Calculations, 272-275. Argument from Mr. Mann's Figures, 275-277. Judgments of Statesmen, 277-279. 'Newspaper Census,' 279. Objections of Dissenters to Denominational Census, 280, 281. Imperfect Christians not to be rejected, 281, 282.

CHAPTER XVI

DIVISIONS AND CAUSES OF OFFENCE, pages 283-293

Theory of Unity of Church and State, 283-287. Causes of Disunion, 287-289. Subdivisions of Dissenters, 288. Divisions within the Church, 289-292. Causes of Offence, 292, 293.

CHAPTER XVII

INVECTIVE AND QUOTATION, pages 294-311

Alleged 'Hindrance to Religion,' 294-296. 'Restraint on Free Action,' 296. 'Worldliness,' 297. 'Exclusiveness,' 298-300. Conservatism in Politics, 300-305. Quotations, 306-311.

CHAPTER XVIII

LIBERTY, EQUALITY, AND THE SCHEME OF DISESTABLISHMENT, pages 312-333

Civil and Religious Liberty, 312-314. Equality, 314-319. The Scheme of Disestablishment, 320-333.

CHAPTER XIX

THE ATTEMPT TO SEPARATE WALES, pages 334-347

The Separatist Argument, 335, 336. Ancient Welsh Church, 335, 336. Dissent in Wales, 337. Position and Work of present Welsh Church, 337-345. The Practical Question, 345-347.

CONCLUSION, 348, 349.

APPENDIX

Extract from Sermon by Rev. E. A. Stafford, preached in the principal Methodist Church of Toronto, 351-353.

INTRODUCTORY LETTER

My dear Mr. Gladstone,

To whatever extent you may retain or may have relinquished your early views of the proper relations between Church and State, the subject (I am persuaded) is one to which you are not and cannot be indifferent. If your later public utterances concerning it have been (as must be confessed) uncertain and enigmatical, this may be due to the exigencies of a political position to which it would be hard to find a parallel in the history of this, or perhaps of any other country. Not even such gifts as yours can enable a Statesman to acquire and maintain boundless popularity, and almost dictatorial ascendency over multitudes of persons of very various political aims, without an abdication of the functions of leadership on some important points, in order, perhaps, to enhance them on others.

In your Address of September 1885 to the Electors of Midlothian, 'the severance of the Church of England from the State' was mentioned as a question, as to which 'the foundations of discussion had already been laid.' You added :—

'I think it obvious that so vast a question cannot become practical until it shall have grown familiar to the public mind by thorough discussion, with the further condition that the proposal, when thoroughly discussed, shall be approved. Neither, I think, can such a change arise, in a country such as ours, except with a large observance of the principles of equity and liberality, as well as with the general consent of the nation. We can hardly, however, be surprised if those who observe that a current, almost throughout the civilised world, slowly sets in this direction, should desire or fear that among ourselves too it may be found to operate.'

These observations afford much scope for reflection. I accept them as an invitation and encouragement to those who, like myself, have strong convictions upon this subject, to take their share in the discussion which you regard as necessary for the information of the public mind and conscience, before the question of a severance of the Church of England from the State can become practical.

1. *What is 'Consent of the Nation'?*

I am not sure that, when you speak of the general consent of the nation, you mean what I should myself mean if I used the same words. I cannot think that such a consent is rightly to be predicated of everything which may be done by a majority, or even by repeated majorities, in the Commons' House of Parliament. It is of course a truism (and I do not suppose that you meant to utter truisms) that such a change as that of which you wrote could not be made without the authority of Parliament; and that, in a technical and constitutional sense, the nation is bound by what Parliament, with the Royal Assent, may do. But, however necessary for the working of a Constitutional system the power of Parliamentary majorities may be, and however clearly it may be the duty of the subjects of the realm to submit to laws so made, it is only in a fictitious and conventional sense that everything so done can be represented as done with the general consent of the nation. There may be and there often has been a clear, sometimes a large party majority in Parliament, returned by an inconsiderable aggregate majority of the total number of votes given by the constituencies. The minority must submit; but when it constitutes nearly half the nation (perhaps more, if women and other non-electors are taken into account), what is done against its will cannot reasonably be said to be done with general consent.

I wish that more consideration than is commonly given to it by party politicians were bestowed upon this distinction. It would be a great moral security against the oppression of classes, and other acts of tyranny and injustice on the part of Representative Assemblies, if it were generally felt, that it can rarely be wise or prudent, and may very often be unjust, to make great changes affecting the interests and the happiness of large numbers of people, and seriously disturbing the balance of social forces, without something approaching to a general consent. The friction and discontent which may, and probably will, attend the working of such measures, when they are the triumphs of party in a war waged by a temporary majority against a temporary minority of the Electorate, may not only prevent them from accomplishing any good which sanguine persons might have expected from them, but may become a fruitful source of public disorders. I cannot help thinking that the subject of which I write is one to which these reflections are particularly appropriate. I am persuaded that, if the question of Disestablishment and Disendowment were to wait until such measures could be carried with the general consent of the nation, in any real sense, it would never 'become practical.' But I cannot divine with equal confidence what may happen if questions of this kind are thrown into the caldron of party politics, when I observe the artificial means by which elections are managed, the underground influences brought to bear upon the choice of candidates, and the way in which some of those who undertake to guide public opinion are accustomed to make all things human and divine bend to party organisation and discipline. If Liberals who care for these things are prepared to postpone them, as often as they are required to fall down before the idol of party; and if Conservatives who care for them proscribe Liberals with whom on this point they agree unless on other points they give up their convictions: things may happen, which a larger measure of patriotism, independence, and openness of mind might have averted.

2. *Is Consent to be Subdivided?*

If I do not misunderstand some of your speeches, you think that the question of Disestablishment in Scotland ought to be determined by Scottish, and not by English or Irish opinion. I presume, therefore, upon the same principle, you think that in England it ought to be determined, not by Scottish or Irish, but by English opinion. It is difficult to interpret such a view otherwise than as having reference to a real general consent of the Scottish, or of the English, people, as the case may be. I hardly suppose you can mean that if a majority (greater or less) of Scottish or of English representatives in Parliament were for Disestablishment in Scotland, or England, the representatives of the other part of Great Britain, and also of Ireland, ought to stand aloof, or simply to follow the local majority, without considering either the wishes and interests of the minority (however large) in the part of Great Britain immediately concerned, or the natural and probable effects elsewhere of the measure, when passed. If, indeed, it were a question of repealing either of those fundamental articles of the Treaty and Act of Union between England and Scotland which provide for the maintenance of the Established Church of each country, it would be a clear breach of national faith to do this without the concurrence of a majority of the representatives of the part of the United Kingdom directly concerned, or (as I should prefer to say) without such evidence of a real general consent of a solid and permanent majority of the people of that part of the United Kingdom, as there undoubtedly was in the case of the Irish Church. But the Act of Union does not contemplate, and national good faith certainly does not require, that the representatives of England or Ireland should assist to repeal or set aside that condition of the Union between England and Scotland which relates to the perpetual maintenance of the Scottish Church Establishment, whenever a majority of the representatives of Scotland in the House of Commons may be found to desire it. To the enemies of all Church Establishments it might, doubtless, be convenient to carry on their campaign by successive operations of sap and mine in different parts of the kingdom, rather than by a general assault : but this method will not recommend itself to practical men who have not that object in view. No one can have the simplicity to imagine that if by such tactics Disestablishment were carried as to Scotland, the Scottish and Irish members of the House of Commons would leave English members to decide the question of Disestablishment in England without their interference; or that the advocates of Disestablishment in England would have the least scruple about carrying it (if they were able) by the aid of Scottish and Irish votes, although a substantial majority of the representatives of England might be on the other side.

3. *Equity and Liberality.*

I note with satisfaction, as far as you individually are concerned, the expression of your opinion that Disestablishment could not take place in this country 'without a large observance of the principles of equity and liberality.' I noted also (with not less satisfaction) what you said on the same point at Edinburgh on the 11th November 1885:—

> 'Many of those who talk about Disestablishment in England, I think, know very little of the subject they are writing about. They frame plans of Disestablishment—plans utterly impossible to be entertained, either at the present or at any other time. I speak of a plan which has appeared in a work called the *Radical Programme*. There is a plan of Disestablishment there, which, even if the people of England made up their minds to disestablish, never could be adopted. But they have not made up their minds. The question, instead of being familiar, is strange to the minds of the mass of the people. They have not accepted the conviction that the Church ought to be disestablished.'

These sentences, written and spoken with the weight of your authority, and with a knowledge of the conditions of the question which few men possess, must doubtless have had (as they ought) great weight with the country. They are a very distinct and emphatic condemnation, as illiberal and iniquitous, of the only plan of Disestablishment yet put forward in England—the plan of the *Radical Programme*—

of the *Case for Disestablishment*—and of the 'Liberation Society.' And yet, to me, they are not quite reassuring.

The people of England (it is most true) have not 'made up their minds to disestablish.' But it is equally certain, that some of those with whom Disestablishment is a principal object have a great deal to do with the management of party organisations for Parliamentary purposes, and have used, and will use, their power in that way systematically for this object. Whether the people of England understand the conditions of the question or not, it is (I fear) only too likely to be thought enough if a Parliamentary majority can be at any time secured. One important step towards the accomplishment of any political design is the advancement of a considerable number of its more prominent advocates to positions of influence and authority in the State; and this (whether through some inevitable necessity, or for any other reason) certainly happened under the Administration which resulted from your success in the elections of 1885.

When you say, that in any practicable scheme of Disestablishment there must be 'a large observance of the principles of equity and liberality,' and that such a plan as that of the *Radical Programme* is 'utterly impossible to be entertained,' I am forced to remember, that what appears to you, who have neither personal nor sectarian rancour against the Church of England, to be equitable and liberal, may appear in a different light to those who are actuated by such motives or feelings, and to the Epicureans in politics, their pliable and ready instruments. This, indeed, we know for certain; for, in the *Case for Disestablishment* (as if your words had been foreseen), it is expressly laid down that in this matter 'equity and liberality are hardly consistent with each other.'[1] And is it not paradoxical to describe as 'impossible to be entertained' a plan put forward with such pretensions and under such patronage as that of the *Radical Programme?* Doubtless, the Association which is the parent of that scheme—as it is of the whole movement for Disestablishment—may not be inflexible as to all its details; they might be willing to consent to some modifications of some of those details if necessary to carry their main object. But what security is there, or can there be, that even so much as this would be necessary, if the authors and patrons of that scheme were at the head of affairs, and in command of a Parliamentary majority? You have many times said that this, if it is to be done at all, must be a work for those who come after you, not for yourself. God forbid that it should be otherwise! The cup is full enough, as it is, to some whose devotion to you, if less demonstrative, was not less sincere than that of other men. Not even to secure the difference between comparatively equitable terms of Disestablishment and the most unmitigated oppression, would I willingly see the name of Gladstone go down to posterity, associated with the direct responsibility for such a measure and all its consequences. But what would be the practical value of your ideas of equity and liberality, and of your condemnation of a certain scheme as illiberal and iniquitous, after power had passed from your hands into those of the authors and abettors of that very scheme, who (at all events) do not regard it as a plan 'impossible to be entertained'? Supposing that situation to arise, the probability surely is, that their measure of equity would simply be the extent of their power.

[1] P. 66. [This publication will in future notes be referred to under the letters *C. D.*]

4. *The 'Current' in the Civilised World.*

You spoke, in your Address of September 1885, of a 'current,' which might be observed to be setting in the direction of a severance of Church from State 'almost throughout the civilised world.' It would have been interesting to know on what facts, and how interpreted, that observation was founded. 'The civilised world' is a large form of expression: it comprehends, I suppose, the English-speaking communities of the United States of America and the autonomous British colonies, the Empire of Brazil and the Republics of Southern and Central America, and the different nations on the Continent of Europe.

5. *United States and British Colonies.*

As to the United States and the British colonies, I am not (of course) ignorant of the stock arguments which are drawn from those sources by politicians of the destructive school, as, for example, in that *Radical Programme* which you so justly reproved; and in the *Case for Disestablishment*, nearly a whole chapter of which (headed 'The Test of Experience'[1]) is devoted to them. I shall be saved the necessity of recurring again to those arguments, at any length, by pointing out their irrelevance now.

In communities where no organic relations between Church and State, such as those now existing in England, have ever existed, or have had time and opportunity to grow up, it is impossible that there should be any current setting in the direction of a severance of those relations: and I should be paying but a bad compliment to your accuracy of

[1] *C. D.*, p. 141.

thought and language if I supposed you to have had those communities particularly in your mind. The fact that in the more recently settled parts of the world the causes which produced Church Establishments in older nations have not yet come, and possibly may never come, into operation, is a quite different thing from a tendency towards the destruction of such Establishments where they have been, under different conditions, a natural and a gradual growth of time. If an attempt had been made to create similar institutions by the originating power of the State in the United States (where there was not so much as an Episcopate till after their independence) or in the British colonies, the analogy of their history in the old world would have been departed from, not followed. Their historical life and character could not have been, by any such means, transplanted or reproduced. But the folly of attempting to force upon a nascent State, or upon States in early stages of development, all the characteristic growths of a national life of many centuries, is certainly not greater than the contrary process of reasoning back to an old country from the different wants and circumstances of a new, and cutting down the organic results and embodiments of its history to the dimensions of a state of national childhood or youth, under conditions entirely dissimilar. Neither you nor I can forecast the future developments of those new British communities, of which the oldest and greatest (the United States) have but lately celebrated the centenary of their independence. Relations between religion and the State, of which there is no sign now, may not impossibly grow up, in any or all of them, hereafter, in the case either of new developments of ecclesiastical power and influence, or of new jealousies of that power and influence on the part of the State. So far as relates to endowment (which some people insist on confounding with Establishment), I know of no obstacle, in any of those communities, to the growth of ecclesiastical endowments—whether land or personalty is immaterial—as the wealth and the liberality and the wants of their Christian Churches may increase. Nor am I aware that in any of them any tendency has yet manifested itself to take away or secularise such permanent endowments, whether of earlier or of later origin, as their Churches have actually possessed: and some such certainly there are. The case of the large endowment of Trinity Church, New York, acquired in the days of British dominion, and respected and protected by the Courts of the United States afterwards, is an example. The case of the Clergy Reserves in Canada, if an apparent, is not a real instance to the contrary. Those were lands which had been set apart by the British Crown under an Act passed in 1790,[1] 'for the support and maintenance of a Protestant clergy' in Canada. No use having been practically made of the greater part of them (which remained waste and unproductive, and unappropriated), their sale by the Colonial authorities was authorised, first in 1825, and afterwards in 1840.[2] A dispute had arisen as to the meaning of the words 'a Protestant clergy;' and the judges advised the House of Lords that they comprehended ministers of the Church of Scotland, and of other Protestant denominations, as well as the Church of England. The Act of 1840 proposed to divide the proceeds of the sales, effected and to be effected, in certain unequal shares, between the clergy of the Church of England, the clergy of the Church of Scotland, and such other 'purposes of public

---

[1] 31 Geo. III., cap. 31.
[2] 6 Geo. IV., cap. 62; and 3 and 4 Vict., cap. 78.

worship and religious instruction in Canada' as might be thought fit by the Governor, with the advice of his Executive Council. But no such division was actually made: instead of it, the whole power of dealing as they chose with those lands and their proceeds was made over, in 1853,[1] by the Imperial Parliament to the Canadian Legislature; and the Canadian Legislature applied them to secular uses. This, therefore, was the case of a public grant, destined for ecclesiastical purposes not accurately defined, which, before it ever practically took effect, or had been actually enjoyed by any Church or denomination, was recalled by the same authority which granted it. But that revocation was not extended to lands, actually assigned and appropriated before 1840 for the endowment, out of those 'Reserves,' of some thirty or forty Anglican Rectories in Upper Canada. The titles to those lands, so acquired, were respected; and the clergy of the Anglican Church were left in possession of them.

In Lower Canada, while that Province was French, the Roman Catholic Church was established, with ecclesiastical corporations, and endowments consisting of the sites and fabrics of churches and parsonages, tithes, and other things. These rights of property were preserved to it upon the cession to Great Britain in 1762-63, and by the Quebec Act of 1774. The Church corporations remained, and still remain in possession of them, undissolved; and, even during the present century, some new ecclesiastical corporations of the same kind in that province have received charters from the Crown. The late Sir Robert Phillimore, when delivering the judgment of the Judicial Committee of the Privy Council in 1774[2] in an important case relating

---

[1] 16 and 17 Vict., cap. 21.
[2] *Law Reports* (Privy Council), vol. vi. p. 206.

to rights of sepulture in a Roman Catholic Churchyard there, said: 'The Roman Catholic Church in (Lower) Canada, though it may, on the conquest, have ceased to be an Established Church in the full sense of the term, nevertheless continued to be a Church recognised by the State, retaining its endowments, and continuing to have certain rights, *e.g.* the perception of *dîmes* (tithes) from its members, enforcible at law.'

Between the confiscation or secularisation of Church endowments, and the discontinuance of annual grants or subsidies out of a public treasury, there is an essential difference of principle. In the former case, the State takes away, and appropriates to itself, the property of a Church ; in the latter, it only ceases to give out of that which is its own, and the disposal of which, from time to time, depends entirely on its bounty. An annual State grant is of necessity precarious ; no legislative Act is required to stop it : on the contrary, a new money vote by Parliament, and a new Act of Appropriation, is in every year necessary for its continuance. In some of the British Colonies, the practice of making annual grants or subsidies (seldom of large amount), for ecclesiastical purposes, did for some time prevail. One example is enough ; and that I will give in the words of the *Case for Disestablishment* :[1]—

'In 1849, amongst the appropriations by Parliament of the public revenues of New South Wales, was a sum of £30,000 per annum for the support of public worship ; and this sum had been distributed amongst the different Christian Churches, according to the number of their members, as shown by the census of 1841, in the following proportions :—

---

[1] *C. D.*, p. 146.

Church of England . . .	£17,581	2 4
Church of Rome . . .	8,510	14 6
Church of Scotland . . .	3,136	9 11
Wesleyan Methodist. . .	771	13 3

In 1850 all State aid to religion was withdrawn.'

The practice of making such grants has been of late years generally discontinued in (I believe) all our colonies, subject to such consideration as has been thought due to the reasonable expectations of individuals; and if, in any of those colonies, Bishops or other dignitaries of the Anglican Church had enjoyed any form of secular dignity of privilege not accorded to the clergy of corresponding rank in other religious bodies, this also has disappeared. In all these cases it is doubtless true, that such slender and insignificant connection between Church and State as resulted from those small subsidies and other privileges has been severed. But the connection so severed was in its circumstances and conditions unlike that of the Church of England with the State of Great Britain; and its unsuitableness to the conditions of colonial society (of which I have already spoken) was the reason for severing it. From any effects or consequences of such a severance of such a connection no inference can be drawn, with the least plausibility or show of reason, as to the effects which might follow from the Disestablishment and Disendowment of the Church of England. I know, of course, that the distinction between permanent endowments like those of the Church of England, and votes or grants of money by Parliament out of the Consolidated Fund, is one which the advocates of Disendowment assiduously labour to confound: but it is impossible for any amount of sophistry or misrepresentation to make things the same which are legally, historically, and practically different. Upon that point I will not anticipate what I may have to say hereafter.

I have given, I think, sufficient reasons why we must look elsewhere than to the United States and the British Colonies for that 'current' of which you spoke. I turn next to that 'new world,' which Mr. Canning described as 'called into existence to redress the balance of the old.'

6. *Southern and Central America.*

The American settlements of the Spaniards and Portuguese had their origin in conquest, not in colonisation, and they carried with them from their birth the ecclesiastical institutions of the countries from which they came. With the single exception of Mexico (where the example of the United States has been followed), no change or (as far as I can learn) tendency to change in the relations of Church and State has resulted from the establishment of their independence, or from the Republican forms of government which all but one of them have adopted. In Brazil (where the Emperor appoints the Bishops, and exercises a power of *veto* upon the introduction of Letters Apostolic or other new ecclesiastical laws), in the Argentine Confederation, in Peru, Chili, Paraguay, Uruguay, and Venezuela, the Roman Catholic religion is established, and its clergy are maintained either by endowments or by salaries from the State.

7. *European Nations.*

It cannot be denied, that there may be observed in most countries upon the continent of Europe some currents of thought, which all who have to take their side upon questions between Church and State will do well to bear in mind. There is a current which sets strongly against dogmatic belief; there is another which may be described as 'anti-clerical.' Neither of these can be described as, in the main, Christian or friendly to Christianity; and I do not suppose you to be in sympathy with either of them, however staunch a defender you may be of liberty of thought, or however strong an opponent of extreme ecclesiastical pretensions.

Whatever has hitherto been done to despoil or impoverish Churches, or any Church, upon the Continent of Europe, is due (as appears to me) to the operation of these two currents of thought, combined with the greed and rapacity of necessitous States and Rulers, and not to any cause at all resembling the political and moral forces which actuate the movement for Disestablishment in Great Britain, and give it such strength and power as it really has. Subtract those forces (in their essence ecclesiastical, sectarian, denominational)—subtract the rivalry and competition of voluntary with Established Churches—and where would the movement among us be? True, indeed, it is, that the anti-clerical, anti-dogmatic, anti-Christian tendencies of the Continent have their representatives among ourselves, ready and forward enough to ally themselves for destructive objects with religious zealots of every or any kind. They think (probably not without reason) that the substantial fruits and trophies of a victory won after an internecine struggle between Churches would remain with themselves. The spectacle of Religious Bodies imitating the false mother, who would rather see the living child cut in pieces than leave it in the arms of her rival, may be to them not unedifying or unwelcome. But, if such a victory were gained, it would not be by the force of a continental current, reaching to and carrying along with it the minds of great numbers of the British people; it would be by religious jealousies of purely British growth. Our example might indeed, and probably would, be felt throughout the continent, as giving a new impulse and encouragement to all the adversaries of Churches and Faiths. Without being ourselves in any sensible degree influenced by those currents of thought, we should be co-operating with and stimulating them.

It was, doubtless, this aspect of the case, from a European point of view, which so much impressed the mind of Dr. Döllinger; whose memorable words, addressed to Canon Liddon[1] on reading the 'Disestablishment' paragraph of your Midlothian Address of 1885, I may be excused for recalling.

'For my part (he said) I think that any such measure should be firmly resisted. It would be a blow to Christianity, not only in England, but throughout Europe.' . . . 'Without maintaining that intimate association with the Civil Power had always been an advantage to religion, or that the existing relations between Church and State in England are of an ideal description, or that, if Disestablished and Disendowed, the Church of England would perish as a religious body, or that she might not, after an interval, enjoy a more vigorous life than now—at least in some respects, he yet held, that the broadest and most serious aspect of such a catastrophe would be that of a blow to the cause of religion throughout Christendom. If such a measure were adopted by a country with a history like that of England, there could be no mistake as to its significance. It would be well understood, alike by the friends and the foes of Christianity,—in Germany, in France, *throughout the civilised world.*'

---

[1] *Times*, October 17, 1885.

Upon this echo of your own words I do not dwell; I am sure that you understand its significance. No one is better able than yourself to estimate the weight of Dr. Döllinger's authority, and the value of his opinion, upon such a subject.

I have spoken of the 'currents' which do exist upon the Continent of Europe; and, no doubt, if the power of States should ever come to be exerted (as that of heathen Rome was) in direct and avowed antagonism to Christianity, this might for a time put an end to all connection between Church and State. But from such a development we are at present a long way off. You have wisely avoided the use of the word 'Establishment' (as to the meaning of which all men may not be agreed), and have spoken of a current which seems to you to be setting in the direction of the 'severance of Church from State.' Is it, then, true that the set of the Continental current is really in *that* direction? Some may perhaps think that it is so in Republican France. Of that I shall speak presently; for the moment I content myself with saying that the facts, down to the present time, have not gone far to warrant that opinion. I can see no sign of any such current in any other country of Europe. Interference with Church revenues there has been in different countries; and in some countries—most of all France—the secular spirit dominant in the State has pressed and still presses with a continually increasing strain upon the Church. But of a tendency in any of those countries towards ecclesiastical independence, towards the 'liberation of Religion from State control,' towards the system of 'a free Church in a free State,' I see no sign.

8. *The Republican Nations.*

In France, during the great Revolution, tithes were abolished and the rest of the property of the Gallican Church was secularised. While the transition from the old to the new order was taking place, the Church was practically under proscription. But that condition of things did not last. The first Napoleon negotiated a Concordat with Rome, which has since been the basis of the relations between Church and State in France. A ministry of Public Worship is to this day one of the regular departments of government in that country, and all the Roman Catholic clergy (numbering about 45,000 in 1884) are direct stipendiaries of the State. In the Budget of 1884 the sum voted for their payment was, in round figures, two millions sterling. I am not aware that this vote has been since materially diminished; though the friction between the Church and the Government of the Republic is undoubtedly great, and the authorities of the State have evinced in many ways a disposition to harass and degrade the Church. The spirit (if not the letter) of the Concordat has been departed from by the Civil Government; the Church has been excluded from its former share in the work of education, and there have been threats of reducing, if not discontinuing, clerical stipends. All this shows a tendency of the civil power to impede and depress the spiritual, which I take to be a different thing from a tendency to 'liberate' it. The relation of the Church in France to the State is still one of dependence; not the less so, because the clergy of some other religious bodies, chiefly Protestants (who in 1884 received about £64,000 of public money), are also State stipendiaries.

It may not be without interest to note the observations

from an economical point of view of M. de Lavergne[1] (whose eminence as a political writer is well known to you) on the effect of French legislation against ecclesiastical endowments in 1789.

'The abolition of tithes has really been of much less importance than is sometimes supposed. The charge has been shifted, but not destroyed; for the cost of public worship at this day to the tax-payers is nearly fifty millions of francs; and the promise made to the country clergy (*curés*) in 1789 to provide them with *minimum* stipends of 1200 francs (£48 per annum) has not yet been fulfilled to all of them. The clergy have lost altogether twenty millions of revenue; but does any one suppose that the tax-payers are gainers to the same amount? I should have no difficulty in pointing out in our present budget, not twenty, but a hundred millions, less usefully spent in the interest of the rural districts than was the produce of the old tithe. On the other hand, the rent paid for land has been increased generally by the amount of the tithe; and the cultivators, properly so called, with the exception of those who farm their own land, have gained nothing.'

Switzerland and France are, at the present time, the only Republican nations of Europe. In Switzerland, the government of the Protestant Church is under the superintendence of the Magistrates of the several Cantons: and, by the Federal Constitution of 1874, the creation of new Roman Catholic Sees without the consent of the Confederation is prohibited: and all disputes arising out of the formation of new religious communities, or schisms in existing religious bodies, are required to be referred to the Federal authorities. In some Cantons, the Churches have endowments as well as State grants. In some, particularly Geneva and Zurich, there has been a party favourable to the severance of Church from State; but the efforts of that party have met with

[1] *Economie Rurale*, etc. (4th ed.), p. 8.

no success; and there is no observable current now setting in that direction. It was in 1878 or 1879, after some previous unsuccessful attempts, that a project of law for the 'abrogation of the budget of worship' was accepted by the Great Council of Geneva; but, by the constitution of that Canton, the minority had a right to demand, and did demand, a reference of the question to a popular vote, in which each individual freeman had to record his personal assent or dissent. The result was, that the 'project' was rejected by such overwhelming numbers, as practically to set the matter at rest.

The Great Council of Zurich, in 1882 or 1883, appointed a Special Commission to report upon the relations of Church and State there: it reported in favour of the continuance of those relations. The people of the Canton were appealed to, and they returned a Council which adopted, by a majority of 132 out of 150 members, a motion, 'that the Cantonal Church should continue in the possession of its rights and privileges.' For complete Disestablishment and Disendowment there were only seventeen, for Disestablishment and partial Disendowment there were only twenty-two votes.

Nothing, I believe, has since occurred to give any encouragement to the revival of these questions in Switzerland.

9. *The European Monarchies.*

Of Russia, and Austria-Hungary, I need hardly speak. There is certainly no current setting in the direction of a severance of Church from State in either of those monarchies. The Greek Church in Russia, and in Austria-Hungary the Roman Catholic, is both established and largely endowed.

In most, if not all, other countries of Europe, Conventual Institutions have been suppressed, and their property taken possession of by the State—a thing which was completely done in England as long ago as the time of Henry the Eighth, and the policy of which stands apart from the general question of Disendowment. But in Russia, Austria, and Hungary, Monastic Institutions, endowed with large estates, still continue.

In every monarchical country of Europe (as well as in France) there is a department of Civil Government called the Ministry of Public Worship, or having corresponding functions under some other name. In Portugal, Spain, and Italy, the Roman Catholic religion is declared, by fundamental laws, to be the Established religion of the State. In Portugal, the clergy have fixed incomes, derived either from endowments or from the State: there are 3769 parishes, with incumbents so supported, and the clergy of the higher orders receive about £66,666 per annum. In Spain, the laws of 1876 (and some of earlier date, still in force) impose upon the nation the obligation of maintaining the priesthood and worship of the Roman Catholic religion. Under a Concordat made in 1859 with the Pope, all Church property in Spain (except churches and parsonages) was sold, and the proceeds exchanged for an equal amount of public debt Certificates, bearing three per cent interest, which substituted endowment the Spanish clergy now enjoy. In Italy (besides the monasteries) a large number of chapters, and non-parochial benefices of secular clergy, were suppressed in 1860 and 1867: but the State, besides leaving the Churches and the parochial glebes untouched, took upon itself the maintenance of the clergy, as a permanent charge, under arrangements not very dissimilar to those of Spain. The property of the suppressed ecclesiastical corporations (estimated to bring in a yearly revenue of £1,238,778 sterling) was transferred to the State domain: but a board, originally called 'Cassa Ecclesiastica,' and now 'Fondo del Culto,' was credited with a corresponding amount of Government five per cent consols; some other Church property, including tithes and ground-rents, being also vested in that Board. The 'Fondo del Culto' is attached to the public department of Grace and Justice, and administered by a director and a council consisting of three senators, three deputies, and three others nominated by the King. Out of the funds of this Board, the annual expenses of public worship, the stipends of Bishops and other dignified clergy, and about £32,000 per annum in aid of the endowments still remaining to the parochial clergy, are paid. The Italian Bishops, nominated by the Pope, cannot enter upon the functions of their office without the Royal consent: and this consent has, of late years, been withheld in many cases, so as to keep Sees for a considerable time vacant.

In Prussia, the higher Roman Catholic clergy are paid by the State; the parochial clergy have endowments; and in the annual budget votes are taken for the payment both of the Roman Catholic clergy and of those of the Evangelical Churches. In all parts of the Prussian monarchy (except the Rhenish provinces, where a Concordat is in force) the Crown exercises some control over the elections of Bishops and the appointment of parish priests; and the Protestant Church is governed by Consistories appointed by the Civil Government, one for each province. The same system prevails, with local variations, in other States of Germany. To take an example: in Wurtemberg the

King (who happens to be a Roman Catholic) is invested by the Constitution with the supreme direction and guardianship of the Evangelical Protestant Church, which is governed by a Consistory of six General Superintendents; and the Bishop of the only Roman Catholic See, though ecclesiastically dependent upon the Archbishop of Freiburg in Baden, is required to act, as to some of the more important matters of diocesan administration, in conjunction with a Church Council appointed by the Civil Government.

In Belgium, Holland, Denmark, Sweden, and Greece, grants of money for the purposes of public worship, and for payment of the clergy, form a regular charge in the annual budgets of State expenditure. In every one of those countries the Church (Roman Catholic, Greek, or Protestant) has definite relations with the State. In most, if not all of them, the national Churches have also endowments of greater or less value. I am not aware that in any of them there is any disposition, on the part of either Government or people, to put an end to this state of things. In Germany I believe that there are only two parties, or schools of thought, which advocate the separation of Church from State—the extreme and most fanatical 'Right' of the Ultramontane Vaticanists, and the extreme and most fanatical 'Left' of the anti-religious Revolutionists; neither of them, nor both together, strong or formidable.

10. *General Results.*

To what conclusion am I led by this examination of the present condition of the relations of Church and State in other civilised countries? To this—that no observable current, either rapid or slow, exists in those countries generally, which ought to exercise or is likely to exercise (unless it be in the direction of that anti-Christian secularism with which English Non-Conformists may be presumed to have as little sympathy as English Churchmen) any serious influence over the course of events in Great Britain. Disestablishment after the Continental fashion would not 'liberate religion from State control': Disendowment after the Continental fashion would make the State paymaster of the Clergy. The European current sets in a direction equally remote from the destructive enthusiasm of our Voluntaries, and from the love and reverence of Churchmen for the Institutions which they hold more precious than their lives. The state of things which now exists throughout Europe is no antiquated relic of the past; it is almost everywhere the product and outcome of the most active movements of our own century—in some countries a very recent product indeed. The opponents, therefore, of Disestablishment in Great Britain may well fight their own battle upon its merits and on their own ground, without being alarmed by the phantom of any irresistible current setting in that direction throughout the civilised world.

In the pages which follow I shall endeavour to deal with the particular facts and arguments relative to the Church of England, which are, in my judgment, material to this great controversy.

I remain, dear Mr. Gladstone,

Ever yours faithfully,

SELBORNE.

PART I

THE CHURCH AND ITS ESTABLISHMENT

CHAPTER I

THE CHURCH OF ENGLAND BEFORE THE REFORMATION

THE assailants of the Church of England put in the front of their battle certain arguments, which they dignify with the names of 'religious' and 'political'; and, having done what they probably think sufficient to justify a hostile attitude, and to raise some adverse prepossessions, they proceed to deal, in their own peculiar fashion, with the facts of law and history: presenting them with a boldness which might be admirable, if it were a little more candid. To those who seek information to guide them to sound judgments, a contrary order may seem preferable—facts first, and arguments afterwards. Many fallacies and misleading assumptions may thus be exposed beforehand, so as to make their refutation, as often as they are repeated, unnecessary.

The fundamental conception of the Church of England, which is constantly put forward by the advocates of Disestablishment, is that of a State Church, a political creation, a Church called into existence by the State, and deriving from the State the essential law of its being. Its defenders are supposed to maintain a political theory of

Christianity; not in the sense (to my apprehension certainly true) that the Divinely-founded Church of our Lord and His apostles was, and ever must be, an organised religious society: but in a sense practically opposed to our Lord's declaration, that His kingdom is 'not of this world.' If there are any persons who maintain such a theory, I am not one of them; I renounce it, as heartily as any 'Liberationist' can do.

Those who put forward this fiction, of the Church of England being a mere State or Act of Parliament Church, rest their historical case upon a denial of the identity of the Church of England before the Reformation with the Church of England after the Reformation—which 'absolute identity' (as Professor Freeman[1] truly says), the facts of history clearly demonstrate. My immediate purpose, in this and the next chapter, will be to exhibit, as concisely as I can, some of the proofs of that identity.

1. *England and Rome.*

It will not, I suppose, be denied, that from the time when Augustin preached Christianity to the heathen Anglo-Saxons, and founded the See of Canterbury (A.D. 596), to the twenty-third year of King Henry the Eighth (A.D. 1532)—for nearly a thousand years—the Church of England preserved unbroken organic continuity. Still less can it be pretended, that the Church founded here by the preaching of Augustin, and organised and extended by him and his successors, was the creation of all or any of the Anglo-Saxon States. Its origin, manifestly, was in the spontaneous missionary efforts of the

---

[1] *Disestablishment and Disendowment* (1885), p. 21. All future references to 'Freeman' are to this work.

One Church (then, at all events, justly called Catholic), which had the Apostles for its teachers, and had come down in unbroken historical succession from their days.

But it has been asserted, that until the time of the Reformation that Church was not 'established by law as the National Church'[1]—that, before that time, 'separate National Churches were unknown'[1]—that 'at the commencement of that period the Church of England, as a separate organisation, had no existence'[2]—that 'it was simply a local branch of the Church of Rome.'[2]

To say that, as long as the unity of Christendom remained unbroken, there was no separation, in the sense of breach of communion, between the Church of England and the Church of Rome and other Churches upon the Continent of Europe, or elsewhere throughout the world, is (of course) a truism; but it is a truism irrelevant to the question, whether the Church of England was not then, as much as at any time since, established by law in England as the National Church, with a separate organisation of its own; and not a mere 'local branch of the Church of Rome.' The justification for, and the consequences of, the subsequent breach of unity in Christendom may require to be considered, in connection with principles which I hope in their proper place to examine: but they have nothing to do with those questions of fact, with which I am at present dealing.

Except as a vague and inaccurate theological generalisation, the phrase 'Church of Rome,' in a context which calls the Church of England before the Reformation a 'local branch' of it, is unmeaning and simply misleading. The fact that in the days of religious unity the Bishop of

[1] *C. D.*, p. 32.   [2] *C. D.*, p. 34.

Rome was regarded as, to some extent, and for some purposes, Primate or Metropolitan Bishop of Western Christendom, was not then understood as denationalising all the Churches of the Western world, either upon the Continent or in England, nor as making them mere branches of the Church of Rome.[1] Every one of them had, as a matter of fact, its own national organisation, separate and distinct from that of the Church of Rome, and its own system of ecclesiastical law and administration—in some things common to it and other Churches, and in other things different,—under the support and sanction of laws, made by its own civil rulers. Nor could the fact, that Augustin, who converted the Anglo-Saxons and founded the See of Canterbury, was a missionary from Rome, have for its consequence any merger or necessary incorporation of the Church which he founded in that of Rome, any more than the Church of Rome itself could properly be described as a 'local branch' of the Eastern Church, because the Apostles who founded it came from Jerusalem. The essential unity of the Church of Christ throughout the world (which in some sense every Christian believes) is consistent with the separate organisation of local or national Churches. There is full intercommunion, at the present day, between the Church of England and the Protestant Episcopal Churches of the United States, Scotland, and Ireland, and of all the British Colonies. But each of them has its own separate ecclesiastical organisation, and would not lose its

---

[1] *C. D.* (p. 33) quotes from the Report of the Royal Commission on Ecclesiastical Courts words which are not really to the purpose. While the unity of Christendom was unbroken it was true of every national Church that it was 'a portion of a much greater organisation'; and 'not *merely* the religious organisation of the nation.' But it had its own organisation as a national Church nevertheless.

identity if that intercommunion were, from any cause, interrupted.

The Church of Rome itself, and its relations to the Church of England and to other European National Churches, underwent important changes during the many centuries which elapsed between the mission of Augustin and the reign of King Henry the Eighth. The whole mediæval system grew up during that interval. If (apart from the breach of ecclesiastical intercommunion which undoubtedly took place at the time of the Reformation, and the moral responsibility for that breach) the authorised doctrine and practice of the Church of England at the present day should be compared with that of the Christian Church generally—including the Church of Rome—in the days of Augustin, it would require a strong application of the theological microscope to discover any really substantial differences between them. Almost, if not absolutely, everything which the Church of England has since rejected as usurpation or corruption was then unknown.

I will mention here particularly two things, and those because they are material to a right conception of the questions which arose between the Church of England and the Church of Rome before, and at the time of, the Reformation. The 'decretals,'[1] falsely ascribed to Isidore, Archbishop of Seville, upon which the entire edifice of mediæval and modern Papal supremacy was built up, were not fabricated till the ninth century (about

---

[1] See Van Espen, *Comm. in jus novum Canonicum*, part ii. pp. 451-475. The forger is known as 'Isidore Mercator.' His work was 'a collection of decretal letters, ascribed to more than thirty Popes, succeeding each other in the first three centuries.'

A.D. 850), nor were they codified by Gratian as the basis of Roman Canon Law till A.D. 1151. Those decretals were the true source of all the subsequent encroachments of the spiritual on the civil power, and on the independent rights of National Churches. The other thing is the temporal power of the Popes; which gradually gave to the Court of Rome the dual character of an Italian State, influencing and influenced by the secular politics of other European States, and at the same time the ecclesiastical centre of Western Christendom. This originated with the donation of the Exarchate of Ravenna to Pope Stephen the Third by Pepin, the father of Charlemagne, in A.D. 755, more than one hundred and fifty years after the foundation of the Anglo-Saxon Church. It was enlarged by further gifts from Charlemagne; from the Emperor Henry the Third in A.D. 1053; and from the Countess Matilda in A.D. 1102; and by conquests, especially under the Popes of the 'Renaissance,' whose unscrupulous worldly ambition and thoroughly secular spirit, during the whole period from Alexander the Sixth (A.D. 1492) until after the breach between England and Rome, was one of the main causes of the Reformation.

There never was a time, even after the development given by Gregory the Seventh and his successors to the principles of the false decretals, when the independence and liberties of the Church of England were not, to a large extent, practically maintained against the encroachments of the Court of Rome, or when its rights and organisation as a National Church were not protected by English law. The legislation of Henry the Eighth's reign against the Pope's pretensions to jurisdiction in this kingdom did but carry to their full consequences, under the circumstances of that time, principles admitted in Anglo-Saxon times, for which Norman and Plantagenet kings had contended, which had been embodied in the Acts of their Councils and Parliaments, and in which the Ecclesiastical authorities of the realm had either actively concurred or at least practically acquiesced. Struggles from time to time arose, sometimes out of the weakness or violence of kings, sometimes out of the zeal or ambition of prelates— William Rufus had to contend for the mastery with Anselm, Henry the Second with Becket; and those prelates sought to shelter or strengthen themselves under Papal authority. King John sunk so low as at one time to surrender the realm of England to be held as a fief from the Pope. Archbishop Boniface defied the civil power under Henry the Third, and Archbishop Winchelsey under his stronger son. But the Church of England was throughout established by law as a National Church, with such power only of interference on the part of the Pope as the laws of England permitted, or did not exclude.

I propose to illustrate and verify this general statement, with reference particularly to the subjects of ecclesiastical liberties, law, and jurisdiction; appeals to Rome; the prelacy and benefices of the realm; bishops in Parliament; and legislation concerning matters of faith.

2. *Liberties, Law, and Jurisdiction.*

It was the Church, not of Rome, but 'of England' (*Ecclesia Anglicana*), of which the 'rights and liberties' were declared to be inviolable by King John's Great Charter,[1] confirmed by Henry the Third. It is 'the holy Church of England' (*seinte Eglise d'Engleterre*), which in the preamble

[1] Matt. Paris (Luard's ed.), vol. ii. p. 589, and 9 Hen. III. cap. 1.

to the Statute of Provisors of 23 Edward III. (A.D. 1350), was described as 'founded in the estate of Prelacy within the realm of England.' The Papal encroachments which that statute was passed to restrain were described as tending to the 'annullation of the estate of the holy Church of England.'

The Establishment of the Church by law consists essentially in the incorporation of the law of the Church into that of the realm, as a branch of the general law of the realm, though limited as to the causes to which, and the persons to whom it applies; in the public recognition of its Courts and Judges, as having proper legal jurisdiction; and in the enforcement of the sentences of those Courts, when duly pronounced according to law, by the civil power. The 'Establishment' (so understood) of the Church in England grew up gradually and silently, out of the relations between moral and physical power natural in an early stage of society; not as the result of any definite act, compact, or conflict, but so that no one can now trace the exact steps of the process by which the voluntary recognition of moral and spiritual obligation passed into custom, and custom into law. Under the Anglo-Saxon kings the ecclesiastical and temporal judges sat together in one Court. It was so expressly enacted by the laws of Edgar[1] and of Canute,[2] which directed the County Court to be held twice a year, and both the Bishop and the Alderman to sit in it, 'each of them there putting in use both God's law and the world's law.' The Conqueror (probably in A.D. 1072) was advised by his Norman prelates that this mode of executing 'the Episcopal laws,' which until his time had prevailed in England, was 'faulty, and not agreeable to the precepts of the

---

[1] Johnson's *Laws and Canons* (Oxford ed. 1850), vol. i. p. 411.
[2] *Ibid.*, p. 514.

sacred Canons;' and, by a mandate in the form of a Charter,[1] issued pursuant to a resolution taken in a council of his Archbishops, Bishops, and Abbots, and 'all the chief men of the realm,' he commanded, and by his royal authority 'enjoined,' that no Bishop or Archdeacon should any longer 'hold pleas in the Hundred Court, or bring spiritual causes to the judgment of laymen,' but that all persons 'impleaded according to the Episcopal laws' should answer before the Bishop, in such place as he should appoint, and should be excommunicated for default of appearance after three citations; the King's and the Sheriff's Courts giving assistance, as need might be, to enforce the excommunication by the secular power.

In the Episcopal Courts, thus separated from the Civil, the ecclesiastical judge had by law the sole cognisance, not only of suits directly concerning religion, and morals, and Church discipline, but also of some others in their nature mixed (according to modern ideas chiefly temporal), as to which the ecclesiastical preceded the civil jurisprudence in establishing the doctrines of moral obligation on which they depended. Such were matrimonial and testamentary causes; to which were added tithe suits, suits relating to consecrated buildings and lands given to churches at the time of their dedication, and other matters arising out of or incidental to these. Of some other things, not less directly concerning the Church — particularly rights of advowson or presentation to benefices — the King's Court took cognisance, whether the parties to the controversy were

[1] See Dugdale's *Monasticon*, ed. 1817-30, vol. vi. p. 1270 (among charters preserved in Lincoln Cathedral). Another copy, preserved in the chapter-house of St. Paul's Cathedral, is quoted by Selden (on Eadmer, *Works*, vol. ii. p. 1634, ed. 1726), and is printed by Wilkins, *Concil.*, vol. i. p. 368.

lay or clerical; providing for the determination of such questions by several forms of civil actions, and excluding in such cases the 'Court Christian.' Whenever an ecclesiastical judge attempted to transgress the limits of his recognised legal jurisdiction, whether under the direct authority of the Pope or on any other pretext, he was stopped by a writ of 'Prohibition,' addressed by the King's Court at Westminster to the parties, and also to the judge; a proceeding which was applicable to all excesses of jurisdiction by any 'inferior Courts' within the realm. If the King's Court, on further examination of the matter, found it to be one in which the Ecclesiastical Court was not really exceeding its jurisdiction, a message, called a 'consultation,' was sent to the spiritual judge, giving him leave to proceed. All this was settled law before the era of Parliaments: it is fully expounded by Bracton,[1] who was one of King Henry the Third's judges.

This division of jurisdictions, and recognition of the proper legal authority of the Ecclesiastical Courts, was confirmed, and the ecclesiastical jurisdiction was in some respects enlarged and in others limited, by statutes[2] passed in the reigns of the three first Edwards. Archbishop Boniface,[3] by Canons made during the troubles of Henry the Third's reign, endeavoured to extend the spiritual jurisdiction; but those Canons were resisted as contrary to law, both then and afterwards. The questions which they raised between Church and State were finally set at rest by a celebrated statute[4] of Edward the Second, 'concerning

---

[1] Fol. 107, and see book iv. *De Exceptionibus*, ed. Twiss, vol. vi.
[2] 13 Edw. I., stat. 1, cap. 5, and stat. 4, cap. 1; 24 Edw. I.; 17 Edw. II., stat. 1, cap. 8; 18 Edw. III., stat. 3, cap. 6, 7, etc.
[3] Coke's *Second Inst.*, p. 599.
[4] *Articuli Cleri*, 9 Edw. II., stat. 1, cap. 1-16.

divers liberties granted to the clergy.' Neither the Pope nor any foreign council was admitted to have a right to make Canons for the English Church. The English Canon law consisted of such Canons and ecclesiastical constitutions as had been lawfully made in England,[1] and of such others, from whatever sources derived, as had been adopted and brought into use in England as part of the customary ecclesiastical law of the realm. Nobody can study the Roman Canon law of the Middle Ages without observing there many things which were never law in England, and any attempt to enforce which would certainly have been met by 'Prohibition.'

The Convocations, in which the inferior clergy of the Church of England, by their dignitaries and elected representatives, have had from the time of Edward the Second a share with the bishops in Synodical action, were institutions peculiar to the English Church.

3. *Appeals.*

The supremacy of the kings of England, 'over all persons and in all causes ecclesiastical as well as civil,' within their dominions, was at all times practically, as well as in principle, maintained by the assertion and exercise of the power of Prohibition.

'Here,' says Sir Matthew Hale[2] (speaking of pre-Reformation times), 'is the clear evidence of the subordination of ecclesi-

---

[1] Coke's *Reports*, 'Caudrey's case,' part v. fol. 32 (*b*); Lord Hardwicke in *Middleton* v. *Crofts*, 2 Atk. *Rep.*, p. 669; Hale on *Royal Supremacy*, p. 13.

[2] MS. of Sir M. Hale on the *Royal Supremacy* in Lincoln's Inn Library (printed at the *Record* Office, 1 Red Lion Square, for private circulation), p. 21.

astical jurisdiction to the temporal, and of the derivation of it; that the Common Law Courts are to judge of the extent of the ecclesiastical jurisdiction, and that where one Ecclesiastical Court invades the jurisdiction of another, there the Common law is to umpire between them.'

As long as there was full intercommunion between the different parts of Western Christendom, there was necessarily free intercourse between the English and Foreign Churches; and the Metropolitan character of the See of Rome (retained from the days of the Roman Empire) always gave to the occupant of that See great influence and moral weight. But this was a different thing from acknowledged lawful jurisdiction and authoritative control. When Wilfrid, Archbishop of York, appealed to Pope Agatho (A.D. 680) against the division of his diocese by Archbishop Theodore of Canterbury with the concurrence of the King of Northumberland, and obtained a judgment in his favour from that Pope and his Council, the judgment was set aside and not acted upon here. Still persisting in his resistance, he obtained from another Pope (John VI.) letters to the effect that a Synod ought to be called to determine the case, and to this the successor of Theodore in the See of Canterbury was willing to consent. But the king objected, and it was not done.[1]

For above five hundred years after Augustin there were no regular appeals to Rome from sentences of Ecclesiastical Courts or Judges in England. The Constitutions of Clarendon,[2] agreed and sworn to, A.D. 1164, by all the prelates and nobles of the realm,—Becket included,—who afterwards obtained a Papal absolution from that oath,—purported to

---

[1] Johnson's *Laws and Canons* (ed. 1850), vol. i. pp. 120, 121.
[2] Wilkins, *Conc.*, vol. i. p. 453.

declare and place on record some of the ancient 'liberties and customs of the Church of England.' In one of them (Art. 8) it was declared that 'appeals, when necessary, ought to be from the archdeacon to the bishop, and from the bishop to the archbishop; and, if justice were not done by the archbishop, the last resort must be to the king, according to whose commandment the cause should be finally determined in the archbishop's Court, without any further process, unless by the king's leave.' The exclusion of appeals to Rome without the king's leave was one of those 'voluntary customs' of the English Church which displeased Archbishop Anselm, and of which he complained in a letter to Pope Urban the Second, written from Lyons, A.D. 1098.[1] From the time when the forged decretals obtained currency in Christendom, the efforts and policy of the Popes were directed against all such national customs; and they were seconded (I do not doubt, from high motives) by the great foreign prelates, who, under the Conqueror and his Norman successors, were promoted to posts of chief authority in the Church of England. That contest lasted through more than a hundred years. The Conqueror himself always maintained friendly relations with Rome; and in his time a dispute concerning precedence between the Metropolitan Sees of Canterbury and York was determined by the award[2] of Pope Alexander the Second's Legate; but expressly, and upon the face of the award, by the king's consent. William Rufus refused to allow Anselm to go as an appellant to Rome, and the bishops as well as barons of the realm then bore testimony, that it was 'a thing unheard of without the king's leave.' The same king resented Anselm's recognition of Urban the Second (there being then an Anti-pope) without

[1] Eadmer, *Hist.*, book ii. p. 43.   [2] Matt. Paris, *Hist.*, A.D. 1072.

his authority, as tantamount to 'an attempt to deprive him of his crown.'[1] Pope Pascal the Second complained[2] that Henry the First would not suffer appeals to be made to him.

It was under Stephen,[3] when the right to the crown itself was in controversy, with civil war raging through the land, and when that king's brother, Henry de Blois, Bishop of Winchester, was the Pope's Legate, that a different practice first came in. Henry the Second, before and during his contest with Becket, endeavoured to recall that concession. 'The supreme devolution of ecclesiastical causes' (says Sir Matthew Hale[4]) 'came but by degrees, and at first by reverent indulgence, to the Pope, and therefore was so eagerly endeavoured by Henry the Second, by the Constitutions of Clarendon, to be restored. But his ill success in that contestation much settled the ecclesiastical jurisdiction.' In King John's time, under Innocent the Third, the Papal power (in this kingdom as elsewhere) reached its zenith. Thenceforward appeals to Rome, in causes within the acknowledged jurisdiction of the Ecclesiastical Courts of England, became common, and were acquiesced in when the laws of this realm were not plainly contravened. But they formed no part of the essential law or original constitution of the Church of England; and they were not admitted except under reservations sufficient to preserve the principle of that original constitution. Even in his act of submission[5] to the Pope after Becket's murder, Henry the Second, while

---

[1] Eadmer, fol. 61. Long afterwards (A.D. 1378), when there was also an Anti-pope, an Act of Parliament (2 Ric. II., stat. 1, cap. 7) was passed, declaring that another Urban (the Sixth) 'was duly chosen Pope, and so ought to be accepted and obeyed.'

[2] Eadmer, fol. 113, 115.

[3] Johnson, *Laws and Canons*, vol. ii. p. 46 (ed. 1851).

[4] *Royal Suprem.*, p. 20. [5] Spelman, vol. ii. p. 99.

promising not to 'obstruct, or suffer to be obstructed, the freedom of appeals in his kingdom to the Pope in ecclesiastical causes,' added the saving clause, that, 'if there were any whom he distrusted, they should be required to give security against seeking anything prejudicial to himself or his kingdom.' In Edward the First's time,[1] under the Common Law, and before the passing of any statute upon the subject, one who had brought in a bull of excommunication against another Englishman, and had published it to the Lord Treasurer, was adjudged guilty of treason, and banished the realm, —narrowly escaping with his life. There were always prohibitions from the Crown to the clergy against attempting, in their convocations or otherwise, anything prejudicial to the King or the realm, and against introducing Papal Bulls having any such tendency. Edward the Third, in letters to Pope Benedict the Twelfth and his Cardinals, dated the 2d May 1337,[2] remonstrated against the admission of an appeal by the Bishop of Winchester from a sentence of the Metropolitan Court of Canterbury, as contrary to law and custom; and by the Statute of 'Præmunire,'[3] passed in the twenty-seventh year of the same reign, any suit to a Foreign Court, 'to answer of things whereof the cognizance pertaineth to the King's Court,' was forbidden under the penalty of outlawry and forfeiture of goods.

4. *Bishoprics and Benefices.*

Before, and down to the commencement of the Reformation, the organisation of the Church of England for the

---

[1] Coke's *Reports*, part v. fol. 12 (c).
[2] Wilkins, *Conc.*, vol. ii. p. 584.
[3] 27 Edw. III., stat. 1, cap. 1.

normal purposes of government and spiritual ministrations (leaving out of sight monasteries and religious houses not attached to Cathedrals), consisted of two Archbishoprics and nineteen Bishoprics, with Chapters (chiefly Conventual) attached to them, and parishes under Rectors or Vicars. All the Archbishops and Bishops, from the times of their first foundation, and all Rectors and Vicars, had in law perpetual corporate succession. The Capitular and Conventual Bodies were also incorporated.

All the Archbishoprics and Bishoprics were regarded as of Royal foundation: the English, because the lands with which they were endowed, whether of Royal or of private gift, were held, not of any subject, but 'in chief,' by title of 'barony,' of the Crown; the Welsh, because similar rights of foundership and patronage were supposed to have been vested in the Princes of Wales, and to have passed from them, by title of conquest or forfeiture, to the English Crown.

Our law books state that all these Bishoprics were anciently donatives of the Crown; that is, the Crown had the direct right of appointment to them without election. It is so stated, not only by Sir Edward Coke,[1] but by King Edward the Third's Judges, in the 'Year-Books'[2] of the sixth and seventeenth years of his reign (A.D. 1332 and 1343). There is a statement to the same effect in the 'Statute of Provisors' (25 Edward III.[3]); and King Edward the Third himself, in a letter[4] written early in his reign to the Pope and the College of Cardinals, stated that his 'progenitors, who long ago established and endowed the Church, used for-

---

[1] *Co. Litt.*, fol. 97 (*a*), 134 (*a*).
[2] 6 Edw. III., fol. 11 ; 17 Edw. III., fol. 40 (*b*).   [3] Stat. 6.
[4] See Selden on Eadmer (*Works*, 1726, vol. ii. part ii. p. 1608).

merly to appoint freely to all vacant Cathedral Churches in the realm, in right of their Crown.'

It is doubtless, on the other hand, true that in the earliest times of the Church of England, before Bishops had civil privileges, or territorial endowments by title of barony, they may have been elected, either by the general body of the clergy of the several dioceses, or by the conventual clergy of the Cathedral Cities. Wihtred, King of Kent, in his 'grant of privileges,' made (according to the Saxon Chronicle) in a Council of his prelates and nobles, A.D. 692, disclaimed the power of appointing Bishops, etc., and seems to have ascribed it to the Archbishop:—

'Let no man in any wise be chosen or consecrated into so sublime an office without the advice of the Archbishop. Kings ought to constitute earls and aldermen, reeves of districts, and judges; and the Archbishop ought to instruct and govern God's congregation, and to choose and appoint Bishops, and abbots and abbesses, and priests and deacons, and to consecrate and establish them.'[1]

It was probably on this early practice that the Chapters or Conventual Bodies attached to Cathedrals founded their claims to be canonically entitled to elect their Bishops. The writer of the history current under the name of Ingulph, Abbot of Croyland (who lived under Edward the Confessor and William the Conqueror), states, that for many years before his time 'there was no free canonical election of prelates; but all the Bishoprics and Abbacies were conferred by the King at his pleasure, by the delivery of staff and ring;'[2]—and that 'the Conqueror distributed among his Normans all the Bishoprics and Prelacies

[1] Johnson's *Laws and Canons* (ed. 1850), vol. i. p. 128.
[2] Fulman's *Rerum Anglicanarum Scriptores Veteres*, p. 62.

of the whole Kingdom.'[1] King Henry the First, at the Council of London held under Anselm A.D. 1107,[2] gave up the practice of Royal or any other manner of lay investiture by delivery of the pastoral staff and ring (symbols of spiritual power), which from the time of Gregory the Seventh had been the subject of deadly strife upon the Continent of Europe: Anselm, on the other hand, consenting, that the Bishops and other Prelates chosen for Sees or Abbeys should before consecration do homage to the King. Few compacts between the Temporal and the Spiritual powers have been so well or so long observed as this, which has never been broken in England to the present day. This compromise was followed in the time of King John, by the admission, on certain terms,[3] of 'freedom of election' to vacant Bishoprics, by the Chapters of the several Cathedral Churches. This (according to King Edward the Third's letter to the Pope and Cardinals, already mentioned), was done 'at the entreaty of the clergy, and out of respect to and at the request of the Supreme Pontiff.' The terms were, that the King should grant his licence to elect, and that the election, when made, should be subject to his confirmation and consent. These reserved powers, together with that of recommending the person whom the King wished to have chosen, left the appointments (in ordinary times) virtually, though not formally, in the King's gift.[4] An example of the forms

---

[1] Fulman's *Rerum Anglicanarum Scriptores Veteres*, p. 70.

[2] Continuation of Ingulph by 'Petrus Blesensis' (Fulman's Collection, p. 126).

[3] Matt. Paris (Luard's ed.), vol. ii. p. 589; and see Edward the Third's letter (Seld. on Eadmer, *ubi supra*), and Statute 25 Edw. III., stat. 6.

[4] In Dugdale's *Monasticon*, vol. vi. p. 1295 (Salisbury Cathedral),

used may be found in letters from the Prior and Chapter of Winchester to King Henry the Sixth,[1] asking for leave to proceed to the election of a Bishop after the death of Cardinal Beaufort; and from the King to the Prior and Chapter, granting them licence to elect, and recommending for their choice 'Master William Waynflete, Provost of our College Royal of our Lady of Eton;' who was, accordingly, elected.

From the first origin of Parliaments, Acts were passed to repel the encroachments of the Pope upon the rights of the King and other patrons in England, in respect of appointments to ecclesiastical benefices.

In the thirty-fifth year of Edward the First (A.D. 1307), it was represented by petition to the Parliament then held at Carlisle, that the Bishop of Rome had assumed to act as if he had been patron of churches and ecclesiastical dignities in England, 'as he was not of right by the law of England;' and that this was to the great prejudice of the realm, and also of 'the estate of the holy Church of England,' and 'against the good disposition and will of the first Founders.' It was thereupon 'ordained, provided, established, and adjudged, that the said oppressions, grievances, and dangers in the realm from thenceforth should not be suffered in any manner.'

The Statute of Provisors (25 Edward III., stat. 6), recited these proceedings in the Parliament of Carlisle, and that the same mischief had nevertheless continued and increased, and it enacted :—

there is a copy of King Henry the Third's Charter of A.D. 1219 to New Sarum, making it 'a free city like Winchester;' in which the King reserved to himself and his heirs 'the advowson of the See, and all other rights during its vacancy, as he had and ought to have in other Cathedral Churches in his kingdom, when vacant.'

[1] Printed in the Appendix to Chandler's *Life of Waynflete*.

'That the free elections of Archbishops, Bishops, and all other dignities and benefices elective in England, shall hold from henceforth in the manner as they were granted by the King's progenitors and the ancestors of other lords, founders of the said dignities and other benefices; and that all prelates, and other people of holy Church' (*i.e.* ecclesiastics), 'who have advowsons of any benefices of the King's gift or of any of his progenitors, or of other lords and donors, to do divine services and other charges thereof ordained, shall have their collations and presentments freely to the same, in the manner as they were expressed by their donors;' and that, if 'the Court of Rome' should in any case have made 'reservation, collation, or provision' of any Archbishopric, Bishopric, dignity, or other elective benefice, 'our Lord the King and his heirs shall have and enjoy for the same time that collation to the Archbishoprics and other dignities elective which be in his advowry' (*i.e.* patronage), 'such as his progenitors had before that free election was first granted by the King's progenitors upon a certain form and condition; as, to demand licence of the King to choose, and after the election to have his Royal assent, and not in any other manner; which conditions not kept, the thing ought by reason to revert to its first nature.'

Further Statutes, in corroboration of these, were passed from time to time afterwards. The Popes never gave up the contest; and, during civil troubles, they sometimes gained advantages over the Crown; but the English Kings and Parliaments, with the consent of the Bishops and Clergy (however unwilling to quarrel with the Pope) still held their ground. The preamble of the last of this series of Statutes (16 Richard II., cap. 5, A.D. 1392), is of considerable historical interest; bearing a close resemblance to some of the well-known preambles of the Statutes of Henry the Eighth.

It recites, at much length, a complaint of the Commons to the King, that the Pope had of late issued processes and sentences of excommunication against English Bishops for acting in obedience to English law, and that he intended to make translations of other English Bishops, some out of the realm, and some to other English dioceses:—

'And so' (the Commons proceeded) 'the Crown of England, which hath been so free at all times that it hath been in no earthly subjection, but immediately subject to God in all things touching the regality of the said Crown, and to none other, should be submitted to the Pope, and the laws and Statutes of the realm by him defeated and avoided at his will, to the perpetual destruction of the sovereignty of the King our lord, his crown and dignity, and of all his realm, which God defend: And moreover, the Commons aforesaid say, that the said things, so attempted, be clearly against the King's Crown and his regality, used and approved of the time of all his progenitors: Wherefore they, and all the King's Commons of the same realm, will stand with our said lord the King and his said Crown and regality in the cases aforesaid, and in all other cases attempted against him, to live and to die.'

They then prayed the King to put the question, severally, to all the lords in Parliament, as well spiritual as temporal, 'how they think of the cases aforesaid, and how they will stand in the same cases with our lord the King, in upholding the rights of the said Crown and regality?' This was done, with the result, that all the lords Temporal declared themselves of the same mind with the Commons: and

'The Archbishops, Bishops, and other Prelates, being in the same Parliament severally examined' (and the proxies of those of them who were absent), 'making protestation, that it was not their mind to say nor affirm that the Bishop of Rome may not excommunicate Bishops, nor that he may' [not?] 'make translation of Bishops after the law of holy Church, answered, and said,—That, if any execution of processes made in the King's Court as before be made by any, and censures of excommunication to be made against any Bishops of England or any other of the King's liege people, for that they have made execution of such commandments' (or, if any such translations of Bishops were executed without the consent and against the will of the King), 'the said lords spiritual will and ought to be with the King in these cases, in lawfully maintaining of his Crown, and in all other cases touching his Crown and his royalty, as they be bound by their ligeance.'

The Statute, of which this was the preamble, imposed the penalties of 'Præmunire' (outlawry, and forfeiture of goods) upon all English subjects who might purchase or procure Bulls from Rome for any of the objects against which it was directed.

5. *Bishops in Parliament.*

This is a fitting place for speaking of the title of the Bishops to sit, as Spiritual lords, in Parliament. It has been controverted among learned men, whether they were summoned to Parliament because they held their lands as tenants-in-chief by Barony from the Crown, or by reason of any custom not founded on tenure. If it were necessary to enter into that controversy, I should myself regard the eleventh Constitution of Clarendon as strong evidence in support of the former opinion. That they were in fact summoned, and did sit with the Temporal lords, from the first commencement of our Parliaments, is certain. Their learning, and their power and influence with the people, naturally made many of them from early times councillors of the Sovereign; and they took part in all the mixed Councils held before the time of Parliaments. The eleventh Constitution of the Council of Clarendon declared, that 'the Archbishops, Bishops, and all other persons of the realm who hold in chief of the Crown, are to have their possessions of the King by title of barony, ... and, like the other barons of the kingdom, they are to have places with the barons in the King's Court, except in cases of life or limb.' King John, by his charter, promised to summon the Archbishops, Bishops, and Abbots, as well as the Earls and greater Barons, to his great Council, whenever a grant of subsidies might be required. The writs summoning the lords temporal and spiritual to every Parliament (which follow to this day the ancient forms) call them together to consider 'urgent affairs' concerning 'the Church' as well as 'the Realm.' Grants of money to the Crown, out of ecclesiastical as well as other revenues, were (no doubt) originally the main object. The presence of the whole clergy, by representation, as a third estate in Parliament (and not of the Bishops only in the House of Lords), was contemplated by Edward the First, in whose reign our Constitution first assumed a settled form. His writs of A.D. 1293[1] and later years commanded the Archbishops and Bishops of both provinces to attend in Parliament, with their Deans and Arch-deacons, and elected representatives of the chapters and clergy of every diocese. But the clergy resisted, objecting[2] that it was uncanonical so to summon them to the King's Parliament, a secular Court. The dispute, after lasting several years, was finally accommodated in the time of Edward the Second; when the provincial convocations were established[3] upon the system which has ever since continued—being summoned, pursuant to Royal writ, by the Archbishops, simultaneously with every Parliament, and

[1] *Parliamentary Writs*, temp. Edw. I. (A.D. 1293), *et seq.*
[2] *Ibid.*, temp. Edw. II., Protest of Clergy, 20th May 1314, and in the following year.
[3] See *Ibid.*, temp. Edw. II., A.D. 1315, p. 158, and A.D. 1318, p. 196.

being dissolved at the same time; but forming no part of the Parliament. The disability of the clergy to sit in the House of Commons is due to the fact that in this way they had their separate representation.[1]

6. *Legislation concerning Matters of Faith.*

The Statutes[2] against heresy (or 'Lollardism') of A.D. 1382, 1400, and 1414, show that before, as well as after the Reformation, the Civil Power interfered by Acts of Parliament and criminal sanctions to enforce the ecclesiastical law, even in points as to which later ages have learnt, by painful experience, to acknowledge and vindicate the freedom of individual conscience. My present object is to deal with facts; not to maintain that all things, either in the Church or in the State of England, have always been right; but to show that no difference of principle, in this respect, came in at the time of the Reformation.

[1] In A.D. 1533 Dr. Nowell, prebendary of Westminster, was returned as member for Looe, but was held incapable of sitting because, 'having voice in the Convocation House,' he could not be a member in the House of Commons.

[2] 5 Ric. II., stat. 2, cap. 5; 2 Hen. IV., cap. 15; 2 Hen. V., stat. 1, cap. 7.

CHAPTER II

THE REFORMED CHURCH OF ENGLAND

I SHALL not concern myself with the motives or the characters of King Henry the Eighth or his successors, nor is it my purpose in this place to justify or to find fault with the Ecclesiastical legislation of those reigns. My purpose is still to deal with facts, and to clear away misrepresentations of matters of fact.

1. *Continuity of the Church.*

Professor Freeman has justly observed[1] that there was not in England, as some people seem to think, some one act done at a definite time, called the Reformation. What is so called is the sum total of certain changes, which extended over many years. The dissolution of the monasteries (for which five successive Bulls of Pope Clement VII. had prepared the way before the rupture of Henry the Eighth with Rome) is beside my purpose. The rest of the ecclesiastical legislation of Henry the Eighth's reign had for its object nothing else than the exclusion of Papal power, and the establishment of the supremacy of the British Crown, not over a new Church

[1] Freeman, p. 21.

then created, but over the old then existing Church of England.

Not one ecclesiastical corporation, except the monasteries—no Archbishopric or Bishopric, no parochial Rectory or Vicarage—was dissolved; none, except certain Conventual Chapters of Cathedrals, and a few Collegiate Churches, were so much even as re-modelled. All their charters, when chartered, all their customary rights and incidents by the Common Law, remained in force without interruption. Their endowments were held as before, by the old tenures and titles. 'There was no moment' (I use Professor Freeman's words[1]) 'when the State, as many people fancy, took the Church property from one religious body and gave it to another. . . . The general taking from one religious body and giving to another, which many people fancy took place under Henry the Eighth or Elizabeth, simply never happened at all.' The Bishops continued throughout to sit in Parliament, not by any new, but by their original title. The jurisdiction of all 'Ordinaries' in England—the Courts of all the Archdeacons, Bishops, and Archbishops, and their officials and commissaries—went on as before, administering the same system of law, in the same causes and matters, with the same assistance from, and subject to the same control by, the King's Courts. The same officers, with the same succession according to regular course of law, performed the same duties and functions. Very few individuals even refused to submit to the new laws then made, or lost their preferments in consequence of them. That new laws should be from time to time made, in matters ecclesiastical as well as civil, was and always had been an incident both

[1] Freeman, pp. 21-23.

of the ecclesiastical and of the civil state, no more involving the dissolution or reconstruction of the one than of the other. The Convocations of the Clergy, constituted and convened as before, continued to meet as before with every Parliament; they synodically agreed to (and generally anticipated) all, or nearly all, measures of importance affecting the Church, which were then taken in Parliament. What was not pulled down was not, and could not be 'reconstructed.'[1] Not a stone of the then existing ecclesiastical organisation in England (the monasteries being only excrescences upon it) was displaced or disturbed.

Even the partisans of the Papacy continued to conform to the Church of England, till the eleventh year of Queen Elizabeth, when Pope Pius the Fifth excommunicated that Queen and her loyal subjects, and took upon himself to give her Crown to the King of Spain. A similar excommunication of Henry the Eighth and those who obeyed his legislation, by Pope Paul the Third, had produced no effect. Gardiner and Bonner, and others of like principles, served that King, submitted to his laws, and accepted or retained preferments in the Church of England, till the very end of his reign. When the separation actually took place in the eleventh year of Elizabeth, the seceders who obeyed the orders of the Pope were (as they have ever since been in England) few and insignificant, in comparison with the great mass of the clergy and lay people who still remained in the English Church. These seceders had no proper ecclesiastical organisation for more than half a century afterwards; and even when Vicars Apostolic were placed over them (one in A.D. 1621, and four in 1688), their government was by immediate delegation from Rome, without any

[1] *C. D.*, p. 34.

diocesan Episcopacy. This state of things continued till the famous 'Papal Aggression,' which led to the 'Ecclesiastical Titles Act' of 1851.

No idea could be more repugnant to the intention and understanding of King Henry the Eighth and his Parliaments (as apparent from their repeated declarations and acts) than that of either creating a new Church, or 'reconstructing' the old. No evidence of the continuity and identity of the Reformed Church of England with the Church of Augustin and of all the centuries after his time could be clearer or more decisive, than that afforded by those Statutes, in which some pretend to find proofs to the contrary.

Twice, in that series of Statutes, the claim to legislate in England concerning 'worldly things and human laws' (as the Act against 'Peter-pence' and Dispensations of 1533[1] describes the subjects of that legislation) was accompanied by a solemn disclaimer of any intention to break ecclesiastical unity. First, in the Act of 1531,[2] against payment of 'first-fruits' to Rome:—'Our Sovereign the King, and all his natural subjects, as well spiritual as temporal,' are there declared to be 'as obedient, devout, Catholic, and humble children of God and holy Church, as any people be within any realm Christian.' And in the Act, just mentioned, against Peter-pence, there is a proviso to exclude the construction, that the King, his nobles or subjects, 'intend to decline or vary from the congregation of Christ's Church in anything concerning the very articles of the Catholic faith of Christendom, or in any other thing declared by Holy Scriptures and the Word of God necessary for their salvation; but only to make an ordinance by

---

[1] 25 Hen. VIII., cap. 21.   [2] 23 Hen. VIII., cap. 20.

policies necessary and convenient to repress vice, and for good conservation of this realm in peace, unity, and tranquillity . . . *insuing much the old ancient customs of this realm in that behalf.*'

The preamble of the Statute 'for Restraint of Appeals'[1] refers to the evidence of 'old authentic histories and chronicles,' as showing that

'this realm of England is an Empire . . . governed by one supreme Head, the King . . . unto whom a body politic compact of all sorts and degrees of people, divided in terms and by names of Spirituality and Temporality, be bounden and own to bear, next to God, a natural and humble obedience ;' and it proceeds to say, that the determination of questions in 'any cause of the law divine' belongs to 'that part of the said body politic called the Spirituality, being usually called the English Church, which *always hath been* regarded and also found of that sort, that both for knowledge, integrity, and sufficiency of number, it *hath been always thought, and is also at this time*, sufficient and meet of itself, without the intermeddling of any exterior person, to declare and determine all such offices and duties as to their rooms spiritual doth appertain.'

The same recognition of the existing Church, its authority and its institutions, pervades the Reformation Statutes; to which (for more convenient comparison of what was then done with the earlier history relating to the same subjects) I shall now refer, under heads corresponding in substance with the divisions of the preceding chapter.

2. *Royal Supremacy.*

It was during the primacy of Archbishop Warham (not Cranmer) that the Convocations[2] of both provinces of

[1] 24 Hen. VIII., cap. 12.
[2] The proceedings of Convocation of the reign of Henry VIII. will

Canterbury and York formally acknowledged the King's 'Supreme Headship' of the Church of England: that of Canterbury unanimously in February 1530-31; that of York in May 1531, under protest from Tunstall, who nevertheless retained his See of Durham. 'Sole Protector and Supreme Head of the Church and Clergy of England' was the title which the King at first desired to have acknowledged, but the Convocation of Canterbury was not prepared to accept this without qualification. The King qualified it by adding the words, 'after God;' for which the Convocations substituted words of their own, 'as far as the law of Christ allows.' The King was satisfied; and in that form the acknowledgment was made. It was not till three years afterwards (A.D. 1534) that the Act of Parliament,[1] which added to the King's style the title of 'the only Supreme Head on Earth of the Church of England,' was passed; and it is plain, from the recitals in that and also in another Statute of the same year, and from other proofs, that the King did not mean to claim any spiritual office or character, or any power different in its nature from what had often before been asserted as belonging of right to the English Crown. That Act itself proceeds upon the recital: 'Albeit the King's Majesty justly and rightfully *is and ought to be* the Supreme Head of the Church of England, and so is recognised by the clergy of this realm in their Convocations.' The other[2] (that as to 'First-fruits') speaks in its preamble of the King as being 'now recognised, *as he always indeed hath heretofore been*, the only Supreme Head

be found in Wilkins, *Concilia*, and they are conveniently summarised in Mr. T. Lewis' recent work, *The Reformation Settlement* (Deighton, Cambridge, 1885).

[1] 26 Hen. VIII., cap. 1.
[2] *Ibid.*, cap. 3.

on earth, next and immediately under God, of the Church of England.'

In the book called *The Institution of a Christian Man*,[1] addressed to the King by all the prelates of the realm in A.D. 1537 (of which a revised edition, under a slightly altered title, was issued by the King himself in A.D. 1543),[2] the spiritual character of the Catholic Church, as a Divine Institution under Christ as its only Head, and of its priesthood, as having from the same source the power of order and of voluntary spiritual jurisdiction, was distinctly asserted; ordination to that priesthood was reckoned among the Sacraments; and the Church of England, and other 'particular' Churches, were represented as branches of that Divine Institution: the authority of Princes and Civil Governments over such Churches being explained and insisted upon, as extending to those things only which were properly the subjects of variable human legislation, and as being the necessary source of coercive legal jurisdiction.

The Act which gave the King the title of 'Supreme Head' was repealed in Queen Mary's time, and was not revived by Queen Elizabeth; who herself disliked that style, though she maintained, as jealously as her father, the power of the Crown over the ecclesiastical as well as the civil state. The first Statute of her reign restored (among other things) the Royal Supremacy; and required an oath in acknowledgment of it to be taken by all office-holders, lay and clerical, within the realm. Finding scruples to be entertained by some persons about this, she explained, by an 'Admonition to simple men deceived by malicious,'

---

[1] See 'Formularies of Faith put forth by authority during the reign of Henry the Eighth' (Oxford, 1825), pp. 21, 75-78, and 101-123.
[2] *Ibid.*, pp. 212, 243-249, and 277-289.

appended to her injunctions of A.D. 1559,[1] that nothing was meant by it, except what was 'acknowledged to be due to the most noble Kings of famous memory,' her father and brother; that it was a perverse and malicious misinterpretation, to infer from it, 'that the Kings or Queens of this realm, possessors of the Crown, may challenge authority and power of ministry of divine service in the Church;' and that she 'neither did, nor ever would, challenge any authority other than was challenged and lately used by the said most noble Kings;' 'which' (she said) 'is *and was of ancient time* due to the Imperial Crown of this realm; that is, under God, to have the sovereignty and rule over all manner of persons born within these her realms, . . . of what estate, ecclesiastical or temporal, soever they be, as no other foreign power shall or ought to have any superiority over them.'

This declaration of the Queen was expressly confirmed by Act of Parliament, in A.D. 1562.[2] And it was followed, in the same year, 1562, by that contained in the Thirty-Nine Articles, then agreed to by the Bishops and Clergy of the Church of England in their Convocations. The thirty-eighth Article, 'of the Civil Magistrate,' is in these terms:—

'Where we attribute to the Queen's Majesty the chief Government, by which titles we understand the minds of some slanderous folks to be offended, we give not to our Princes the ministering either of God's Word or of the Sacraments (the which thing the Injunctions also lately set forth by Elizabeth our Queen do most plainly testify): but that only prerogative, which we see to have been given to all godly Princes in Holy Scripture by God Himself, that they should rule all states and

---

[1] Cardwell's *Documentary Annals*, vol. i. pp. 199-201. See Hallam's *Constitutional History*, vol. i. p. 133, note (ed. 1832).

[2] 5 Eliz., cap. 1, sect. 14.

degrees committed to their charge by God, whether they be ecclesiastical or temporal, and restrain with the civil sword the stubborn and evil doers.'

The Church of England, therefore, claimed in 1562 (as she has ever since claimed, for the Thirty-Nine Articles are still part of her law) to have a spiritual mission and authority, a ministry of the Word and Sacraments, neither derived from nor communicable to the State; and she acknowledged in the Head of the State that power only, over ecclesiastical persons and causes, which she believed to be within the rightful province of all Christian Governments. And to this claim on the part of the Church, and this limitation of the rightful Supremacy of the Crown in matters ecclesiastical, the Parliament and State of England also distinctly assented; because eight years afterwards, in the thirteenth year of the Queen, an Act[1] was passed which is still in force, requiring subscription to those Articles from all the Clergy of the Church of England, and making any substantial contradiction of their doctrine incompatible with office in the Church.

3. *Liberties, Law, and Jurisdiction.*

The policy of the Court of Rome, aided by the connivance of our Kings (to whom it was always convenient to be on good terms with so great a moral and political power), and the influence upon our clergy of the Roman Canon Law, had enabled the Popes to establish a large system of practical interference with the liberties of the Church of England; chiefly by means of dispensations, and bulls purporting to grant or to confirm titles, exemptions, privileges,

---

[1] 13 Eliz., cap. 12.

and nominations or elections to Church offices, and by various kinds of pecuniary exactions. Papal bulls of confirmation were constantly obtained, even for things as to which the primary and exclusive power of the Civil Government was most indisputable. Thus, in A.D. 1138, Pope Innocent the Second, in a bull[1] granted to the then Bishop of Lincoln, confirmed the title of the See of Lincoln to lands, granted to it by several kings of England and other donors; and also to a remission by the king of one-third of certain military service, which the Bishop's predecessors had been accustomed to render in Lincoln Castle, and its transfer to the Bishop's castle at Newark. King Henry the Seventh[2] did not disdain to accept from Pope Innocent the Eighth a Bull in confirmation of his Statutory title to the English Crown. All these things were fruitful sources of revenue to the Papal treasury. They were all cut off, as usurpations, by the legislation of Henry the Eighth. The clergy did not recover all that the Pope lost: for 'first-fruits,' and 'tenths,' were given by Parliament to the King. But the relief to the clergy was great.

On another point, still more important, a liberty long withheld was by the Reformation restored to the clergy; not, indeed, in Henry the Eighth's reign, but in that of his son. It had been only by slow degrees that the requirement of celibacy was imposed upon those of the clergy who were not bound by monastic vows. It was attempted in the time of Dunstan: but Pope Gregory the Seventh was the first (A.D. 1074) to forbid the people to attend the

---

[1] Printed by Dugdale from the Cotton MSS. (*Monasticon*, vol. vi. p. 1277; Lincoln Cathedral).
[2] Bacon's *History of Henry VII.*

ministrations of married[1] priests: their sons also were placed under canonical disabilities. In England, marriage had been so general among the clergy, that Pope Pascal the Second, writing to Archbishop Anselm in A.D. 1100, took notice of that fact, and that 'the greater and better part of the English clergy were clergymen's sons;'[2] for which reason he considered, that (as to them) the observance of the Roman rule must be dispensed with. In a Synod held at Westminster under Anselm,[3] two years after the date of this letter (A.D. 1102), Canons were first passed forbidding the English married clergy to live with their wives. In the first year of Edward the Sixth (December 17, 1547), Convocation[4] resolved, that the compulsory celibacy of the clergy ought not any longer to continue; and in the following year (A.D. 1548) an Act of Parliament[5] was passed, taking away 'all laws positive, canons, constitutions, and ordinances, theretofore made by authority of man only, which did prohibit or forbid marriage to any spiritual person or persons.'

In the general system of ecclesiastical law and jurisdiction, administered by the Church Courts in England, no change was made, except that the use (which had arisen out of the Legatine power) of direct citations to the Provincial, passing over the Diocesan Courts, was taken away.[6] By

---

[1] Matt. Paris, A.D. 1074: 'Uxoratos sacerdotes a divino amovit officio, et laicis missas eorum audire interdixit.'

[2] Wilkins, *Concil.*, vol. i. p. 377. Archbishop Lanfranc's Canons of 1076, while endeavouring to put a stop for the future to the marriage of the clergy, expressly permitted those already married, who 'lived in castles and villages,' to retain them.—Johnson's *Laws and Canons* (ed. 1851), vol. ii. p. 18.

[3] Johnson's *Laws and Canons* (ed. 1851), vol. ii. pp. 25, 26.

[4] Wilkins, *Concil.*, vol. iv. pp. 15, 16.

[5] 2 and 3 Edw. VI., cap. 21.   [6] 23 Hen. VIII., cap. 9.

the Statute 'for Restraint of Appeals,'[1] the cognisance of 'all causes testamentary, causes of matrimony and divorce, rights of tithe, oblations, and obventions,' was recognised as 'appertaining, by the goodness of princes of this realm, and by the laws and customs of the same, to the spiritual jurisdiction of this realm.' By the Statute of tithes[2] (A.D. 1535), payment of tithes, etc., was required to be made by all the King's subjects, 'according to the ecclesiastical laws and ordinances of the Church of England, and after the laudable usages and customs of the parishes and other places' in which each man dwelt.

It was not until the present reign that the cognisance of testamentary and matrimonial causes, and the remedies for recovery of tithe rent-charge, were transferred to the temporal Courts. It is an inexcusable mis-statement of fact, to say that, either on account of abuses, or for any other reason, the 'Legislature, early in the present reign, swept most of the ecclesiastical Courts away.'[3] Nothing of the kind has been done. The exercise of coercive jurisdiction has, indeed, been limited to the Courts of the Bishops and Archbishops (who still appoint their own Judges, and retain the power of acting personally in their dioceses); and certain peculiar jurisdictions have been abolished. In other respects the spiritual jurisdiction remains in substance unchanged; its forms of procedure only having been revised and regulated.

In A.D. 1532, the Commons having complained in Parliament of alleged excesses of power by the clergy, the Convocation, pursuant to request from the King, made (under the presidency of Archbishop Warham) the famous 'Submission,' on which the Statute of A.D. 1533,[4] 'for the

---

[1] 24 Hen. VIII., cap. 12.
[2] 27 Hen. VIII., cap. 20.
[3] C. D., p. 51.
[4] 25 Hen. VIII., cap. 19.

Submission of the Clergy,' was grounded; the object being to secure the Royal Supremacy against the introduction, by foreign influence or otherwise, of new ecclesiastical laws not already accepted in the realm, nor assented to by the Crown. The Convocation then promised, for the whole 'priesthood' of England, that no new Canons should thereafter be made without the King's license; and they prayed (as the King had also desired) that a Royal Commission might be issued to revise the English Canon law. The Statute, on both points, followed the Submission; and provided against any canons being made contrary to the King's prerogative royal, or the customs, laws, or statutes of the realm. Commissions for the revision of the existing canons were accordingly issued, both by Henry the Eighth and by Edward the Sixth; but no result followed from them. The Canon law, which had been received and in use here before the time of Henry the Eighth, remained (and still remains) in force in our ecclesiastical Courts, except so far as it may have been varied by later Canons duly made, or by Statute law. The principle on which its authority rested (and still rests) in England, was solemnly declared in the preamble of the Statute of A.D. 1533[1] against Peterpence and Dispensations:—

'This your Grace's realm, recognising no superiority under God but only your Grace, hath been and is free from subjection to any man's laws, but only to such as have been devised, made, and obtained within this realm for the wealth of the same, or to such other as, by the sufferance of your Grace and your progenitors, the people of this your realm have taken at their free liberty, by their own consent, to be used among them, and have bound themselves by long use and custom to the

---

[1] 25 Hen. VIII., cap. 21.

observance of the same; not as to the observance of the laws of any foreign prince, potentate, or prelate, but as the customed and ancient laws of this realm, originally established as laws of the same by the said sufferance, consents, and custom, and none otherwise.'

It is here, perhaps, that the Royal powers of 'Visitation' over the ecclesiastical estate, which in the reigns both of Henry the Eighth and of Queen Elizabeth were founded upon the Supremacy, ought to be mentioned. They were of a judicial nature.[1] The Act of Queen Elizabeth, which revived most[2] of the Statutes repealed by Queen Mary, and restored the Supremacy over all legal jurisdictions, ecclesiastical as well as civil, within the realm, enabled that Queen and her successors to exercise corrective and other powers of visitation by Courts of Commissioners, having authority concurrent with and independent of the ordinary ecclesiastical Courts. Under that Statute, the 'High Commission Court' was established, which continued till the troubles of Charles the First's reign. It was then, with universal approval, abolished; and the Crown was thenceforth disabled from calling into existence any other extraordinary Court of a like nature. But the judicial powers conferred upon Queen Elizabeth, and exercised till 1641, were subject to an important limitation, contained in

---

[1] It has often been represented that the Statute which gave this Visitatorial power to Henry the Eighth (in which heresy was included) annexed to the Crown all such authority as the Pope had or claimed to have. I am unable to discover any ground for such an interpretation. The power given is only to visit, and correct, all such errors, etc. 'which *by any manner of spiritual authority or jurisdiction ought, or may lawfully,* be reformed,' etc. It was a large power, and might have been much abused; but the Popes claimed more. (26 Hen. VIII., cap. 1.)

[2] The Act just mentioned (26 Hen. VIII., cap. 1), was *not* revived.

the 40th section of the Statute[1] which gave them :—viz., that no Court of the Queen's Commissioners should have power to adjudge anything to be heresy which had not previously been so adjudged, either by one or more of the first four General Councils, or by some other General Council founding its determination upon express words of Holy Scripture; or which might not afterwards be determined to be heresy 'by the High Court of Parliament, with the assent of the Clergy in their Convocation.' The rule, therefore, for the determination of matters of faith, was to be taken from those ecclesiastical decrees which had always been accepted as of authority in the Church; and if new legislation concerning such questions should at any time be found necessary, it was not to take place without the Synodical consent of the Church of England, given in the proper constitutional manner by the Clergy in Convocation.

4. *Appeals.*

The practice of Appeals to Rome, which came in under King Stephen, was put an end to by the Statute passed for that purpose in A.D. 1532.[2] That Statute was a necessary consequence of the King's Supreme 'Headship,' which the Clergy, in the Convocations of both Provinces, had acknowledged in the preceding year: and the principle on which it was founded was expressly re-affirmed in A.D. 1534 by both Convocations,[3] by a Resolution (passed unanimously in the Northern Province, and in the Lower House of Canterbury by a majority of 34 to 4), 'that the Pope of Rome hath no greater jurisdiction given him in Holy Scripture by

---

[1] 1 Eliz., cap. 1.   [2] 24 Hen. VIII., cap. 12.
[3] Wilkins, *Concil.*, vol. iii. pp. 769, 782.

God in this Kingdom of England than any other Foreign Bishop.' So far, the usage of the Church of England was brought back to what it had been before King Stephen's time. This being done, the future course of appeals had also to be regulated: and this was, at first, attempted by the same Statute, which made the decisions of the Archbishop's Court final, except when the King's interest might be concerned, and in that case gave a further appeal to Convocation. The unsuitableness of such a body as Convocation for judicial functions, and the reasons (equally obvious) for giving to private persons the same right of appeal which was thought necessary for the King, led to a change in the next year (A.D. 1533); when provision was made[1] for a final appeal, in all cases, from the Court of the Archbishop to the 'King in Chancery;' that is, to Judges, nominated or delegated from time to time by commissions issued in the King's name out of the Court of Chancery. These Courts of Commissioners acquired the name of 'Delegates;' and that system of Appeals continued in use till the reign of William the Fourth; when the authority of the Courts of Delegates in ecclesiastical causes was transferred by Statute[2] to the Judicial Committee of the Privy Council.

There was very little, if any, difference in principle between the Appeal to the 'King in Chancery,' given by the Act of 1533, and the old custom of the Church of England before the allowance of Appeals to Rome, as declared by the eighth article of the Constitutions of Clarendon. The

[1] 25 Hen. VIII., cap. 19.
[2] 2 and 3 Will. IV., cap. 92, and 3 and 4 Will. IV., cap. 42. This change was made on the recommendation of a Royal Commission appointed in 1830 to inquire into the Ecclesiastical Courts, among whom were the then Archbishop of Canterbury and Bishop of London, and all the ecclesiastical judges of any repute.

procedure, also, under that Statute, was (in form as well as substance) very nearly identical with that which had prevailed before the Reformation as to 'Free Chapels,' exempt from ordinary ecclesiastical jurisdiction;[1] which were always subject to Visitation by the King's Chancellor (personally or by commissary), with an Appeal to the King, by Commission of Review. It is needless to add, that there cannot possibly be any difference in principle between an Appeal to the King in Chancery, given by Statute in A.D. 1533, and an Appeal to the King in Council, given by Statute in A.D. 1832: the latter may, or may not, be a better Court than the former; but there cannot be any difference in principle.

5. *Bishoprics and Benefices.*

The law of the Church of England as to presentation and admission to Capitular and parochial benefices, and as to rights of patronage, and the remedies for their disturbance, was not altered at the time of the Reformation. But a Statute was passed in A.D. 1533,[2] to secure to the Crown the right of nomination to all English Bishoprics. It did not prescribe any new course or form of proceeding for that purpose, or for the consequent acts, from election to consecration. The Royal license for election, with a letter missive naming the person whom the King desired to have elected, was still to go, 'as of old time had been accustomed:' but it was made obligatory, under heavy penalties, to elect the person nominated by the King. A later Statute,[3] passed in Edward the Sixth's reign, to abolish the form of election, and to make all Bishoprics once more (as our law-books say

---

[1] See Sir Matthew Hale's *Treatise on the Supremacy*, p. 18.
[2] 25 Hen. VIII., cap. 20.   [3] 1 Edw. VI., cap. 2.

they were before the time of King John) donatives of the Crown by letters patent, was among the Acts repealed by Queen Mary, and not revived by Queen Elizabeth. The Act of 1533 was revived: and by that Statute appointments to Bishoprics are governed to this day. I shall consider elsewhere the objections which have been often made to the principle of an election in form, which is not free in substance: for the present, it is enough to observe, that the direct nomination of Bishops by the Crown, which was law in Edward the Sixth's time, was but a recurrence to an ancient usage; and that, under the manner of elections which prevailed from King John's time till the Reformation, the general (if not invariable) practice had been, for the King to recommend, and for the electors to choose the person recommended. The constitution of the Episcopacy of the Church of England was therefore not altered in substance by the Statute of 1533, whatever exception may be taken to the penalties, or to the form.

In Henry the Eighth's time, upon the suppression of the greater monasteries, six Conventual Churches (those of Westminster, Gloucester, Bristol, Peterborough, Chester, and Oxford) were made Cathedrals of an equal number of new Bishoprics, then first erected. All the Bishops of those new Sees were placed, in all respects, upon the same footing with the old: the Conventual bodies of those cities (as well as of Canterbury, Durham, Winchester, and several other old Sees) being then converted into Deans and Chapters. In the same reign the See of Sodor and Man, previously independent, was brought within the Province of York. Westminster soon afterwards ceased to be a separate Bishopric. Seven more English Bishoprics have been erected within the last fifty years, most of them quite recently, and an eighth is about to be erected. It is unnecessary to say, that such additions to the number of Bishoprics are not only consistent with the identity of the Church, but result naturally from its strength and growth.

6. *Bishops in Parliament.*

The Bishops of the new Sees erected in Henry the Eighth's time sat (like those of the older Sees) in the House of Lords; as the Abbots, into whose places all but one of them came, had done before them. It was otherwise with the Bishop of Sodor and Man; the lands with which that See was endowed being held, not of the King directly, but of a subject, who nominated the Bishop, till 1829, when the lordship of the Isle of Man was purchased by the Crown. By an Act passed during the present reign, to prevent an increase in the number of lords spiritual upon every creation of a new Bishopric, the title of the greater number of the Bishops to sit in the House of Lords has been so far modified, as to suspend the writs of summons to those newly consecrated, until they come, by succession in order of seniority, within the limited number; the Bishops of the new Sees being admitted, on those terms, to sit like the rest.

If I here take notice of a reference which I find (in the book called *The Case for Disestablishment*) to King Henry the Eighth's Statute 'for placing the Lords,'[1] it is rather because it may illustrate the nature and value of the 'historical argument,' into the service of which such matter has been pressed, than for any other reason. That Statute[2]

---

[1] *C.D.*, p. 39. The same chapter of that book contains references to many of the Statutes which I have mentioned; to which the account of those Statutes here given is a sufficient answer.

[2] 31 Hen. VIII., cap. 10.

regulated the places and the precedence of all the lords, temporal as well as spiritual. So far as it gave certain great officers of State (if peers) precedence over others of the same or higher rank, whether spiritual or temporal, it did nothing strange or new. It is quoted only because it placed Lord Cromwell and his successors (if there had been any) in the post of Vicegerent 'for the good exercise of the most Royal dignity and office of Supreme Head on earth under God of the Church of England,' on the same form or bench in the House of Lords with the Bishops, and above the Archbishop of Canterbury. Whatever might be 'the Royal dignity and office of Supreme Head,' nothing was added to it by that ceremonial honour. No place could be fitter than the House of Lords for the external recognition, in any form and manner which pleased the King, of the Royal Supremacy 'over all persons, ecclesiastical as well as civil,' within his dominions. So much as this was, no doubt, meant; but certainly nothing more.

7. *Doctrine, etc.*

The legislation of King Henry the Eighth's reign, so far as it related to doctrine or worship, had in it little or nothing of a reforming character. It was contained chiefly in two Statutes; that of A.D. 1533-34,[1] 'for punishment of heresy,' which confirmed the persecuting Acts of Richard the Second and Henry the Fifth against the Lollards, and that of A.D. 1539[2] (the Act of the 'Six Articles'), for 'abolishing diversity of opinions;' which object it sought to obtain (with 'the consent,' recited in the preamble, 'of the Clergy in their Convocations,') by enforcing under severe penalties

---

[1] 25 Hen. VIII., cap. 14. [2] 31 Hen. VIII., cap. 14.

the doctrine of Transubstantiation, the practice of refusing the cup to the laity, clerical celibacy, vows of chastity and widowhood, private masses, and auricular confession. Both these Statutes were repealed[1] in the first year of Edward the Sixth; and were, of course, never re-enacted.

There was also indirect legislation, bearing on the same class of subjects, by two other Statutes of Henry the Eighth's reign; the one of A.D. 1539,[2] giving the force of law to all the King's Proclamations, past or future (not as to religion only, but on all subjects whatever), which might neither affect rights of property, nor be at variance with any existing law or custom of the realm; the other of A.D. 1542-43,[3] for 'the advancement of true religion, and the abolishment of the contrary.' This latter Statute expressly confirmed the Act of the Six Articles, and placed the use of the English Bible by the common people under various severe restrictions; proscribing Tyndale's translation, as 'crafty, false, and untrue;' and prohibiting books 'against the Holy Sacrament of the Altar,' or in favour of Anabaptist opinions. It also prohibited under penalties any contradiction, by books or otherwise, of any 'doctrine,' or 'godly instructions or determinations,' which had been since A.D. 1540, or at any time afterwards during the King's life might be, set forth by the King. The force of law may have been in this way given, during the short time while that Act remained on the Statute Book, to 'the King's Book,'[4] published in A.D. 1543 under the title of *A necessary Doctrine or Erudition of a Christian Man*, which (as already stated) was a revised edition of the

---

[1] By 1 Edw. VI., cap. 12.
[2] 31 Hen. VIII., cap. 8, and see 34 and 35 Hen. VIII., cap. 23.
[3] 34 and 35 Hen. VIII., cap. 1.
[4] 'Formularies of Faith' (Oxford ed. 1825), p. 212.

Bishops' book of 1537. Neither of those books contained any substantially new doctrine; they mitigated some of the abuses and superstitions associated in the popular mind with those usages and practices, which it was reserved for later reigns to abolish; and they vindicated and explained, as has been elsewhere stated, the Royal Supremacy, and the position of the Church of England as independent of Rome.

I am not aware that anything else of a doctrinal character, except the First Book of Homilies (published in A.D. 1547 with full ecclesiastical as well as Royal sanction), was set forth by King Henry the Eighth's authority after A.D. 1540. The powers given, both by the Proclamations Act of 1539 and by the Statute of 1542-43, were of a character which no reasonable man could justify, either from an ecclesiastical or from a civil point of view; and they might have been (though I do not know that they were in fact) seriously abused. One of the first and best things done in Edward the Sixth's reign was to repeal[1] both those Statutes; they were never afterwards revived. The law, doctrine, or constitution of the Church of England is not now, and never has been practically, affected by either of them.

All that was done under Edward the Sixth, as to doctrine and ritual, was to restore Communion in both kinds to the laity; to remove image-worship, and some other observances deemed superstitious; and to settle, for the public services of the Church, one book of Common Prayer in the English tongue. The book of Common Prayer afterwards underwent several revisions; and controversies have been raised about it, which make it convenient to reserve that subject for a separate chapter.

[1] 1 Edw. VI., cap. 12.

The restoration of Communion in both kinds to the laity was unanimously agreed to by Convocation[1] in A.D. 1547; so reverting to the primitive Christian usage which had prevailed universally in England, as elsewhere, till the beginning of the twelfth century,[2] and the departure from which was never authoritatively sanctioned till the Council of Constance, A.D. 1415.[3] A Statute passed in the same year gave to the reform, so synodically determined on, the force of law.

There has been no later legislation on any subject connected with the doctrine of the Church of England, except the Statute of A.D. 1570, enforcing the Thirty-nine Articles agreed to eight years before by the Convocation of A.D. 1562. Of those Articles I need here say no more, than that their doctrinal determinations were on a number of points raised by the controversies of that time, of which by far the greater number had been open questions in the Church of Rome itself (so far as creeds, catechisms, tests, and terms of Communion are concerned), until the Council of Trent,[4] of which the first Session was held after the commencement, and the last towards the close, of the English Reformation.

[1] Wilkins, *Concil.*, vol. iv. pp. 15, 16.

[2] Mr. Lewis (*Reformation Settlement*, p. 81, note), quotes correctly the following from Cardinal Bona, a Roman theologian of high authority:—' Always and everywhere, from the very beginning of the Church till the twelfth century, the faithful communicated under the species both of bread and of wine; and it was by degrees, at the beginning of that century, that the use of the cup began to be discontinued, the greater number of Bishops forbidding it to the people from fear of irreverence,' etc. (Bona, *Rerum Liturgicarum*, lib. ii. cap. 18, p. 444, ed. 1671).

[3] The decree for this purpose was passed in the thirteenth Session of that Council.

[4] The Council of Trent assembled 13th December 1545, and was brought to a close 3d December 1563.

The only points authoritatively dealt with by earlier mediæval Councils were some of those relating to the Sacrament of the Lord's Supper; these also had been open until the Council of Constance, A.D. 1414,[1] unless the Confession[2] with which the Acts of the Fourth Lateran Council (A.D. 1215) begin ought to be regarded as equivalent to a formal declaration of the dogma of Transubstantiation; as some have thought it.

[1] The Council of Constance, in its eighth Session, condemned the tenets of Wicliff; the five first charges against whom were (in substance), that he denied the doctrines of Transubstantiation and of the Mass.

[2] This 'Confession' was not a Synodical determination of the Council, as on any controverted point, but was recited by the assembled divines, at the outset of their proceedings, after the manner of a creed; and it contained, among other things, an enunciation of that doctrine, the word 'Transubstantiated' being used.

CHAPTER III

THE BOOK OF COMMON PRAYER

THE use of the first Book of Common Prayer (A.D. 1549), and of the Second Book (A.D. 1552), was enjoined by the Acts of Uniformity,[1] passed in those years. Under Elizabeth, the use of the Prayer Book of 1552 was restored, with exceptions which (but for controversies recently raised as to one of them) would be insignificant.

It has often been asserted, by Roman Catholic and other controversialists who impute what they call 'Erastianism' to the Church of England, and also by some within the Church of England itself, who appear to think this no reproach, that the authority which settled the Books of Common Prayer, both of 1549 and of 1552, was Royal and Parliamentary only, without any Synodical concurrence of the Church, as represented in Convocation. On subjects such as this, even the best and fairest men are apt to be swayed in their examination of historical evidence (unconsciously, no doubt) by the inclination of their own opinions; and no one can complain of the opponents of the Church, if they accept somewhat easily the conclusions of partisans within the Church which seem to tell for their argument. There have been few more accomplished or more excellent

[1] 2 and 3 Edw. VI., cap. 1, and 5 and 6 Edw. VI., cap. 1.

men in the Church of England, within our own generation, than Arthur Stanley, Dean of Westminster, whom I had the privilege to number among my friends. But he was eccentric in his ecclesiastical opinions; and, although in intention as honest as any man possibly could be, his critical faculty upon questions of this kind was not exact or dispassionate. He is quoted[1] in the *Case for Disestablishment* as an authority, as to 'the extent to which the State has regulated the doctrines, rites, and ceremonies of the Established Church without any reference to Convocation.' So far as relates to the successive revisions of the Book of Common Prayer, I propose in this chapter to state the true facts, and the evidence bearing upon them. Dean Stanley himself was satisfied (though some other respectable controversialists,[2] equally inclined to magnify the province of the State in matters of religion, have not been) that 'the first Act of Uniformity, in the reign of Edward the Sixth, had the sanction of Convocation;' but (he said) 'the second Act of the same reign was passed without that sanction, and so also was the Act of Elizabeth, and the Prayer Book of James the First.'

1. *The Registers of Convocation.*

If the Registers of Convocation had been kept during

[1] *C. D.*, p. 52.
[2] Heylyn, who desired to find a justification for the proceedings of Archbishop Laud and Charles the First in the matter of the Scotch Liturgy, adopted (in his *Cyprianus Anglicus*, p. 307) the opinion that Edward the Sixth 'durst not trust his Clergy' with any voice as to the *First* Book (that of 1549), 'but acted sovereignly therein of his own authority; not venturing that Book to his Convocation, but only giving it the strength of an Act of Parliament.' As to the Second Book, he appears to have thought otherwise.

the reign of Edward the Sixth, so as to show what business was done at each sitting, there could have been no question as to the concurrence or non-concurrence of that body in the settlement of the Prayer Book of 1549, or the revision of 1552. But they were not so kept. Their evidence goes no farther than to show that Convocation was sitting, both in 1548-49 and 1551-52, at times when that particular business might have been before it. Fuller and Heylyn, writers of the seventeenth century, examined those Registers before the Fire of London, in which some of them (those of the Upper House) were destroyed. Fuller[1] says: 'The journals of the Convocation in this King's reign I have carefully perused, which are no better than blank paper; containing only the names of the members therein daily meeting, without any matter of moment (yea, any matter at all), registered to be performed by them.' Heylyn[2] says: 'The Acts of the Convocation' [of 1552] 'were so ill kept, that there remained nothing on record touching their proceedings, except it be the names of such of the Bishops as came thither to adjourn the House.' To infer that, because nothing was recorded, nothing was done, would be very unreasonable, even if there had been no proof to the contrary: but there is proof to the contrary, not only as to other matters, but as to this matter itself. I will state, as shortly as I can, its nature and effect; and first, as to the Book of 1549.

2. *King Edward's First Prayer Book.*

'The Papists' (I quote from Strype) 'were very angry

---

[1] Fuller's *Appeal*, part ii. p. 78 (quoted by Archbishop Wake, *State of the Church and Clergy of England*, p. 578). *Church History*, pp. 420, 421.

[2] *Hist. of the Reformation*, p. 121.

to see their old superstitious ceremonies laid aside: and those that came after laboured all they could to asperse and enervate it, by calling the religion a *parliamentary religion* (so Dr. Hill), and the Church of England, thus reformed, a *parliament Church*. As though it were forged and framed in Parliament by secular men, and that ecclesiastics, whose chief business it had been, had not been consulted therein. But in truth and reality it was not so. For the consideration of this Book of Common Prayer, together with other matters of religion, was committed first of all to divers learned divines; and what they had concluded upon was offered the Convocation. And, after all this, the Parliament approved and gave it their ratification. The which is more fully showed and declared by the pen of a very knowing and learned man.'[1]

The 'knowing and learned man' to whom Strype here refers was Dr. Abbot, Archbishop of Canterbury under James the First, who wrote thus,[2] in answer to Dr. Hill:—

'The religion which was then, and is now, established in England is drawn out of the fountains of the word of God, and from the purest order of the Primitive Church. Which, for the ordinary exercise thereof, when it had been collected into the Book of Common Prayer by the pains and labour of many learned men and of mature judgment, it was afterwards confirmed by the Upper and Lower House. Yet not so, but that the more material points were disputed and debated in the Convocation, by men of both parties; and might further have been discussed, so long as any popish divine had ought reasonably to say. . . . And then, it being intended to add to ecclesiastical decision the corroboration of secular government, according to the ancient custom of this kingdom (as appeareth by record from the time of King Edward the Third), the Parliament, which is the most honourable Court of Christendom, did ratify the same.'

---

[1] *Eccl. Memorials*, vol. ii. part i. p. 137.
[2] Dr. George Abbot, *Reasons which Dr. Hill hath brought for the Upholding of Papistry*, etc. (Oxford, 1601), p. 104 (in answer to Dr. Hill's third 'Reason').

Archbishop Abbot was born in 1562, only thirteen years after the time to which this circumstantial statement relates. He could not, of course, be a witness to the facts from personal knowledge, but he was thrown, by the circumstances of his life, into close intercourse with those in whose time these things happened. His predecessor in the See of Canterbury, Bancroft, who was ten years older, and so much nearer the time, in a Sermon preached at 'Paul's Cross' against the Puritans, in A.D. 1588, stated, that King Edward's First Communion Book 'was carefully prepared, and confirmed by a Synod.' And these statements are confirmed by evidence of the highest authority, contemporary with the events themselves.

Preparations for the establishment of 'a convenient and uniform order of service in the Church'[1] had been made towards the close of Henry the Eighth's reign: and in A.D. 1547 the Lower House of the Convocation of Canterbury presented an address[2] to the Upper House, asking, that 'no Statutes concerning matters of religion and causes ecclesiastical should pass without their assent;' and also, that 'the books' (which they understood or supposed to have been prepared) 'might be seen and perused by them, for a better expedition of Divine service to be set forth accordingly.' The Convocation of 1547 was, therefore, favourable to the work: and there could be no reason of prudence or policy, practice or precedent, for refusing their request, so far (at all events) as 'the books' were concerned.

The first Act of Uniformity passed through Parliament in January 1548-49. In the summer of that year the Princess Mary (afterwards Queen) objected to the use of the

---

[1] Wilkins, *Concil.*, vol. iv. pp. 15, 16.
[2] Cardwell's *Synodalia*, vol. ii. pp. 419-421.

English Communion Service, and wrote to the King (22d June 1549) that 'the law made by Parliament was not worthy the name of a law.' The King's Council dictated an answer to that letter, to be communicated to the Princess by Dr. Hopton, her chaplain; in which they said, 'The fault is great in any subject to disallow a law of the King, a law of the realm, by long study, free disputation, and *uniform determination of the whole clergy* consulted, debated, and concluded.'[1]

In the month following (July 1549) the King addressed a circular letter[2] to the Bishops, requiring them to take active measures for putting the Act of Uniformity in force. The Book of Common Prayer is stated in that document to be set forth 'by the agreement and assent,' not only of the nobility and Commons and Bishops in Parliament, but also 'of all others the learned men of this our realm in their Synods and Convocations.'

In the same year, discontent manifested itself against the Book in Devonshire; and the King gave an answer[3] to a petition from that county, in which he stated, that the Book was '*by the whole clergy agreed*, yea by the Bishops of the realm devised;' and reproved the discontented, as opposing themselves to 'the determination of the Bishops *and all the clergy.*'

It is not wonderful that evidence such as this convinced even Dean Stanley of the assent of Convocation to the Book of 1549.

---

[1] Foxe's *Acts and Monuments*, vol. ii. p. 45.

[2] The copy sent to Bonner (still at that time Bishop of London) is in Wilkins, *Concil.*, vol. iv. p. 35; another copy, sent to Thirlby, Bishop of Westminster, is quoted by Strype, from the Register of that prelate (Strype, *Eccl. Mem.*, vol. ii. pp. 211, 212).

[3] Foxe's *Acts and Monuments*, vol. ii. p. 14.

3. *King Edward's Second Book.*

As the preparation of the Book of 1549 was preceded or accompanied by proceedings on the subject in Convocation, so also was its revision, in A.D. 1550.

Heylyn, who saw the Registers which were afterwards destroyed in the Fire of London, found in them a note of a debate in the Upper House, and a communication by them to the Lower, of which he gives the following account:—[1]

'In the Convocation which began in 1550, the first debate amongst the prelates was of such doubts as had arisen about some things contained in the Common Prayer Book, and more particularly touching such points as were retained, and such as had been abrogated, by the rules thereof; the forms of words used at the giving of the Bread; and the different manner of administering the Holy Sacrament; which being signified unto the Prolocutor and the rest of the Clergy, who had received somewhat in charge about it the day before, answer was made, that they had not yet sufficiently considered of the points proposed, but that they would give their Lordships some account thereof in the following Session. But what account was given, appears not in the Acts of that Convocation; of which there is nothing left on record but this very passage.'

It is certainly not a reasonable inference from this state of the (now destroyed) Register, either that the Clergy of the Lower House were unwilling to take that part in the business opened to them, to which they had been expressly called by the message of the Bishops, or that their promise to proceed with it in the following Session was not fulfilled. The work of revision was conducted (as that of

[1] Heylyn, *Hist. of Reformation*, p. 107.

1548-49 had been) by a Commission of Bishops and divines; and the result of their labours (subject to amendment) was printed in September 1551.[1] The Convocation sat on the 14th October and the 5th November 1550, and again, *de die in diem*, from the 24th January 1551-52 till the middle of April 1552,[2] when it and the Parliament were both dissolved. The Bill for the Second Act of Uniformity, giving the force of law to this Revised Book as finally settled, was not brought into the House of Lords till the end of March or the beginning of April; it passed that House, and was sent down to the Commons, on the 6th of April 1552. The Convocation, therefore, had very abundant time and opportunity to consider and approve the Book printed in September 1551, with such amendments as may have been made or suggested in it, before any Bill was introduced into Parliament; and, in the absence of evidence to the contrary (of which there is none), the reasonable presumption is, that they did so. All the evidence which there is supports that presumption. Archbishop Bancroft, in the Sermon[3] at 'Paul's Cross' already spoken of, described the Revised Book as 'published with such approbation as that it was accounted the work of God.' The next Convocation (that of 1552-53) agreed to the Forty-two Articles[4] of Religion of that year; one of which (the thirty-fifth) declared the Book

---

[1] See Joyce's *England's Sacred Synod*, pp. 478-479.

[2] Wilkins, *Concil.*, vol. iv. (A.D. 1551-52).

[3] P. 53 (*Miscellaneous Sermons*, bound under letters B A, in British Museum).

[4] Cardwell's *Synodalia*, vol. i. pp. 1, 15 (where they are both Latin and English). These Articles, in English, with the Catechism prefixed to them in the original print of A.D. 1553, and a facsimile of the original title-page, are also in the Parker Society's *Two Liturgies*, etc. (Cambridge, 1844), pp. 486, 526.

of 1552, together with the Ordination service at the same time set forth, to be agreeable to sound doctrine, and 'therefore to be received, approved, and recommended to God's people, with all readiness of mind and thanksgiving, by all faithful members of the Church of England, and especially by the ministers of the Word.' The Book is described in that Article as 'recently delivered to the Church of England by the authority of the King and Parliament, and containing the manner and form of Prayer, and of the administration of the Sacraments, in the Church of England,'—a description accurate in fact, and agreeable to the respect paid in those times to the authority so mentioned: but certainly not implying that Convocation had borne no part in the work. If Synodical assent had been formally wanting, the adoption of that Article itself would have been enough to give it;—it proves, that there could not have been any reason, founded upon any supposed hostility of the Clergy to that revision, for not following up, in the usual manner, the invitation to co-operate in the work which had been given them in 1550: nor is it at all consistent with probability, that if any such slight had been put upon them, the next Convocation, which assembled in the year after the Second Act of Uniformity was passed, would have in that solemn manner recorded its approval.

These Forty-two Articles were published in 1553[1] (in the same volume with a Catechism, having a history of its own, not material to be here stated) by the King's authority.

---

[1] The state of the controversy and evidence concerning them is fairly summed up by Dr. Cardwell in his note to *Synodalia*, vol. i. pp. 3-7. But the Parker Society's republication of the text of 1553 best exhibits the internal evidence.

On the title-page[1] of that volume the Articles (not the Catechism) are expressly stated to have been 'agreed upon by the Bishops and other learned and godly men in the last Convocation of London in the year 1552 ;' and this is repeated in the sub-title,[2] at the head of the Articles themselves. Some writers, extending to those Articles a question which was raised, as to the 'Catechism' only, in the first Convocation[3] of Queen Mary's reign, have sought to throw doubt upon the accuracy of that statement; suggesting that nothing more may have been meant by it, than that the 'learned and godly men' referred to acted under some delegation of power from the Convocation of 1552-53. This notion was examined, and justly rejected, by Archbishop Wake;[4] who proved that these Articles were not only agreed to, but were subscribed by the clergy present in the Convocation of 1552-53 itself, by an express statement to that effect, positively made on one side, and admitted on the other, in a public controversy as to the lawfulness of the prescribed rites and ceremonies, which arose a few years later, in 1566, and to which some of the clergy who had subscribed those Articles in 1552-53 were parties. And when the Convocation of 1562 entered upon the business which ended in the settlement of the present Thirty-nine Articles of the Church of England, the Prolocutor of the Lower House, on its behalf, asked the Upper House to authorise the delivery, to a committee

---

[1] Parker Society's *Two Liturgies*, etc., p. 486.   [2] *Ibid.*, p. 526.
[3] Foxe's *Acts and Monuments*, fol. 1460. Wilkins, *Concil.*, vol. iv. p. 88.
[4] *State of the Church and Clergy of England*, pp. 599, 600. And see Strype's *Memorials of Cranmer*, part ii. chap. xxvii., and Appendix No. lxiv. Also Parker Society's *Miscellaneous Writings and Letters of Cranmer* (Cambridge, 1846), vol. ii. pp. 439-441, and note (*b*) to p. 441.

which the Lower House had appointed, for examination, of 'the Articles lately set forth *by the Synod of London* in the time of King Edward the Sixth :'[1] to which request Archbishop Parker, as President, assented. The Convocation of 1562 could not have been ignorant whether they were so set forth or not.

It is, therefore, certain, that the Revised Book of 1552 received Synodical authority before the end of Edward the Sixth's reign and the accession of Queen Mary: nor can I see room for any reasonable doubt that it received that authority, not by way of ratification only in 1552-53, but also before the promulgation and Parliamentary sanction of the Book in the preceding year. I have thought it worth while to exhibit, both as to this and as to the First Book, the exact state of the existing evidence; which appears to me to be of much greater importance than opinions or doubts of writers of the seventeenth and eighteenth centuries, such as Heylyn, or Fuller, or Collier, and those who may have followed them in later times. If it were a question of the comparative weight due to opinions, I should not myself consider any of those writers of greater weight than Archbishop Wake, or Strype; but it is really a question, not of opinions, but of reasonable deduction from evidence; which (as far as it goes) is all on one side. To me, it is fully sufficient to prove the affirmative conclusions as to both Books, which I have stated: while, in support of the contrary view, that both or either of King Edward the Sixth's Books had Parliamentary authority only, and not that of Convocation, there is nothing beyond the absence of entries decisive of the question, one way or the other, in the

---

[1] Wilkins, *Concil.*, vol. iv. p. 76.

Registers of Convocation; as to which, all that is necessary has been said.

4. *Queen Elizabeth's Book of* 1559.

It is insisted, however, that at all events Queen Elizabeth's Act of Uniformity of 1559 (which restored, with three slight qualifications, the use of the Book of 1552) was an Act of the Civil power alone, without Synodical concurrence. Those who lay stress on this either forget what had taken place in Queen Mary's time, or attribute more importance than is really their due to the variations in the Book of 1559, and the Statute of that year, from the Book of 1552.

In the first year of Queen Mary's reign an Act[1] had been passed by Parliament alone—without any sort of ecclesiastical concurrence, not even that of the Pope, for the reconciliation with Rome was of later date—for restoring throughout the Queen's dominions 'all such divine service and administration of the Sacraments as were commonly used in the realm of England in the last year of the reign of King Henry the Eighth,' and prohibiting the use of 'any other kind or order of divine service or administration of Sacraments;' many of the Statutes, as to religion, of the two preceding reigns, being at the same time repealed. The Reforming Bishops and clergy were, soon afterwards, deprived of their Sees and benefices, and some of them were put to death; adherents of the Papacy being put into their places. In 1554, when the Queen had married Philip of Spain and made him partner of her Crown, the kingdom was reconciled to the Pope, under a 'Submission' embodied

---

[1] 1 Mary, Sess. 2, cap. 2.

in an Act of Parliament,[1] more abject and degrading than anything which had taken place in England since King John's time. It was the necessary result of this counter-revolution that, on the accession of Elizabeth, all the places in Convocation were filled by strong Papists;[2] and to reverse the Act which prohibited the use of the Prayer Book of 1552 by the same authority which passed it, that of Parliament alone, was a measure not even in form derogatory to the independent spiritual rights of the Church of England, while it was practically rendered necessary by the circumstances of the time. If this had been done without changing anything in that Book, no question (I suppose) could ever have been raised about it. But it was thought desirable, after consulting some leading divines, to restore the Book of 1552, not absolutely, but with a few (and those very slight) qualifications; and it is out of these only, that the question, such as it is, arises.

To represent Queen Elizabeth's Act of Uniformity as having imposed upon the Church a new Book of Common Prayer, because of those variations from the Book of 1552, is to lose sight of substance in accident. What were they?—First, there was a wise and charitable omission of a special 'suffrage' against the Bishop of Rome, which had been in the Litany of 1552; secondly, there was a combination of the words of the two Books, of 1549 and 1552, in the delivery of the Consecrated Elements to Communicants at the Holy Communion; and, lastly, there was

---

[1] 1 and 2 Phil. and Mary, cap. 8.
[2] See the Acts of the Convocation of the first year of Queen Elizabeth, in Cardwell's *Synodalia*, vol. ii. pp. 493, 494, affirming unequivocally the doctrines of Transubstantiation, the sacrifice of the Mass, and the Papal Supremacy.

a proviso for retaining, until 'other order should be taken by the Queen's authority,' those 'ornaments of the Church and the ministers thereof' which had been in use under the Act of 1549, some of which had been altered or discontinued by the Book and Act of 1552.[1] For the present purpose it is not material, whether, as to these 'ornaments,' or any of them, 'other order' was, or was not, afterwards taken by the Queen's authority; that (as is well known) has been the subject of judicial decisions on the one hand, and of controversial arguments against those decisions on the other. If the judicial decisions are regarded, the exact order, as to these matters, of the Book of 1552 was, in 1566, re-established in all the parish churches of the kingdom. Those who pay no regard to such judicial decisions are of opinion that, in theory (though it was not so in practice), the order of 1549 was permanently restored by the Statute of 1559. In either way, the variations of 1559 brought nothing into the Service Book which had not, either in 1548-49, or in 1551-52, been there before. All the rest of the Book remained as it was; no doctrinal question was involved in the alteration of the Litany, or in that of the Communion Service; and, as to the 'ornaments of the minister,' the use of those directed by the Book of 1552 continued, practically, to prevail in the Church, and was afterwards, by the canons of 1604, expressly enjoined. Variations of such a nature, even if made with less regularity than might have been requisite in ordinary times, could neither affect the general Ecclesiastical position of the Church, nor bring in a new principle. Such as they were, they were universally acquiesced in during the whole of Queen Elizabeth's reign; and, if to any mind their Synod-

[1] 1 Eliz., cap. 2.

ical ratification might still appear necessary, that authority was added to the Book containing them (subject to what has been said as to 'ornaments'), by the Canons passed in 1603-4.

5. *Changes in* 1604.

The trivial changes, made in the Prayer Book after the Hampton Court Conference, had the authority, not only of King James the First's Ratification and Proclamation,[1] but also of the Canons of the following year,[2] which directed the strict observance of the Prayer Book so altered. Parliamentary authority they had none, unless by a strained and doubtful construction of the 26th clause of Queen Elizabeth's Act of Uniformity.

6. *The Book of* 1662.

The last Revision of the Prayer Book, after the Restoration, was entirely the work of Convocation, as appears on the face of the Act of Uniformity of 1662.[3] The Book, as then altered, was sent by Convocation to the King, and by the King, exactly as he had received it from them, to Parliament, with a recommendation that it should be appointed

---

[1] Cardwell's *History of Conferences*, etc. (Oxford, 1841), pp. 217, 225. The King's 'Ratification,' in which all the particular alterations and 'explanations' made by Archbishop Whitgift and his brother Commissioners are specified, is dated the 9th February 1603-4: the Proclamation, enjoining the use of the Book so altered, is dated the 5th March following.

[2] Cardwell's *Synodalia*, vol. i. pp. 164, *et seq.* (see Canon 14, *ibid.*, p. 171). The Convocation which passed these Canons entered upon the consideration of them on the 2d May 1604, and finished it later in the same year. (*Synodalia*, vol. ii. pp. 587-590.)

[3] 14 Car. II., cap. 4.

to be used in all the Churches of the Kingdom. Not one word of it was changed during its passage through Parliament,[1] except two or three clerical errors of the transcriber, which, when discovered, were corrected by certain Bishops, specially deputed by Convocation for that purpose. The House of Commons, while asserting unanimously its right (which no man did or could deny) to debate the matter of 'the amendments made by the Convocation in the Book of Common Prayer, and sent down by the Lords to that House' (if it had thought fit so to order), resolved,[2] by a majority of ninety-six to ninety, not to exercise that right. Dean Stanley said, that 'the Act itself never came before Convocation.' Of course it did not, and could not; Bills depending in Parliament are always debated there, and not elsewhere; and when passed they are law.

No further legislation affecting the Church of England in any matter of doctrine or ritual has taken place since 1662, except some relaxations of the Acts of Uniformity, and a new Lectionary or Table of Lessons, all agreed to by Convocation. The 'political services' (all but one now discontinued) never constituted part of the Liturgy of the Church of England. They were (like the observance of days of public fasting or thanksgiving, and prayers for particular occasions, under Orders in Council) examples of that deference and respect to the Sovereign, as representing the State of this Christian nation, upon which any Church, Established or not, and with or without legal obliga-

---

[1] I do not go here into detail as to this matter, having done so with much minuteness in another work, *Notes on some Passages in the Liturgical History of the Reformed English Church* (Murray, 1878), pp. 58-65.

[2] *Commons Journals*, 16th April 1662.

tion, may most properly act, without the least derogation from its just independence or spiritual character. It is, indeed, doubtful, perhaps more than doubtful, whether in all these cases there was legal obligation; but the authorities of the Church and its ministers did as became them, in never raising that question. Nor is the principle affected by the customary forms, under which the wishes (or, if that word be preferred, the commands) of the Sovereign have, in such cases, been expressed.

CHAPTER IV

PRINCIPLES CONSIDERED

1. *Establishment.*

MR. GLADSTONE, in his book on the *Relations of Church and State*, published in 1838, enumerated[1] under nineteen heads those things which he regarded as together (at that time), constituting or significant of 'the Nationality of the Church of England.' Six of these were signs of the public recognition of Christianity, as represented by the Church, on the part of the Sovereign and of the State. Two were the Acts of Union with Scotland and Ireland, which guaranteed the permanence of, but did not otherwise affect, the Establishment of the Church. Two consisted of oaths and declarations (since abolished), which Parliament had imposed on certain classes of persons, as (supposed) safeguards for the Church. One was the law of compulsory Church rates, also since abolished. One related to the Universities, then standing in closer relations to the Church than they do now. Two others related to temporalities; of which I shall speak under the head of Endowments. All these may be regarded rather as separable accidents of greater or less importance, significant of or consequential upon the relations otherwise constituted between Church

---

[1] First edition, chap. vii. pp. 238-240.

and State, than as entering into the very substance of those relations; and the same might, perhaps, be said of the seats of Bishops in the House of Lords (which Mr. Gladstone also mentioned), and of their nomination by the Crown (which he did not). There remain, of his nineteen heads, those which relate to law, legislation, and judicature; viz. the summoning of the Convocations by Royal writs—the part taken by Parliament in Ecclesiastical legislation—the restrictions placed by the State upon the enactment of Church laws—and the authority of the Ecclesiastical Courts. Of all these (which do constitute the essential terms and conditions of the 'Establishment' of the Church) I have spoken, historically, in the preceding chapters.

It is desirable to understand rightly the meaning of words in common use; false conclusions are often conveyed or insinuated through their misinterpretation. The words, 'established by law,' as applied to the Church of England, mean nothing different from what they would mean if applied to any foreign Churches,—say, of Italy, or of Spain; though, in different countries, the particular forms and conditions of establishment, as well as the tenets of the Churches established, differ. They do not anywhere mean that the Church was founded, or set up, or moulded into its actual form, by the State; but, that the temporal legislature has recognised and added certain sanctions to the institutions and laws of the Church. One of the leading senses of the verb 'establish' is, 'to settle in any privilege or possession, to confirm;'[1] and of the noun 'Establishment,' 'confirmation of something already done, ratification.' The use of these words, with reference to

[1] See Johnson's *Dictionary*.

the Church of England, in Acts of Parliament and other public documents, has always been according to that sense. The earliest instance of it which I have noticed is in the Statute of 'Provisors,'[1] by which Parliament 'ordered and established,' that the elections to Bishoprics and other elective Church dignities should be as they had been 'granted by the King's progenitors, and the ancestors of other lords, founders of the said dignities,' without Papal interference. The use of the same word in Queen Elizabeth's Act of Supremacy,[2] as to the Royal jurisdiction, is exactly similar. In the Acts of Uniformity[3] of 1552 and 1662, the expressions, 'establishing the Book of Common Prayer hereto annexed,' and 'the Liturgy of the Church of England as is now by law established,' relate plainly to the legal sanction given by those Acts to the use of the Books referred to in them. The 'Bills for establishing of true religion' mentioned in the Journals of the House of Commons for the 24th February 1606[4] cannot be supposed to have been intended to set up a new form of religion in that year. In the Royal Declaration of 1662, prefixed to all subsequent editions of the Thirty-Nine Articles, 'the doctrine and discipline of the Church of England now established,' and 'the Articles established,' were spoken of; plainly signifying that the doctrine, discipline, and Articles in question had then the force of law; not that they had originated in acts of State. 'The Protestant Reformed religion established by law,' in William the Third's Coronation oath,[5] was an expression which no one could have then understood to imply, that the 'religion,' so established, was a thing of political inven-

---

[1] 25 Edw. III., stat. 6.   [2] 1 Eliz., cap. 1.
[3] 5 and 6 Edw. VI., cap. 1, and 14 Car. II., cap. 4.
[4] Referred to in *C. D.*, p. 47.   [5] 1 Will. and Mary, cap. 6.

tion. And when, after the Revolution of 1688, the phrases, 'the Church of England established by law,' 'the Church as by law established,' 'the Church of England as now by law established' (with other variations), became current,[1] the meaning was always the same. Nothing can be more contrary to the fact than to represent that form of speech (whether used popularly, or in public Acts and documents) as 'a brief but compendious method of declaring, that the Church of England *is what it is as the result of the action of the Legislature which founded it and shaped it throughout.*'[2] If any proof of the perverseness of that interpretation were needed, beyond the historical facts mentioned in the preceding chapters, it would be found in the Act of Union[3] between England and Scotland, embodying the separate Acts passed in both kingdoms, as to their respective national Churches; in both which similar phrases are used. The English Act speaks of 'the true Protestant religion professed and established by law in the Church of England, and the doctrine, worship, discipline, and government thereof.' The Scottish Act in like manner speaks of the 'worship, discipline, and government of the Church of this kingdom' (*i.e.* of Scotland) 'as now by law established.' Nobody, I suppose, will say that the Presbyterian worship, discipline, and government of the Church of Scotland had been 'founded,' or 'shaped,' by merely civil legislation; though it did not appear to that Church, any more than to the Church of England, to be inconsistent with the spiritual character and authority which it claimed, to receive the support of such temporal sanctions as the State could give.

[1] *C. D.*, p. 47. [2] *Ibid.*
[3] 6 Ann., cap. 11 (commonly numbered cap. 8).

2. *Reasons for Establishment.*

The reasons for, and the advantages of, the Establishment (as distinguished from the endowments) of the Church have always appeared to me (as I believe they do to most Churchmen at the present day) to be stronger and greater on the side of the State than on that of the Church. But the fact that they are so is no reason for imputing to the Church unfaithfulness to her spiritual mission and principles, either because in past times, under the circumstances of those times, she accepted or acquiesced in those relations with the State of which the existing terms of Establishment are the result; or because she still thinks it the course of wisdom and duty to abide by those terms, for the sake of the public good which is in many ways promoted by them, and to avoid the great evils which most certainly would accompany or follow from Disendowment. Disestablishment without disendowment—a renunciation by the State of such powers of control as are involved in Establishment, without a total or large secularisation of the endowments of the Church—is a measure which nobody now proposes, and which I, therefore, need not consider.

In considering these questions I prefer practical to theoretical arguments. I do not, and cannot, take my stand upon any mystical view,—such, *e.g.*, as that the State is 'a person,'[1] with a corporate conscience, 'cognizant of matter of religion;' though I do not at all doubt, that respect paid to true religion, and recognition of its principles, and of the Forms and Institutions in which they have been historically embodied, by the public authority of the State,

---

[1] Gladstone, *The State in its Relations with the Church* (First edition, 1838), pp. 9, 37.

may be, and in England at the present time is, a source of strength and support both to Church and State, for the proper work and duty which each has to do. The mainstay of all law, civil as well as ecclesiastical, is (and must be) the moral sense of mankind; religion, wherever it is truly professed, is (and ever must be) powerful in the direction and reinforcement of that moral sense. Both powers, the Ecclesiastical and the Civil, are (according to the view of those who accept Christianity) in their origin divine; each has its proper province; the persons over which each exercises its authority are to a great extent the same; and there is, by the unchangeable laws of nature and Providence, a large middle or common ground between them. Each will best perform its proper work within its own province when it works in harmony with the other. So far, I think, most Christians ought to be agreed; they certainly would be, but for the disturbing influences of that spirit of division, which was happily unknown in the days when the Establishment of the Church of England began.

In saying this, I do not depart from the opinion (quoted in the *Case for Disestablishment*)[1] which I expressed in the House of Commons, upon the Second reading of the Irish Church Bill in 1869, that there might be a severance of the political relations of the Church with the State, without any 'abnegation of national Christianity,' or 'national apostacy;' and that the religion of a nation is really neither more nor less than the religion of the people, who constitute the nation; which (however it might eventually be affected) could not, in the case of any individual person, be directly or

[1] *C. D.*, pp. 136, 137.

immediately changed by the passing of any Act of Parliament for the Disestablishment of the Church. But it does not follow that, although there might be no 'national apostacy,' there would not be an enormous public mischief; or that the effect, in a religious point of view, either immediately or consequentially, upon that large floating mass of weak or unsettled belief or opinion, which is always influenced by the preservation or disturbance of the balance of the moral forces which hold society together, might not be very powerful for evil.

Regarded apart from their higher moral and social effects, the relations between the Church of England and the State, which constitute the Establishment of the Church, are in their true nature securities taken by the State against possible excesses of uncontrolled ecclesiastical power, rather than privileges conferred upon the Church by the State. The power and influence, in any country, of a great Church (such as the Church of England is now, and would not cease to be, even if it were disestablished and also disendowed) is and must be great. It is a thing necessarily to be taken account of by the rulers of any nation. We are not without experience, very near home, of the disturbance of social and political systems, which may be caused or fomented by such a power, if its spirit is hostile to the State; which, through human infirmity, a policy hostile to itself on the part of the State may easily make it. In times when there was no balance to the power of the Church of England from opposing forces of Non-Conformity, and when its use of that power was liable to be affected by foreign influence, the State had reasons, not now equally applicable, for treating its laws and institutions as matters to be recognised, and to some extent regulated and controlled, by the public law of the land. Some of the laws made upon, or as consequences of, that principle, have been long since repealed ; of others, the practical application has been largely limited and relaxed : but much remains, which has never hitherto been regarded by the Rulers of the State as unimportant to its interests ; and with which (if I rightly understand their views) even the advocates of Disestablishment would be generally unwilling to dispense, leaving the Church in possession of her endowments.

From the recognition of the Ecclesiastical Law and Courts, as part of the public law, and public tribunals, of the realm, the principle of those terms and conditions of the Establishment of the Church which affect legislation and judicature follows, if not of necessity, at all events reasonably and intelligibly. To allow that which is regarded as public law, and which is enforced by public tribunals, to be enacted, repealed, or altered, in any matter of substance, without previous licence, or subsequent assent and confirmation of the Civil Power, would be to admit a dual system of government within the realm, not less inconsistent in principle with the independence of the Supreme authority of the State than the Foreign Power which was rejected at the Reformation. At all the numerous points of contact between Church and State, in respect of temporal rights dependent on or affected by ecclesiastical jurisdiction, office, or duty, the power of regulation by the Civil Legislature must come in ; the greater those interests, the stronger and the more widely-extended the religious society to which they belong, so much the more frequent must be the occasions for its exercise. When Civil Legislation has once taken place concerning any ecclesiastical matter—Synods, Courts, benefices, appointments, dioceses, parishes, formularies—any change as to the same matter must of necessity require the authority of, or confirmation by, the Civil Legislature. An Appeal in ecclesiastical causes to a Royal Court is on sound judicial principles a reasonable consequence of the recognition of the ecclesiastical Courts as public Courts of the realm, and of the Sovereign as 'over all persons, and in all causes, ecclesiastical as well as civil,' within his dominions Supreme.

In like manner, if the nomination of Bishops by the Crown is not a necessary, it is at least a natural and reasonable consequence of their public authority, as chief administrators and Judges of Ecclesiastical law, and of their places as Lords Spiritual in the House of Lords. Whatever may be thought of the reasonableness, on the part of the State, of enforcing by severe penalties this right of nomination to Bishoprics, while forms of election are retained, those forms are not (as is often represented) a mere mockery, nor could they be abolished without the loss of some real security against improper appointments. The time has not been, and is not yet, when Churchmen worthy of the name may not be found in those electoral bodies, and in the highest places of the Church, ready to suffer loss of goods, or worse evil, rather than elect or consecrate, under secular compulsion, persons known to be disqualified for so sacred an office. The spirit which animated the Seven Bishops in their resistance to the unlawful commands of James the Second is not dead among us: and its existence, with the necessity (where there is an electoral body) for election, and for consecration, is a great safeguard against the nomination of really unfit persons. Some instances have occurred of nominations unacceptable (whether for good or bad reasons) to parties within the Church. They have been few in number: but the remonstrances which they provoked were enough to show that a power of rejection in the last resort is not, even as the law now stands, a thing without value: while, on the other hand, the results of the same nominations go far to justify a state of the law which does not leave that power, uncontrolled and irresponsible, in the hands of bodies which might sometimes be too much influenced by temporary excitements and passing gusts of opinion. It may (to say the least) be doubted, whether a system of free election by capitular bodies, or even by all the clergy of a diocese, would work as smoothly and well, in the general run, and upon a large scale, as the system of nomination by the Crown does under the existing law.

3. *The 'Religious Argument.'*

But it is said (I suppose seriously) that all such relations of the Church to the State as those which are summed up in the term 'Establishment' are, from a religious point of view, unscriptural and unlawful; 'directly opposed to the word of God;' an 'invasion of the prerogatives of God.' These bold dogmas are put forth in the front[1] of the *Case for Disestablishment*, as having been declared in the year 1844 by a 'Conference,' at which the Society for (what is now called) 'the Liberation of religion from State patronage and control' was formed; and we are informed, with laudable candour, that the movement for Disestablishment had its origin in these 'religious considerations;' that, although 'the purely political aspects of the question have [since] necessarily come into greater prominence,' 'the essentially

[1] *C. D.*, pp. 1, 2.

religious character of the movement remains unchanged;' and that 'the motives and principles, thus explicitly avowed by the founders of the Society, are those of the great majority of its present supporters.' Confessedly, therefore, the movement has now, and has always had, a theological and a sectarian basis; it is founded upon interpretations of or inferences from Scripture, not accepted certainly by members of the Church of England, and which no reasonable man is likely to accept upon the authority of that Society; upon dogmas, which brand with their anathema the general belief and practice of all Churches and States in Christendom, from Constantine the Great to the present day.

Anything more frivolous than the arguments[1] offered from Scripture in support of these dogmas it is impossible to conceive. In the Jewish 'Church-State,' which had a complete code of moral, ceremonial, and political laws, with coercive sanctions of great severity, all legislation on those subjects by temporal rulers is assumed to have been excluded. If the assumption (hardly consistent with what David and Solomon did as to the Temple Services) were correct, its bearing upon the relations of Christian Churches to Christian States which have no similar code, and in which the powers united under the Jewish Theocracy are divided, would not be self-evident. 'The payment of tithes' (we are told, by a singular inversion of the arguments sometimes used by divines upon that subject), although enjoined by the Mosaic law, 'was not enforced, but was wholly left to the conscience.' I know no ground for that assertion; but if it were true, the powers of Christian legislators could not be circumscribed by the practice of the Jews. The

[1] *C. D.*, pp. 7-10.

examples of Royal interference among the Jews in matters of religion are very summarily disposed of:—'Jewish princes, ignorant of the law of their God, or regardless of its directions, may have legislated about religion and used force in promoting it; but their disobedience to the Divine will does not invalidate the teaching of the Scriptures.' Whether the Reformations of Jehoshaphat, Hezekiah, and Josiah were in this writer's view, I know not; doubtless he was at liberty to draw his own inferences from what he read in the Old Testament, as much as the framers of the thirty-eighth Article of the Church of England (subscribed for nearly a century by Non-Conformist ministers as well as Churchmen) were to find there authority for the line which they drew, between things properly spiritual, and those ecclesiastical matters in respect of which they acknowledged the prerogative of 'chief government' to be in Princes. But it exceeds all bounds of modesty as well as reason, when theological dogmatism like this is put forward as a ground for disestablishing the Church of England.

The references to the New Testament[1] are, if possible, more idle still. It cannot be pretended that any code of laws, as to ritual, worship, or ecclesiastical discipline, by which the future practice of all Christian Churches or Christian Rulers of States was to be in all things exclusively governed, is contained in the New Testament. Principles, and doctrines of faith and morality, there are; there is a record of the Great Facts on which the Christian faith depends, of the institution of the Sacraments, and of the foundation and early days of the Church. The Church was sent into the world to apply those principles, to teach those

[1] *C. D.*, pp. 10, 11.

doctrines, to bear perpetual testimony to those Facts, to administer those Sacraments, and to extend and perpetuate her own organisation. But in the use of suitable means for those purposes, under the various circumstances in which she might have to fulfil her mission, she was placed under no restraints, except those necessarily implied from the original law of her being. That our Lord's kingdom, as Head of His Church, was spiritual and not temporal, seems to be a good argument against encroachments, such as those of the Papacy, of spiritual upon temporal Rulers, or against attempts to extirpate religious error by force:—it is not an argument, either that the power of Temporal Rulers is not 'ordained of God,' or that all ecclesiastical matters must be exempted from the supremacy of the Civil Power within its own province, or that there may not be temporal legislation concerning ecclesiastical matters which the Church may lawfully submit to and obey. That 'in the commission'—(not directory as to *any* mutable accidents of the work to be done)—'which Christ gave to His Apostles, there is not a trace of any thought of the establishment of the Christian religion by the State,' is true, but irrelevant: it no more warrants the inference, that such relations as constitute establishment might not naturally, rightly, and beneficially grow up between Churches and States consisting of Christian people governed by Christian Rulers, than it warrants a similar negative argument against Presbyteries, Consistories, or Conferences, buildings set apart for religious worship, creeds, catechisms, liturgies, formularies of faith, music in Churches, or any other matters not expressly prescribed or prohibited in Scripture. That 'the first preachers of the Gospel never asked kings or rulers for their patronage,' when there were no Christian Kings or Rulers to ask, is intelligible enough; but it does not follow that their successors in later times were departing from their principles, when they came into or acquiesced in relations with Christian Kings or Rulers, naturally arising, and deemed to be advantageous for the free course or the extension of the work of the Church.

I have bestowed upon this (so-called) religious argument more space than it deserves. I have only done so, because it is characteristic of the movement in the service of which it is used; and because we are told, that 'the motives and principles,' which depend upon this argument, are 'those of the great majority of the present supporters' of the Liberation Society.

4. *The Practical Question.*

The Church is a Society placed by its Divine Founder *in* the world, though the spirit by which it is, or ought to be, actuated and animated is not *of* the world. From the things of the world it neither is, nor by any possibility can be entirely separated; all its outward accidents, all the material instruments and appliances by the aid of which it works, do and must belong to that category.

It is not necessary, in order to justify the present position of the Church of England, to maintain (in Dr. Döllinger's words[1]) 'that intimate association with the Civil power has always been an advantage to religion,' or 'that the existing relations between Church and State in England are of an ideal description.' Where, in this world of probation and imperfection, or in that Church of which our Lord said that both 'the tares' and 'the wheat' must 'grow together until the harvest,' can we meet with anything which *is* 'of an

[1] Canon Liddon's letter to the *Times*, Oct. 17, 1885.

ideal description'? It is enough, as far as principle is concerned, if the relations existing between Church and State in England are such as a true branch of the true Church, faithful to its spiritual mission, may lawfully accept or acquiesce in. If so, the only remaining question on the religious side is, whether it is better for the spiritual work of the Church that those relations should continue (subject to such modifications as changes of times and circumstances may naturally bring about, or admit of, for good), or that they should be severed in the way desired by the advocates of Disestablishment? This is a purely practical question. It depends, not on dogma, not on technical rules of ecclesiastical polity, but upon the balance of those practical considerations, which affect everywhere the work of the Church.

If, under the Tudor Sovereigns, or at any other time, there were encroachments, potential or actual, by State legislation upon the spiritual province of the Church, these are not now material, unless the same state of things still continues. If they were submitted to when they ought to have been resisted, that was only an instance of the liability to human infirmity and error, from which the Church of England does not claim an exemption which she denies to other Churches. But the Church of England has never surrendered, or acknowledged the power of any State authority to take away, the spiritual gifts and powers inherent in the office and character which she claims as a true branch of the Catholic Church of Christ. Both Church and State were agreed (as I have already shown) even in very arbitrary times, in so limiting the acknowledgment by the one and the assertion by the other of the Royal Supremacy, as to exclude matters admitted to be properly spiritual. No State legislation in England ever affected the Creed, or the Orders of the Ministry of the Church, otherwise than by adding certain sanctions of law to what the Church had from the beginning received:—no such legislation as to doctrine or worship—certainly none which is now in force—took place, except in confirmation of what had already been determined and agreed to in Synods of the Church. The Statutes against Lollards, and the Act of the Six Articles, were oppressive and intolerant; so also were later Acts against Popish recusants. But none of these innovated upon the doctrinal position of the Church, while they remained in force; and they have all, long since, happily been repealed. The exorbitant powers given to Henry the Eighth to issue proclamations and declarations concerning doctrine defaced the Statute-book for a very few years; they had no lasting or practical effect. The extraordinary jurisdiction given to the Crown by Queen Elizabeth's Act of Supremacy (strictly limited, as to questions of heresy,) also came to an end more than two centuries ago. And the coercive powers of ecclesiastical law, which (through false principles too long prevalent in all nations, and in the greater number of sects as well as Churches) were employed to enforce outward religious conformity where there was not inward agreement, have been long since, and are now, restrained to their true province,—that of compelling the clergy of the Church to perform those obligations which they have voluntarily undertaken, which every Church and religious Society has, and necessarily must have, the right to enforce against its ministers; and maintaining in some other respects, as between professed members of the Church, its internal discipline.

Questions of principle, such as I have been considering, must be the same for Non-Conformists and for Churchmen:—they cannot depend upon the magnitude of the scale on which they may be applied. In a future chapter I shall examine some of the bearings on this part of the subject of the history of Non-Conformity in England.

5. *Corruption and Reform.*

In the preceding historical chapters it was shown that the organic continuity and identity of the Church of England has never been interrupted from the time of Augustin to the present day. Enlargement and local extension; endowment; increase in the number of Bishoprics, and in the ranks and degrees of parochial or other beneficed clergy; adaptation of machinery and modes of operation to the requirements of time, place, and circumstances; disciplinary and other legislation, and its effect upon the conditions of tenure of offices and benefices;—all these things are the ordinary and natural incidents of vitality, energy, and growth; not proofs of the loss of organic or spiritual identity, but the reverse.

It cannot be questionable, except from a Roman point of view, that a national or particular Church may contract corruptions, and fall for a time into errors or superstitions, doctrinal or practical, without losing its spiritual any more than its organic identity; nor, on the other hand, that, if this has happened, such a Church may again, without in either sense losing its identity, reform itself, and cast off all or any of those abnormal accidents. Once grant that the things cut off were not good in themselves, and were not original or essential conditions of the constitution of the Church, and Dean Hook's saying, that a man whose face has become dirty may wash off the dirt and yet remain the same man that he was before, undeniably applies.

As to the effect of the lapse of a particular Church into that kind and degree of error which in theology is called heresy, no question can arise, except with those who believe it to be heretical. The doctrines and practices which the Church of England rejected at the Reformation were mediæval, not primitive; they were unknown (even if germs of some of them may have existed) when the Church of England was founded by Augustin, and for ages afterwards; the historical origin of most of them can be and has been traced. Those who justify them do so on the ground of theological development; those who maintain them as authoritative do so upon the authority of the Roman Church; those who believe them (as Protestants generally do) to have been erroneous or superstitious, cannot regard their correction as heretical, or treat it as exceeding the powers of self-government and self-reform inherent in particular Churches. If the Pope were admitted to be, by divine right, the supreme, infallible, and absolute governor of all true Churches, it might doubtless follow, that the rejection of his authority was heresy, and that the sentences of Interdict and Excommunication pronounced against England by Paul the Third and Pius the Fifth deprived the Church of England of the character of a true Church. But this no Anglican, or other Protestant, believes. Those who do not hold that dogma cannot believe that the continuity or identity of the 'Orthodox' Greek Church was broken (spiritually or theologically, more than organically) when Pope Leo the Ninth excommunicated Michael

Cerularius, patriarch of Constantinople, and all who adhered to his communion; although there has ever since been a difference of doctrine, regarded on both sides as material, and a schism and breach of communion, between the Eastern and the Western Churches. What is true, in that respect, of the 'Orthodox' Greek Church, is equally true of the Church of England.

That there were *some* powers of self-government, self-development, and self-reform, inherent from the beginning in the Church of England, no student of its history can deny. The admission of Papal control, so far as it took place, was at first intermittent and tentative;—even when most fully developed, it was never without checks, limitations, and exceptions. What was so admitted at one time could (unless there were some divine law to the contrary) be excluded at another. Whether that step was justifiable in principle is a question which cannot depend upon the mere occasion which led directly to it. Whatever might be Henry the Eighth's motives, the pretensions of the Court of Rome had then become so exorbitant as to justify resistance, unless they were really founded in Divine right. No better proof of this could be desired than that supplied by those 'Bulls' themselves, by which the breach between Rome and England became complete. That of Paul the Third[1] (dated in September 1535, and published in December 1538), besides condemning Henry the Eighth and all his adherents to eternal perdition, and placing all his dominions and all churches within them under interdict, was a sentence depriving the King of his Crown and dominions, and all his loyal subjects of all their rights of property, which all comers were authorised to take from them;—it

[1] *Bullarium Romanum*, tom. i. (Paul III., Const. 7).

absolved all the King's subjects from their oaths of allegiance, and commanded all his judges and other officers and servants to refuse him obedience on pain of excommunication: —it prohibited every sort of commerce with him or his adherents, by buying, selling, marketing, carriage of provisions or other goods, or otherwise in any way of business: —it declared forfeited to the first takers the goods of those who might carry on such intercourse. In the event of the King still continuing obdurate, it required all the nobility and lay people of his realm to rise against him and expel him, by force of arms if necessary, from his dominions: and it forbade all other Kings and Emperors either to make treaties or compacts with him, or to observe them, if made; the Pope taking upon himself to cancel and annul all such treaties or compacts, present and future; and the Rulers of all nations were enjoined to make war upon him, and so reduce him to the obedience of the Roman See.

The Bull of Pope Pius the Fifth[1] (A.D. 1570) in like manner purported to deprive Queen Elizabeth of her throne, and to absolve all her subjects from their allegiance; requiring them, on pain of excommunication, to refuse obedience to her laws. In the preamble of that Bull, the Pope's claim of universal dominion was thus set forth:—

'The Most High, to whom is given all power in heaven and earth, has committed to one alone on earth (that is), to Peter, the Prince of the Apostles, and to the Roman Pontiff, his successor, the absolute government of the one Holy Catholic and Apostolic Church, out of which there is no salvation. Him only has God set up as Prince over all nations and all kingdoms, with power to pluck up and pull down, to scatter and destroy, to plant and build, in order to

---

[1] *Bullarium Romanum*, tom. ii. p. 324.

preserve in the unity of the Spirit, and present safe and whole to the Saviour, a faithful people united in the bonds of mutual love.'

In the English Reformation, as in all other great movements, there was doubtless loss as well as gain. Emancipation from those vast Papal pretensions was not attainable, except at the cost of a breach of the relations of free intercommunion which had always, until then, subsisted between the Church of England and the Churches which still obeyed the Pope's authority. And if it be true, as the poet[1] has said, that in that stormy time

> 'Green leaves, with yellow mixed, were torn away,
> And goodly fruitage with the mother spray,'

it was not possible (as he also said), in order to avoid that loss, to retain in the Church, by some insincere compromise, acknowledged errors and abuses. It is not for those who believe the gain, upon the whole, to have been greater than the loss, to borrow from the Roman armoury weapons against the English Church. Unless the central position of Rome is true, it must have been as much within the power of the Church of England (spiritually and theologically, as well as formally and organically) to give its people the English Bible and the Book of Common Prayer, to reclaim for its clergy the right of marriage, and for its laity the right to communicate in both kinds, and by the Thirty-nine Articles to reject those opinions and practices which they condemn, as it was for the Church of Rome, without becoming a new Church, to give to such of the same opinions and practices as were approved by the Council of Trent an authoritative character which they never had before; turning them (as

---

[1] Wordsworth, *Eccl. Sketches* (Sonnet 21).

was then done by the new creed of Pope Pius the Fourth,[1] and the Catechism of his successor Pius the Fifth) into articles of faith, necessary terms and conditions of communion. The popular notion involved in the common use of the words 'Roman-Catholic' and 'Protestant,' as descriptive of the Church of England before and after the Reformation, loses sight of the many centuries of the earlier life of the Church of England before mediæval developments came in; and also of the wide difference between floating opinions and practices, prevalent for a time but not irreversibly imposed or fixed by any binding authority, and the same or similar opinions and practices, after they have been stereotyped in a dogmatic form by an authority claiming absolute power. The former were not original or necessary elements of the faith or worship of the Church, but accretions to it, the products of later times and circumstances; and they might depart as they came. The latter, having been transformed into necessary and immutable articles of the professed faith of Churches, could not be got rid of, as long as the authority which so transformed them might be accepted as supreme.

This difference impressed itself upon the mind of a remarkable man and very independent thinker, Richard Hurrell Froude, during his visit to Italy in 1833. In a conversation as to the possibility of reconciliation between the Churches, with a Prelate then at the head of one of the Colleges in Rome, he found, 'that not one step could be gained without swallowing the Council of Trent as a whole,' to the decrees of which the modern Roman Catholic

---

[1] *Bullarium Romanum*, tom. ii. (Pius IV., No. 88). Also printed at pp. 208-210 o *Canones et decreta S.S. Œcumenici Concilii Tridentini* (Leipsic, 1837).

Churches were 'committed finally and irrevocably;' although (as the same Prelate admitted to him), 'many things, *e.g.* the doctrine of the mass, which were fixed then, had been indeterminate before.'[1] The words in which Mr. Froude summed up the position of modern Roman Catholics (omitting an unnecessary adjective) were, '*Tridentines every-where.*'[2]

All that has been said represents, of course, an English, not the Roman point of view. I do not wish to dogmatise, or to speak of the Roman or any other form of Christian religion in terms of contumely or reproach. But it is necessarily from an English point of view that this controversy must be conducted. And, from that point of view, I make bold to say, that no member of the Church which has come down from Augustin, the first Archbishop of Canterbury, to the present day, and which counts among its later lights such men as Herbert, Hooker, Taylor, Bull, Butler, Berkeley, and Keble, need be ashamed even of those generations of his spiritual ancestry which lived in dark times, and partook more or less (as all men are apt to do) of the faults of their times. Among them are many of the noblest names which have adorned and illustrated the history of England; men of sanctity in the midst of corruption, of peace in the midst of war; supporters of freedom against tyranny, of justice against violence; patrons and examples of learning in days of ignorance; statesmen and counsellors of kings; builders of cathedrals and churches; founders of colleges and schools; precursors, and honest opponents too—heroes, martyrs, and victims—of Reform. Neither for the earliest, nor for the middle, nor for the later days of our Church—neither for its Conservatives nor for

---

[1] Froude's *Remains*, vol. i. pp. 306, 307.   [2] *Ibid.*, p. 434.

its Reformers—can we claim (God forbid the presumption) immunity from weakness, faults, failures, and abuses, greater or less. This is the common lot of humanity, from which neither Churches, nor sects, nor States, will ever be delivered by any reforms. But the unavoidable mixture of evil in human things, even when most allied to that which is Divine, is no reason why we should desire to break the links which bind the present to the past, 'the living generations with the dead;'[1] or why we should not rejoice in all the good which there was in the days of our forefathers, as well as in our own.

[1] Wordsworth, *Thanksgiving Ode.*

PART II

CHURCH ENDOWMENTS

CHAPTER V

ORGANISATION AND PROPERTY

1. *Organisation.*

BEFORE entering particularly upon the subject of endowments, it may be desirable to state shortly the general facts as to the present organisation of the Church of England, and the numbers and emoluments of its clergy.

There are altogether thirty-three Bishoprics (including Sodor and Man); or thirty-four if Gloucester and Bristol (now united) are reckoned as two. Measures are in progress for the separation of those Sees; and also for the erection of an additional Bishopric at Wakefield.

Of these Bishoprics, twenty-eight have Cathedrals, with Deans and Chapters; six (Sodor and Man, St. Albans, Truro, Liverpool, Newcastle, and Southwell), though their principal Churches have been made Cathedrals, have no Chapters. The Collegiate Churches of Westminster and Windsor (of which the former was for a few years, in the sixteenth century, a Bishop's See, and the latter stands in a special relation to the Sovereign) have also Deans and Chapters. The Cathedral and Collegiate Clergy consist of 30 Deans, 131 Residentiary Canons, and 119 Assistant Ministers, designated by the various names of Minor Canons, Vicars Choral, Priest-Vicars, and Chaplains. All these receive stipends. There are also Honorary Canons and Prebendaries, receiving no payment. To the diocesan organisation of the Church belong 84 Archdeacons; some of whom are Canons of Cathedral or Collegiate Churches; and most of whom receive, for their duties as Archdeacons, moderate stipends out of Church funds in the hands of the Ecclesiastical Commissioners.

The entire number of parishes in England and the Channel Islands and Isle of Man, now under Rectors, Vicars, or Perpetual Curates (according to the most accurate reckoning which I have been able to make, counting for this purpose united parishes as if they were one, and excluding proprietary chapels and chapels of ease), is 13,739;[1] of which 57 are in the Channel Islands and the Isle of Man. Of the remaining 13,682, 8467 are old, and the rest new parishes. By old parishes I mean those which were founded before the Reformation; by new, those which have been since formed (chiefly within the last hundred years) by the subdivision of large and populous places. Of the old parishes, 4998 are Rectories (Churches which were never united or 'appropriated' to any monastery or other non-parochial Corporation, or which, if at any time so united or appropriated, were afterwards re-endowed with the 'great tithes' of their parishes); and 3469 Vicarages, or Churches which were so united or appropriated, and of which the duties were from that time forward performed by 'Vicars,' appointed originally as deputies of the Appropriators, and having now

---

[1] In *C. D.* (p. 59), the number of parishes is estimated as 'about 15,000 in all.' That estimate probably reckons united parishes, as if there were no union. My own estimate has been corrected, by the help of returns from the Archdeacons, down to the present time.

assigned for their maintenance the tithes, called 'small tithes,' of some particular kinds of produce.

Of the whole number of parishes, 1050 are in Royal, 4257 in ecclesiastical, and 8023 in lay patronage. Of 300, the patronage is divided:—as to 230, between the Crown and ecclesiastical patrons; as to 25, between the Crown and lay patrons; as to 45, between lay patrons and ecclesiastical. There remain 109, as to which I have no precise information; but the greater number, if not all of them, may be presumed to be new parishes, in the gifts of the incumbents of the mother-churches, out of whose original parishes their districts were taken. Under the description of Royal patronage, I include the Lord Chancellor's livings, those of the Duchy of Lancaster, and those in the gift of the Prince of Wales: under that of ecclesiastical, all livings in the gift of ecclesiastical Corporations, aggregate or sole: under that of lay, all livings in the gift of Colleges in the Universities and other lay Corporations, or of any bodies of trustees, as well as private individuals.

1. *Aggregate Church Income.*

The aggregate amount of the stipends of the Bishops, the Capitular clergy, and the Archdeacons, as now fixed by law, is £352,847, viz.—

Bishops	£166,300
Deans and Canons	146,836
Minor Canons, etc.	24,385
Archdeacons	15,326
	£352,847

To state with equal exactness the incomes of the parochial clergy is not possible; because they are liable to vary from year to year,—so far as they are derived from land, according to its letting value,—and so far as they depend upon tithe rent-charges, according to the average prices, during the last seven years, of wheat, barley, and oats. They are stated in the Clergy List for 1884, in figures which (as I have cast them up) amount altogether to £4,457,782. If this might be taken as representing, approximately, the aggregate annual value of all the parochial benefices in England, it would give, when added to the former figure, £4,810,629 as the total (approximate) amount of the aggregate incomes of all the beneficed clergy, great and small, of the Church of England. Both from the information which I have been able to collect, and from my own experience as a dispenser of Crown patronage from 1880 to 1885, I am satisfied that this estimate is considerably in excess of the whole income, from all sources, of the Church of England at the present time.

It is necessary (in order to judge of this) to see what the figures given in the Clergy List do, and what they do not, include. In the *Case for Disestablishment*, it is said,[1] that 'it is believed they take no account of fees and pew-rents,' and that the Clergy List 'understates the value of the livings to the extent of from ten to twenty per cent.'[2] Whether, at any time of greater agricultural prosperity than the present, the figures given in the Clergy List may have been too low, is a point on which I have not (and it is also

---

[1] *C. D.*, p. 64.
[2] *Ibid.* So loose are the statements of this book, that they do not always agree with each other. On this point it is said, at p. 115, to be 'well known that the Clergy List gives the incomes of the parochial clergy at from ten to *twenty-five* per cent less than their actual value.'

tolerably plain that the author of this work had not) the knowledge necessary for the formation of a trustworthy opinion. But the experience to which I have referred enables me to state with confidence, that the value of the livings in 1884 is not at all understated, but is overstated (by how much I cannot say) in the Clergy List of that year, from which my own figures are taken.

As to fees and pew-rents (which form but an inconsiderable part of the clergyman's income anywhere, except, perhaps, in some metropolitan and other urban churches, chiefly those erected under the Church-building Acts between 1818 and 1840), I have no reason to doubt, that they are included, generally, in the figures given in the 'Clergy List.' I know that they are so included in some particular cases with which I am acquainted; and I believe it to be so generally. And this, properly considered, is matter for deduction from the total figure, £4,457,782, when the question is, what income is received by the Church from endowments? Fees, certainly, could not be appropriated to the State, by any measure of disendowment; nor could pew-rents, unless the churches, generally, were secularised, and let out for rents; it being an object (with churchmen at all events) rather to get rid of pew-rents wherever it can justly and prudently be done, than in any degree to extend that system.

On the other hand, it is true, that the residence-houses of the Bishops and other clergy are not, in the Clergy List, reckoned as productive of income; which, in fact, they are not; though, of course, a house rent free has its money value. Mr. Frederick Martin,[1] in a work[2] prepared for the 'Liber-

---

[1] *C. D.*, p. 63.
[2] Entitled *The Property and Revenues of the English Church Establishment.*

ation Society' in 1877 (with a fairness commendable when compared with some later calculations, to which I shall presently refer) brought up his estimate of the total amount of the incomes of the dignified and parochial clergy, at that time, to £5,383,560, by adding to the other figures (derived by him, probably, from the Clergy List) certain estimated yearly values of their residence-houses; the 'glebe-houses' of the parochial clergy being valued by him—I know not on what *data*—at £750,000. I neither assume at present the correctness of that estimate, nor the reverse; but what he added prevents me from placing the same confidence in Mr. Martin's opinion which I do in his good faith; because he said:[1]—'In this estimate no account is taken of extra Cathedral revenues, nor of the disbursements of Queen Anne's Bounty, nor of the surplus income of the Ecclesiastical Commissioners; the aggregate of which cannot be under three quarters of a million sterling.'

'Extra Cathedral revenues' can only mean some possible excess in the value of lands reassigned by the Ecclesiastical Commissioners to certain capitular bodies, over the fixed incomes, for which those lands were intended to provide. Whether there was ever any such excess I know not; but this I know for certain, that there is a deficiency, and not an excess, at the present time. The Chapters, for example, of Winchester, and of Gloucester (to which separate estates were reassigned) have for some years past been unable to pay the full amount of the fixed incomes of the Deans and Canons.

As for the disbursements of Queen Anne's 'Bounty,' they consist of loans for building purposes, repayable with interest (and, therefore, not constituting any item of clerical income); and of permanent augmentations of small livings,

[1] *C. D.*, pp. 63, 64.

which are all included in the figures given in the Clergy List for the value of the benefices so augmented.

As for the 'surplus income of the Ecclesiastical Commissioners,' it has been expended from time to time in the augmentation of poor livings; and those augmentations, down to 1884, are all included in the figures of the Clergy List for that year. On comparing my own figure of £4,457,782 (the aggregate of the annual values of parochial benefices, as given in the Clergy List of 1884) with £4,277,060 (the figure given by Mr. Martin in 1877 for the incomes of the parochial clergy), it will be seen that there is an increase, since 1877, of £180,722. That increase represents, not only the whole amount of the augmentations made since 1877 by the Ecclesiastical Commissioners, but also those by Queen Anne's Bounty, and by private benefactions. The private benefactions, to meet the augmentations by the Commissioners and the Bounty Board, may be safely taken at not less than one-fifth of that amount. By the Report of the Ecclesiastical Commissioners for the present year (1886), it appears that they had at the close of 1885 a balance in hand, sufficient to make an appropriation in the present year, productive of a further addition of £15,000 per annum to the incomes of the parochial clergy: but so far are they from having a surplus of annual revenue at the present time, that their receipts during the year 1885 did not balance their expenditure.

Instead, therefore, of the 'three-quarters of a million sterling,' which Mr. Martin supposed might be added to his estimate of Church revenue in 1877, there is (down to the present time, without making any deduction from the Clergy List figures, and including the augmentations proposed to be made by the Ecclesiastical Commissioners during the present year) only a total sum of (at the most) £195,480; the whole of which (except £15,000) is included in the figures which I have given from the Clergy List.

I will now state my reasons (confirmed by my own experience) for the conclusion that large deductions must be made from those figures.

The incomes of the parochial clergy are derived (1) from tithe rent-charge; (2) from glebe lands, and lands or money-payments assigned in lieu of tithes in certain parishes; (3) from augmentations by the Ecclesiastical Commissioners and Queen Anne's Bounty; and (4) from modern private benefactions, in the form of rent-charges or invested funds.

As to the tithe rent-charge, all the facts are certainly known. By the Report of the Land Commissioners for 1883,[1] the total amount of tithe rent-charge throughout the kingdom (at par value) was stated to be £4,053,985 : 6 : 8½. But of this not less than £962,289 : 15 : 7¼ was in the hands of lay impropriators (including under that description schools and colleges, etc.); leaving only £3,091,695 : 11 : 1¼, for ecclesiastical owners, of which £678,987 : 1 : 1¾ is payable to the Ecclesiastical Commissioners, in right of Bishops and Chapters, and the rest, £2,412,708 : 9 : 11½, to the incumbents of parishes. To this may be added £8000, which, by a return prepared in the Office of the Land Commissioners in 1882, is shown to be the balance of increase over decrease, down to that time, of Extraordinary tithe, viz., tithe upon hops and the produce of orchards and market gardens, etc., which was [2] liable to exceptional increase or diminution, according to the enlargement or reduction of those particular kinds of cultivation. The

---

[1] See *C. D.*, p. 59.
[2] An Act to remove that anomaly has passed in this year (1886).

total, therefore, of Ecclesiastical tithe rent-charge is (at par) £3,099,695 : 11 : 1¼. But, in 1886, the value of this rent-charge, upon the averages of the preceding seven years, according to which it is payable, was only £90 : 10 : 3¾ per cent [1]—in other words, it was depreciated, by the decline in the value of agricultural produce, more than 9 per cent below par. By that depreciation the £3,099,695 : 11 : 1½ had become (in 1886) reduced in value to £2,805,653 : 13 : 6, a total loss of £294,041 : 17 : 7½ ; of which something more than seven-ninths fell on the parochial clergy, and the rest on the Ecclesiastical Commissioners.

Subtracting from the aggregate (£4,457,782) of the incomes of the parochial clergy as given in the Clergy List for 1884 £2,412,708 (from which this deduction of above 9 per cent is to be made), there remains £2,045,074. It appears, by the Ecclesiastical Commissioners' Report for the present year, that the total annual value of all the grants hitherto made by them (including some, unproductive of income, which may be neglected) is reckoned by them at about £739,000 per annum. Deducting this, there remains (to represent the annual value of glebe and other lands, augmentations by Queen Anne's Bounty—in their total amount not large—modern private benefactions, fees, and pew-rents) £1,306,074. The greater part of this must certainly represent rents of land, which of late years have undergone, generally, an enormous and still progressive reduction, falling with especial severity upon the clergy; who, in many parts, especially of the eastern and midland counties, are very much dependent upon that source of income; and who, in too many cases, have had the land thrown upon their hands

[1] See Mr. George Taylor's *Tithe Commutation Table* for 1886 (the last table, p. 6).

without tenants, not having themselves the capital necessary to farm it. I have not yet seen any estimate of the annual value of glebe lands which exceeds £400,000 (the estimate of Mr. Arthur Arnold); or of other lands and annual payments allotted or made payable to the parochial clergy in lieu of tithes, which exceeds £320,000; and this I suspect to be quite an excessive estimate. Adding these sums together, and deducting them from the £1,306,074, there would remain £586,074 per annum, certainly too large an amount to represent the aggregate of the augmentations by Queen Anne's Bounty, modern private endowments, pew-rents, and fees.[1]

It is impossible to avoid the conclusion, that the total of £4,810,429 exceeds the utmost money value of the whole endowments (exclusive of Churches and residence houses) of the Church of England at the present time.

3. *Extravagant Estimates.*

When we turn from these facts to what is paraded in the *Case for Disestablishment*[2] as 'the most recent estimate of the value of Church property'—that of Mr. Arthur Arnold, in 1878—the strain put upon a man's disposition to give credit to everybody else for good faith is very severe. That controversialist, professing to take 'an independent view of the subject,' and 'accepting all responsibility for his figures,' 'submits them with some confidence.' They bring out a total of £7,502,602 'revenue,' and £183,503,050 'capitalised value,' which he estimates as 'the amount of the fund at

---

[1] £167,147−14,409 + 151,000 = £303,738 (see post, pp. 161, 162, 165). Pew-rents and fees cannot amount to the difference, £282,336.

[2] *C. D.*, p. 64.

the disposal of the State in the event of disendowment;' adding, 'with regard to the capitalised value, I am of course aware that the estimate is very moderate.' Now, this (so called) estimate not only proceeds upon an arbitrary valuation of Church lands and residence-houses (without reference to the sums which the Bishops and other clergy actually receive), and adds to this £361,860 per annum (capitalised at £9,046,500) for 'property omitted from the New Domesday Books'—whatever that may mean—and £21,000 (capitalised at £525,000) for 'Churchwardens' etc., lands;' but it coolly takes, from the Preface to the 'New Domesday Books,'[1] £5,000,000 as the estimated annual value of tithes (capitalised at £125,000,000); when the authentic return of the Land Commissioners for 1883 (quoted only five pages before[2] in the *Case for Disestablishment*) shows £4,053,985 : 6 : 8½ to be the whole amount of the commuted tithe rent-charge, lay and clerical, throughout the kingdom; *all* which is here ascribed to the Church as a 'fund at the disposal of the State in the event of disendowment;' though the same report shows that, of that sum, £962,289 : 15 : 7¼ belongs to lay impropriators, leaving £3,091,695 : 11 : 1¼ only as the total amount of ecclesiastical tithe. Whether the *Case for Disestablishment* adopts and endorses Mr. Arnold's estimates, or only uses them to stimulate an appetite for public plunder, I cannot clearly make out; the preceding context, in which the figures of the Land Commissioners and of Mr. Frederick Martin are given, seems inconsistent with the former supposition; but the follow-

---

[1] See *C. D.*, p. 58. This incorrect figure is not in the *Return of Owners of Land* (itself disfigured with very many inaccuracies) of 1873, but is taken from a 'preface' to a republication of it, thus designated.

[2] *C. D.*, p. 59.

ing passage, which swells Mr. Arnold's total by £2,000,000 more, as the assumed annual value (to let, I suppose) of our Cathedrals and Parish Churches, is founded upon it :—

'In neither of these estimates, it will be observed, is there any reference to the value of the ecclesiastical edifices, the churches and cathedrals throughout the country. But, as they form an important part of the public property appropriated to the Church of England, any estimate of the value of that property which excludes them is clearly defective. In 1818 the number of churches was about 11,700; and the annual value of these buildings and the cathedrals together cannot fairly be estimated at less than £2,000,000. Making the necessary additions to Mr. Arnold's totals above given, the result is reached, that the Church of England is annually subsidised out of public property to the extent of £9,500,000; and that the capitalised value of the property thus appropriated is more than £220,000,000.'[1]

Of the assumptions here made, that all the Churches and other property of the Church of England are 'public' (by which the writer evidently means ordinary State property), and that everything which the Clergy of the Church enjoy, from the income or use of Church property of any kind, is an 'annual subsidy out of public property,' a refutation will be offered in the following chapters. I have, so far, been dealing only with the question of fact, as to the actual or approximate amount of the annual value of the whole endowments of the Church.

4. *Proportion of Means to Work.*

Whatever that amount may be, it is not all net income : it is subject to important deductions.

[1] *C. D.*, p. 65.

The number of working Clergy in charge of the 13,739 parishes of the Church of England (or of Chapels of Ease or Mission Churches, etc., included within them) is 13,824. The number of their Assistant Curates is 5795. The total number of working parochial clergy is, therefore, 19,619.[1] The incomes of the beneficed clergy are subject to heavy local rates; and out of them have also to be paid the stipends of most of the 5795 curates by whom they are assisted, whose services are, generally, indispensable.

If the sum of £4,457,788 per annum (derived from the Clergy List) were equally divided among all the incumbents of all the parishes, it would give less than £330—if equally divided among all the working parochial clergy, it would give less than £228—to each. It is not divided in either of these ways; nor, indeed, would it be reasonable that it should be: for, even if there were one common fund to be distributed, regard ought to be had to the variety of the work to be done, and to the inequalities in the size, population, and wants of different parishes, and other circumstances. A large proportion of the beneficed clergy have incomes very much less than £330 per annum: on the other hand, the number of those benefices of which the emoluments, when compared with local wants, may reasonably be thought excessive, is by no means great.

With respect to the Bishops and other dignified clergy, the amount of their incomes has been recently fixed, after much consideration, by the Legislature; and it has been fixed on a scale certainly not more liberal, upon the whole, than that on which our Judges and other officers of State are paid. The expenses of those offices are very great, not only

---

[1] These figures are taken from an excellent publication, *The Official Year-Book of the Church of England* for 1886, p. 517.

in travelling (which is constant) and becoming hospitality, but in promoting and taking the lead in all sorts of Church work, and other charities and good deeds, both public and private. And it may be said of them generally, with truth, that in all these things they set, as they ought to do, to other men, an example honourable to themselves, and most useful to the Church and nation.

5. *What is meant by 'Church Property'?*

It may be well here to add a few words in explanation of the collective phrase 'Church property,' or 'property of the Church of England.'

There has never been any general or simultaneous endowment of the Church of England: no property has ever become vested by law in the whole Church of England, which, although it is an aggregate of many ecclesiastical corporations, is not itself a corporation in law. Professor Freeman[1] has said accurately:

'People talk as if "Church property" were the property of one vast Corporation called "The Church." In truth, it is simply the property of the several local churches, the ecclesiastical corporations sole and aggregate, bishops, chapters, rectors, and vicars, or any other. The Church of England, as a single body, has no property.'

Elsewhere[2] he says:

'If we wish to argue this question on its true ground, we must put out of sight the popular notion that at some time or other the State determined to make a general national endowment of religion. . . . If there ever was a time when the State determined on a general national establishment of religion, we

---

[1] Freeman, p. 16.   [2] Freeman, pp. 18, 19.

must suppose it to have been at the time of the conversion of the English nation to Christianity. But the conversion of England took place gradually, when there was no such thing as an English nation capable of a national act. The land was still cut up into small kingdoms, and Kent had been Christian for some generations at a time when Sussex still remained heathen. If any act which could be called a systematic establishment and endowment of the Church ever took place anywhere, it certainly took place in each particular kingdom for itself, not in England as a whole. The Churches of Canterbury and Rochester undoubtedly held lands while men in Sussex still worshipped Woden. But it would be an abuse of language to apply such words as systematic establishment and endowment to the irregular process by which the ecclesiastical corporations received their possessions. The process began in the earliest times, and it has gone on ever since ; and nothing was done systematically at any time. This king or that earl founded or endowed this or that church in which he felt a special interest, and from this it naturally followed, that one church was much more richly endowed than another.'

Without giving due attention to these facts, the nature, origin, and history of ecclesiastical endowments, and the questions of public justice and equity depending upon them, would be liable to be misunderstood. But there is, nevertheless, a true sense, consistent with these facts, in which the property of all the ecclesiastical corporations may be spoken of as belonging to the Church of England, considered as one organised religious society or community, which, from small beginnings, gradually extended itself over the whole country. In that general society or community, all those corporations, and all their several offices, functions, and duties, are bound together, summed up, and united:—they are not isolated, they are connected parts and organs of one whole ; they exist, and have always existed, for its purposes and its services, and for those only.

The case of the Church of England, in this respect, is not different from that of the Wesleyan body, or of any Non-Conformist denomination, having local and particular trusts and endowments, but not one general trust or endowment for the whole denomination. The general body is endowed, not collectively, but in its several parts; it has an interest in the endowment of every part. These considerations do not affect questions depending directly upon the original title to particular endowments; but they do affect, on principles well understood in our law, ulterior questions, relating to such modifications of the form or manner of enjoyment, and such applications of surplus funds not required for the primary objects of any endowment, as may be from time to time made by competent authority.

CHAPTER VI

FABRICS AND LANDS, ETC.

THE property of the Church of England (understanding that expression in the sense which has been explained) may conveniently be classed under the different heads of (1) Fabrics of Churches, with their consecrated enclosures, and their plate, furniture, and other accessories; (2) Parsonage-houses and glebes; (3) Lands belonging to Bishoprics, and to Cathedral and Collegiate Churches; and (4) Tithes; or lands, money-payments, or rent-charges, in lieu or commutation of tithe. Rights of patronage, resulting from these endowments, have also to be considered. Of these (except tithes or their equivalents, which is a subject so large as to require separate treatment) I now propose to speak.

There are, besides those things which I have enumerated, a large number (in all 4228,[1] of which 362 are permanent) of unconsecrated buildings—mission-rooms, school-chapels, iron churches, etc.—used for Church of England services under licenses from the Bishops; and in most parishes there are Church-schools, with suitable buildings for teachers and scholars. All these are so identified with the organic system and settled ministry of the Church, that they must

[1] *The Official Year-book of the Church of England* (1886), p. 518. (I have deducted the consecrated buildings.)

necessarily be to a very large extent affected (indirectly, if not directly) by any measure of disestablishment and disendowment. Their circumstances vary much; some might, perhaps, be regarded as Church property, being held on permanent trusts; the greater part, probably, are private property, or are maintained, on a footing not necessarily permanent, by voluntary subscriptions. They are not included in Mr. Martin's estimate of the value of the property of the Church; and, if included in that of Mr. Arnold, it can only be under one or other of his indefinite heads, of 'Churchwardens' etc., lands,' and 'property omitted from the new Domesday-book.'

Of customary offerings, oblations, and fees (which from their nature could not enter into any scheme of disendowment), no account need here be taken.

1. *Churches.*

There are in England 14,558 Parish Churches, and 1110 Chapels of Ease; in the Isle of Man seventeen Parish Churches, and twenty-four Chapels of Ease; in the Channel Islands forty Parish Churches, and three Chapels of Ease; altogether 15,752 consecrated buildings[1] (besides Cathedrals), set apart for the perpetual worship and religious uses of the Church of England by irrevocable gifts, and dedicated by the most solemn religious acts to the service of Almighty God for ever.

[1] I am indebted for these figures to the Archdeacons of England and of the Isle of Man, who have furnished the number in each Archdeaconry at my request. The excess of the number of parish churches over my reckoning of the number of parishes is explained by the fact that 876 parishes, having separate churches, are united to others; and, in my reckoning of parishes, I have counted two or more united parishes as one.

Few ecclesiastical edifices now existing in this country are, as to any considerable or conspicuous parts of their fabrics, of earlier than Norman, most of them are of later times. But most of the Cathedrals, and many of the older parish churches, have replaced earlier buildings dedicated to the same uses (often upon the same sites) at various periods —sometimes long before the Conquest. Almost all these churches have undergone alterations, renovations, and additions, at different times. They are monuments of the Christian zeal of many generations of Churchmen: the Christian dead, of many generations, sleep around them. Words are inadequate to express the feelings of affection and reverence with which they are, generally, regarded by Churchmen.

The magnificence of our Cathedrals, their central diocesan character, and the uninterrupted succession of the Capitular or Conventual bodies which have always been connected with them, have led to the preservation of fuller memorials of their history than has been possible in the case of old parish churches. We know the names of the Bishops and other great Churchmen, who, chiefly out of their own resources or those of the corporations with which they were connected, (not, however, without frequent aid from lay contributors), built the Cathedrals of Canterbury, York, Durham, Winchester, Ely, Lincoln, Lichfield, Wells, Exeter, Worcester, Norwich, Hereford, Rochester, and other cities. Bishop Poore built Salisbury Cathedral, partly out of his own means, partly by the aid (according to the chronicler Matthew Paris[1]) of many of the nobles of the realm, and of King Henry the Third, who laid the foundation-stone, and was present at the consecration. Westminster Abbey was twice rebuilt by kings, Edward the Confessor, and Henry the Third;

[1] Under date A.D. 1237.

Henry the Seventh's chapel was added to it, with a special endowment, under the will of that King; Sir Christopher Wren's two western towers were added in the eighteenth century, out of coal-duties granted by Parliament. Out of the same coal-duties (granted in A.D. 1671 to the Corporation of London to rebuild that part of the city which was destroyed by the great Fire, and continued by Acts of the three succeeding reigns) the present fabric of St. Paul's Cathedral was erected. Those monies out of coal-duties were the only Parliamentary funds granted for church building in England before 1818.

Other splendid churches, formerly conventual, were made parish churches on the dissolution of the monasteries—among them, Southwell, Beverley, and Wimborne minsters; St. Alban's, Tewkesbury, Evesham, Malmesbury, Sherborne, Romsey, Christchurch, Waltham, Howden, and Selby Abbeys. These had been erected by the founders or superiors of the religious houses to which they originally belonged, as Cathedrals were (generally) by their Bishops. And in several districts of England parish churches, of more than usual grandeur and architectural beauty, abound; monuments, probably, of the power and influence of the greater monasteries of those districts, such as Crowland, Peterborough, and St. Edmund's Abbeys in the east, and Glastonbury in the west. Many of these, and all the commoner sort of plain and simple, but venerable and solemn churches of old parishes, were originally built by the lords of manors and other land-owners, who gave the sites with the adjoining consecrated ground for the service of God, at or before the times when the parishes were formed.

That a great majority of these founders were private persons (though some were ecclesiastical corporations, and some kings) may be inferred, with reasonable certainty, from the large amount of Church patronage which now is, and from ancient times has been, in lay, and the comparatively small amount which has been, and is still, in Royal hands. In making this comparison, I do not (of course) lose sight of the facts, that some part of the patronage of ecclesiastical corporations came to them by gifts from kings; that of the benefices, formerly appropriated to monasteries (some of which are now in lay, and some in ecclesiastical patronage), part—by no means the greater part—also came to those monasteries from Royal patrons; and that, of the 8023 benefices now in lay patronage, 119 have recently passed from the Crown into lay hands, under a late Act of Parliament.[1] On the other hand, many of the churches of which the patronage came to the Crown upon the Dissolution of the Monasteries were Vicarages, of which the Rectories had been appropriated to the dissolved monasteries by lay patrons. Giving such weight as is due to these facts, on both sides, the conclusion which I have stated remains untouched.

Of the particular history of these parochial foundations very little has been recorded. It was long ago observed by Sir William Dugdale,[2] that 'we are not only without all knowledge when our churches were first founded and endowed, but are very much to seek touching many of their presentations and institutions within the compass of time in which we are sure that such there were.' It is probable that the gifts, both of sites and of endowments of parish churches, made before the Conquest, were usually by word of mouth and symbolical delivery before witnesses, without any written title-deeds. The general use of charters

[1] 26 and 27 Vict. cap. 120.
[2] *Antiquities of Warwickshire*, p. 14 (ed. 1730).

first came in with the Normans :[1] and even where written documents may have existed, they were liable, in course of time, to be lost through neglect, in the absence of any provision for their proper custody, or for their due transmission from the representatives of a deceased incumbent to his successor.

Those churches of metropolitan parishes, which had been destroyed by the Fire of London in A.D. 1666, were rebuilt out of the proceeds of the coal-duties granted by Parliament (as already mentioned) in 1671. The same duties were continued till 1724, for the purpose (among other things) of building fifty new churches in London and Westminster, and providing residences for their incumbents.

Of the churches built or restored in more recent times, I shall speak hereafter.

All the parish churches and chapels of ease in England have their appropriate fittings, furniture, and ornaments, suitable for the worship of Almighty God according to the order of the Church, and their fonts and communion-plate, hallowed by the most sacred of uses. Whatever is most valuable in them has generally been the offering of individual piety or munificence, or has been provided by private contributions. These things are necessary or suitable for the present uses of those sacred buildings; they are unsuitable (as a rule) for any other use; and the very thought of turning them to profane uses would be to most minds revolting.

2. *Parsonage-Houses and Glebes.*

From the time when parishes were first formed, a

[1] Ingulph's *Hist.*, p. 70 (Fulman's *Rerum Anglicanarum Scriptores*).

'manse,' or house of residence for the incumbent, with a glebe or portion of land attached to it, was the indispensable accompaniment of a parish church. The word 'manse' included both those things. 'The assigning of these at the first' (says Bishop Gibson[1]) 'was of such absolute necessity, that without them no church could be regularly consecrated.' They were regarded by the canon law (in England, as elsewhere[2]) as accessories, of common right, to the church. Archbishop Anselm's Canon[3] of A.D. 1102, 'that churches be not consecrated till all necessaries be provided for the priest and it' (*i.e.* for the church), did but confirm the earlier rule and practice. Whenever, therefore, any lord of a manor or other land-owner desired that a parish should be constituted within or out of his estate, and that a church should be consecrated for it, he had to provide (with other things necessary), a suitable house and glebe to the satisfaction of the Bishop, for the perpetual use of the incumbent, free from all secular services. All ancient parish churches had (and still retain) their parsonage-houses and glebes, by gift from the first founders. In the modern formation of new parishes, this rule has been departed from. Many of these have no parsonage-houses; few, if any of them, have glebes.

3. *Episcopal and Capitular Estates.*

The English Bishoprics existing at the time of the Conquest, and their Capitular Bodies (including under that

---

[1] *Cod.*, p. 661.
[2] Lyndwode, *Provinc.*, p. 254; and see Spelman, *De non temerandis ecclesiis*, pp. 8, 9, sect. 5.
[3] Johnson, *Laws and Canons* (ed. 1851), vol. ii. p. 27 (Canon 16).

term the Priors and Convents of several Cathedrals, afterwards converted into Deans and Chapters), had all, when Domesday Book was compiled, large landed possessions. These had come to them from many different sources: some by purchase; the greater part by gift. Among the givers were Kings of Kent, Mercia, Wessex, and all the other kingdoms of the Heptarchy; and of England, as united under Egbert and his Anglo-Saxon and Danish successors. There were also Queens, Princes, Princesses, Bishops, and other Ecclesiastics; noblemen, and other private lay persons. Many particulars of those early gifts are contained in extracts from charters and other documents of title belonging to those corporations, collected in Sir William Dugdale's *Monasticon*.[1]

The English Sees were at that time fifteen: Canterbury, York, London, Durham, Winchester, Rochester, Worcester, Lichfield, Hereford, Wells, and Exeter (which still remain in the same Cathedral cities without change, Lichfield having been for a time removed, but afterwards brought back again), and Sherborne, Selsey, Dorchester in Oxfordshire, and Thetford. These four were respectively translated, during the Conqueror's reign, by Royal and also Synodical[2] authority, to Salisbury,[3] Chichester, Lincoln, and Norwich, retaining the titles to their endowments, and taking their Capitular bodies with them.

Of these fifteen sees and capitular bodies, those of Can-

---

[1] My references are to Messrs. Caley, Ellis, and Bandinel's edition of this work, of which the different volumes appeared at intervals from 1817 to 1830.

[2] See Johnson, *Laws and Canons* (ed. 1851); vol. ii. p. 14 (Council of London, A.D. 1075; Canon 3).

[3] Old Sarum; from which it was removed to its present site, under Henry the Third.

terbury, London, Durham, Winchester, Rochester, and Selsey, and (after their translation) Salisbury and Lincoln, were much indebted to Royal munificence.[1] Royal gifts, though less considerable in extent and value, were also bestowed upon York, Worcester, Wells, Lichfield, Exeter, and Norwich.[2] But in all, or most of these cases, the private benefactions were large, and in general preponderated. Among the donors of lands to Canterbury[3] (favoured beyond all other Sees by Kings, of whom more than twenty made gifts to it before the Conquest), were three Queens, and the Black Prince; eleven Archbishops; three other clerical benefactors; twenty-four lay noblemen. All these private gifts were allowed and confirmed by the Sovereign, whose permission or consent to them appears to have been necessary in Anglo-Saxon, as well as in later times.

The endowments of the Abbey of Ely[4] (erected into a Bishop's See in A.D. 1109), were derived almost wholly from private sources. The foundress, a princess of the East Angles, settled upon it the whole isle of Ely; and the names of more than thirty other private benefactors (lay and clerical) appear in its charters or evidences of title. Three Anglo-Saxon kings also made gifts to it.

The Bishopric and Capitular body of Carlisle[5] were

---

[1] See Dugd., *Mon.*, under those names: vol. i. pp. 89, 93-98; 153, 161 *et seq.*; 189, 210 *et seq.*; 232, 237 *et seq.*;—vol. vi. p. 1159, 1162 *et seq.*; 1266, 1269; 1292, 1264; — and Dugd., *St. Paul's Cathedral* (Ellis' ed. 1818).

[2] Dugd., *Mon.*, vol. i. pp. 567, 584 *et seq.*;—vol. ii. pp. 274, 285, 513, 525, 527, 539;—vol. iv. pp. 1, 3, 6, 13 *et seq.*;—vol. vi. pp. 1172, 1175 *et seq.*; 1238, 1240 *et seq.*

[3] *Ibid.*, vol. i. pp. 93-98.

[4] *Ibid.*, p. 457 *et seq.*   [5] *Ibid.*, vol. vi. pp. 141, 144.

founded and endowed by King Henry the First, and received further donations from some of his successors. I have not ascertained the particulars of such private gifts as may have been added to them.

The Welsh Bishoprics[1] (which were all ancient) were not united to the Province of Canterbury till after the Conquest. They were then greatly impoverished, and so continued until the approximate equalisation of the revenues of the greater numbers of Bishops, through the agency of the Ecclesiastical Commissioners, which has taken place during the present reign.

The Abbeys of Peterborough, Gloucester, Chester, and Bristol, were erected into Bishops' Sees, with Deans and Chapters, in A.D. 1541-42.[2]

Peterborough Abbey[3] was founded about A.D. 650 by Penda, King of Mercia, and had at the Conquest very considerable possessions, derived from the gifts of seven Anglo-Saxon Kings, and many private donors, of whom nineteen are named in its charters. These were augmented in Norman times by large additional purchases of land, under seven Abbots.

Gloucester Abbey[4] was founded by Wulfhere and Ethelred, Kings of Mercia, in A.D. 680, and received some additions to its estates from later Kings. But the greater part of its lands came from gifts by private lay donors, of whom twenty-nine are named in a charter of confirmation by King Stephen,[5] dated A.D. 1138.

---

[1] Dugd., *Mon.*, vol. vi. pp. 1217, 1218, 1297, 1301, 1302 (and see Haddan and Stubbs' *Councils*, etc., vol. i. pp. 202-295, and 308).

[2] King Henry the Eighth's Charters of Foundation of all these sees are printed in the *Monasticon*.

[3] Dugd., *Mon.*, vol. i. pp. 344, 375 *et seq.*

[4] *Ibid.*, vol. i. pp. 531, 544-550.   [5] *Ibid.*, p. 551.

Chester Abbey[1] was founded by Elfleda, Countess of Mercia, in the reign of King Athelstan, and received some of its endowments from Kings Edmund and Edgar, and from Leofric, Earl of Chester, and other laymen, in Anglo-Saxon times. After the Conquest, large additional grants of lands, tithes, and appropriated churches were made to it by Hugh Lupus, the first Norman Earl of Chester, and by eighteen of his chief barons under his license. One of his successors in the earldom added further gifts.

St. Augustine's Abbey at Bristol[2] was founded by Robert Fitzhardinge, Mayor of Bristol, about A.D. 1120; and its endowments were given almost entirely by members of the Fitzhardinge and Berkeley families.

The See of Oxford,[3] founded in A.D. 1545 (with a Dean and Chapter, part of the Collegiate foundation of Christ Church), was endowed by King Henry the Eighth out of the revenues of the Priory of St. Frideswide (whose church is the Cathedral) and other Priories and Nunneries, for the suppression of which Cardinal Wolsey (intending them for the endowment of his own 'Cardinal College') had obtained a Bull from Pope Clement the Seventh.

Ripon[4] and Manchester[5] were Collegiate Churches, with Deans and Chapters, before they became Bishops' Sees in 1836. Ripon had been an Abbey, founded about A.D. 661 by Wilfrid, Archbishop of York, with some aid from private benefactors, and from a King of Northumberland. It received a new constitution, after the Conquest, from Aldred, Archbishop of York, who endowed it largely with lands.

[1] Dugd., *Mon.*, vol. ii. p. 370 *et seq.*
[2] *Ibid.*, vol. vi. pp. 363, 365.
[3] *Ibid.*, vol. ii. pp. 134, 142, etc.
[4] *Ibid.*, p. 131; and vol. vi. pp. 1367-68.
[5] *Ibid.*, vol. vi. p. 1423.

The Collegiate Church of Manchester was founded in the reign of Henry the Fifth by a private gentleman, Thomas de la Warr. It was suppressed under Edward the Sixth, but was afterwards restored. The endowments of the Bishops of both these Sees are derived from the surplus of Episcopal and Capitular estates, under the management of the Ecclesiastical Commissioners.

The Bishoprics of St. Albans and Truro were founded in 1877, the former by a division of the diocese and revenues of the See of Rochester, the latter by a division of the diocese, with some contribution from the revenues of Exeter, and with aid, in both cases, from private subscriptions. The Bishoprics of Liverpool, Newcastle, and Southwell, were founded in the years 1880, 1882, and 1884 respectively; being endowed principally by private subscriptions, with some aid from the revenues of the Sees of Chester, Durham, Lincoln, and Lichfield.

Of Westminster Abbey,[1] it is enough to say that it was founded early in the seventh century by a citizen or petty chieftain of London, and at various times received endowments from Anglo-Saxon and later kings, as well as from private persons, and by means of purchases of land made by some of its Abbots. The Collegiate Church of Windsor is a royal foundation of Edward the Third, afterwards augmented by Edward the Fourth and Henry the Eighth.

4. *Patronage.*

Of the rights and powers exercised at different times by the Crown in respect of appointments to Bishoprics, what is necessary has been said in former chapters.

---

[1] Dugd., vol. i. p. 265 *et seq.*

The founders of parish churches had power, when parishes were first formed and endowed, to determine in whom the right of 'advowson' (*i.e.* of presentation to the benefice when vacant) should be vested. Sometimes they gave, or afterwards transferred that right to Bishops or other Ecclesiastical corporations; in most cases, they retained it themselves; and, when they did so, it was a heritable right, passing, on death or alienation, to their heirs or successors in estate.

These rights of founders, and their origin in the endowment of churches, were referred to and recognised in public Statutes, of which I will here mention three.

The petition against Papal encroachments, on which the Statute of Carlisle[1] (A.D. 1307) proceeded, referred to the foundation and endowment of the 'prelacies' and other churches of the realm by the King and his progenitors, 'and the earls, barons, and other nobles of the realm, and their ancestors;' and it asserted the right of the King, and the earls, barons, and nobles, 'as lords and advowees' (*i.e.* patrons), to the custody during vacancy, and the presentations and collations to such benefices and churches.—The Statute of Provisors[2] (A.D. 1350) was passed to secure elections to the higher church dignities, 'in the manner as they were granted by the King's progenitors, and the ancestors of other lords, founders of the said dignities,' etc.; and also to secure freedom of presentation to all other benefices 'of the King's gift, or of any of his progenitors, or of other lords and donors, . . . in the manner as they were enfeoffed by their donors.'—In the preamble to the Statute 'for Restraint of Appeals'[3] (A.D. 1532), it is recited, that for

---

[1] 35 Edw. I., Sess. 4, cap. 3 (see Statute next cited).
[2] 25 Edw. III., St. 6.   [3] 24 Hen. VIII., cap. 12.

the due administration of their offices and duties by the clergy of 'the English Church,' and 'to keep them from corruption and sinister affection,' the 'King's most noble progenitors, and the antecessors of the nobles of this realm, have sufficiently endowed the said Church, both with honours and possessions.'

CHAPTER VII

TITHES, GENERALLY

1. *Their Origin.*

BETWEEN tithes, and the other property of the Church of England, there is this difference: that, while the other endowments were, in every sense and in every way, occasional and voluntary, the payment of tithes originated in the acknowledgment of a moral or religious obligation, supposed to be incumbent on Churchmen generally; which, after acquiring first the force of custom, and afterwards the sanction of ecclesiastical law, passed, with the rest of that law, into the national jurisprudence of our own and other Christian countries.

'The nearest approach,' says Professor Freeman,[1] 'to a regular general endowment, is the tithe; and this is not a very near approach. The tithe can hardly be said to have been granted by the State. The state of the case rather is, that the Church preached the payment of tithe as a duty; and that the State gradually came to enforce that duty by legal sanctions.'

Before the payment of tithe was enjoined by any Church canons, there was no difference between it and any other voluntary offerings or contributions of Churchmen for

[1] Freeman, p. 19.

the services and charities of their religion. That Christians should give to the Church out of the increase of their goods, 'as God had prospered them,' was an Apostolical precept.[1] The precedents of the Mosaic law, and of earlier patriarchal usage,[2] were not binding upon Christians: but they naturally suggested the tenth part, both to the clergy in their exhortations, and to the people in their practice, as a suitable measure for such gifts. Whether Selden[3] was right in supposing this not to have been customary till towards the end of the fourth century (when there is evidence of it in the works of St. Ambrose and St. Augustine), may be doubtful; but it is not material. It certainly became so more than two hundred years before the first foundation of the Anglo-Saxon Church. When the observance of this custom came to be enjoined (like other things regarded as religious duties) by the public Acts of Councils and Churches, these for a long time had, in England as elsewhere, such authority only as the regulations of any Church or religious society must always have over its own members. When the State, according to the measure of the authority which Church law from time to time acquired in particular countries, added a Civil to the Ecclesiastical sanction, this was in recognition and acknowledgment of the previously accepted customary obligation, and of the corresponding customary rights. It was not the creation, by way of tax, of a new burden: much less was it the grant of a new title, as out of any public fund or revenue. The tithe was never at any time a public fund or revenue. And the sanction so given,

---

[1] 1 Corinth. xvi. 2.
[2] Genesis xiv. 2; and xxviii. 22.
[3] *History of Tithes*, chap. v.; *Works*, vol. iii. p. 1096 (I quote from Wilkins' edition of Selden's Works, A.D. 1726).

whether by the ecclesiastical or by the temporal law, to the existing and generally recognised obligation, was a different matter from the appropriation of particular tithes, by way of endowment, to particular churches or other ecclesiastical corporations.

If there were no other proof that this is the true account of tithes, and that they had not their origin in any secular enactment or grant, the mere fact that suits for the 'subtraction' or non-payment of tithes were, till very modern times, of ecclesiastical cognisance only, without any concurrent jurisdiction in temporal Courts, might be enough for that purpose.

In tracing the history of the processes by which our parish churches, and other ecclesiastical corporations, came to be endowed with tithes, it is necessary to bear in mind that the customs of all parts of Western Christendom were not the same; and that, in the laws founded on those customs, both ecclesiastical and temporal, there were corresponding differences. The customs of Rome and of Italy were not the same as those of France or Spain; the custom of England was not the same with that of Ireland. The laws of Charlemagne, which added civil sanctions to the ecclesiastical customs of his Empire, never had any force here. Selden's reply [1] to one of the 'Animadversions' of his critic Dr. Tillesley upon his *History of Tithes* is as much in point now as it was in his own time :—'He tells you of France here, to oppose only what I say of England; and the Capitulars, that were for the old Empire and France, are urged to it. You should look better about you, Doctor, and remember, that France is not England.'

[1] *Works*, vol. iii. p. 1383.

2. *Continental Customs.*

There was anciently, before there were any special endowments with tithe, or any ecclesiastical or temporal laws upon the subject, one common fund or treasury in each diocese, under the administration of the Bishop, into which the tithes and other offerings of the faithful were brought. From the Cathedral city, as a common centre, missionary or itinerant clergy went out to preach and administer the Sacraments throughout the diocese, in such places, and with such provision for their charges and maintenance, as the Bishop might appoint.[1] As to the distribution of the funds brought into the diocesan treasury, different usages prevailed in different parts of Western Christendom. In the Church of Rome,[2] and those to which it gave the rule, there was a customary division into four parts; one for the maintenance of the ministry; another for the relief of the poor; another for the repair of Churches; and the remaining fourth for the Bishop. In some dioceses of the French, Spanish, and some other Churches,[3] the division was into the three former only of those parts, the Bishop taking no share. In some German Churches,[4] the Bishop claimed and retained the whole for himself.

There is no proof, or reason to believe, that any such division of tithes was ever customary in practice—it may safely be affirmed that none such was ever enjoined by law—in any part of England. I shall have occasion to refer to this subject hereafter, when I notice some statements about it which have been circulated by the advocates of Disestablishment.

[1] Selden, vol. iii. p. 1206.
[2] *Ibid.*, p. 1121.
[3] *Ibid.*
[4] *Ibid.*, p. 1130.

3. *Anglo-Saxon Canons and Laws.*

When Augustin, the founder of the Anglo-Saxon Church, asked Pope Gregory the Great (whose missionary he was) to advise him how the offerings of his converts should be distributed,—not particularly mentioning tithes,— he was answered, that,[1] although it was the custom of the Apostolical See to charge Bishops, on their consecration, to make that fourfold division which has been mentioned, it would be best for him, in the infancy of the Anglo-Saxon Church, to live together with such of his clergy as were unmarried, and to imitate as far as possible the community of all things which was practised under the Apostles.

That the Bishops in England received tithes from the people as early as A.D. 747, appears probable, from a letter[2] written about that time by Boniface, first Archbishop of Mentz (an Englishman, and the apostle of Germany), to Cuthbert, Archbishop of Canterbury. But there was no canon or other law here upon the subject before A.D. 785, when two Italian Bishops (the first 'Legates,' who ever came here from Rome) were sent to this country by Pope Adrian the First. They brought with them letters, recommending for the adoption and observance of the Anglo-Saxon Church a number of Constitutions or Injunctions, ready prepared in the Latin language, under twenty-nine heads: all which (being duly explained) were accepted and agreed to by the Archbishop of York and the Bishops and Clergy of his province, at a Council held in the north of England, with the assent of Aelfwald, king of Northumberland; who, with

---

[1] Bede, *Eccl. Hist.*, book i. chap. xxvii.; and Haddan and Stubbs, *Councils*, vol. iii. p. 19.

[2] Haddan and Stubbs, vol. iii. p. 380.

K

many of his nobles, was personally present. The Legates then travelled southward, accompanied by ambassadors from that prince; and another Council was held at Chalchyth (now generally supposed to be Chelsea), at which the same Constitutions or Injunctions were in like manner accepted and agreed to by the Primate and other Bishops of the Southern Province, with the assent of Offa, king of Mercia (then present with several of his nobles), and Kenulph, king of Wessex; who did not, however, like Offa, set his hand to the acts of that Council, and perhaps may not himself have been there.

One (only one) of these Constitutions or Injunctions related to tithes; and, being characteristic of the way in which the subject was dealt with then and afterwards, I think it worth while to give the translation in full :—

'As to paying tithes, it is written in the law, "The tenth part of all thine increase :"—" If thou bring thy first-fruits into the house of the Lord." Again, by the prophet; " Bring ye all the tithe into the storehouse," etc. As a wise man says; "No man can justly give alms of what he possesseth, unless he hath first separated to the Lord what He from the beginning directed to be paid to Him." And on this account it often happens, that he who does not pay tithes is himself reduced to a tenth. Therefore we do solemnly enjoin, that all take care to pay the tenth of all that they possess; because that peculiarly belongs to God; and let them live, and give alms, out of the nine parts; and we advise, that alms be given in secret; because it is written, "When thou givest alms, sound not a trumpet."'[1]

An idle story is told by some of the old chroniclers, and has been repeated by some uncritical writers[2] in more

[1] Seld., *Hist. Tithes*, chap. viii. (vol. iii. pp. 1179-81); Johnson, *Laws and Canons*, vol. i. p. 277 (Canon 17); Blackstone's *Commentaries*, vol. ii. p. 25.

[2] *E.g.* Dean Prideaux, *Original and Right of Tithes*, chap. iv. p. 102 (2d ed. 1736).

modern times, about a supposed grant of all the tithes of his kingdom to the Church, by the same King Offa, by way of penance for a murder which he had committed. For this, there is no historical foundation. Another error, as to a similar grant in A.D. 855 by a later king, Ethelwolf,[1] rests upon a misconstruction (as learned men are now agreed) of a document not really relating to tithes.

Of later constitutions or laws, I shall mention all which are material, omitting mere repetitions (in succeeding reigns) of some of those enactments.

Athelstan,[2] king of all England, by orders made in a Council of Bishops (A.D. 925), directed his own 'reeves' to pay tithes; adding, that all Bishops should do the same; and grounding this order on certain texts of Scripture, and of St. Ambrose.

By a law of King Edmund,[3] passed in a national Synod of both the Archbishops and many Bishops at London (A.D. 944), the penalty of excommunication was denounced against those who would not pay their tithes.

King Edgar's laws[4] (supposed to have been made

---

[1] See Dean Prideaux, *Original and Right of Tithes*, chap. iv. p. 103; whose work (see *C. D.*, p. 55) has been reprinted by the Liberation Society,—perhaps, because he said, that on this charter of Ethelwolf 'the civil right of tithes in this land had its main foundation.' The *C. D.* (p. 188) gives this charter up; quoting Haddan and Stubbs, vol. iii. p. 636, note. That note hardly does justice to Selden; who, though he accepted Ingulph's interpretation of the charter, stated the question fairly, as one of doubtful construction (Seld., *Works*, vol. iii. pp. 1182-84).

[2] Johnson, *Laws and Canons*, vol. i. p. 339; Seld., *Hist. Tithes*, vol. iii. p. 1186.

[3] Johnson, *Laws and Canons*, vol. i. p. 366; Seld., *Hist. Tithes*, vol. iii. p. 1187.

[4] Seld., *Hist. Tithes*, vol. iii. p. 1189; Johnson, *Laws and Canons*, vol. i. pp. 409, 410.

about A.D. 970) were the first which recognised rights of particular Churches to tithes; I shall recur to them, when I speak of the formation and endowment of parishes. They were also the first to appoint definite times and seasons for their payment, and to provide the means of enforcing it by temporal penalties. The king's reeve and the Bishop's reeve, and the mass-priest of the 'older' or principal church, were to go together to any defaulting occupier, and take from him the whole produce; of which he was to receive back only one-tenth; the other eight-tenths (after paying its tithe to the 'older' or principal church) being forfeited, in equal shares, to the lord and the Bishop. This law was repeated by Canute,[1] and is also found in the collection of Anglo-Saxon laws, sometimes erroneously[2] ascribed to Henry the First.

To this summary of the material parts of the extant public acts of Anglo-Saxon times on the subject of tithes (for I reject the constitutions[3] ascribed to Ethelred the Unready, which I shall hereafter mention), it is proper to add, that in the collection of the 'laws, rights, and customs' of his new subjects, made and confirmed by William the Conqueror (sometimes called laws of Edward the Confessor),[4] the first place is given to 'the laws of the holy mother, the Church:' among which is one enumerating titheable matters, and providing for the recovery of tithes in the Bishop's Court, with aid (if necessary) from the Court of the King.

---

[1] Johnson, *Laws and Canons*, vol. i. p. 506.
[2] See Thorpe's *Ancient Laws*, vol. i. pp. 520, 641.
[3] See *post*, pp. 149, 151, 152.
[4] Johnson, vol. i. p. 534.

4. *Special Endowments with Tithe.*

Whether from any variance between law and practice, or from laxity in the administration and enforcement of the law (as is intimated in those laws of William the Conqueror, to which reference has just been made), or from any other cause, it is certain, that the lords of the soil were, during the whole of this period, under very little restraint or control as to the manner in which they should fulfil the generally recognised religious obligation of paying tithes. It is a common saying in our law-books,[1] that 'before the Council of Lateran, any man might give his tithes to what spiritual person he would.' The form in which this doctrine (as ancient, certainly, as the reign of Edward the Third) is stated by modern writers will be found in Blackstone's *Commentaries*,[2] and in the following extract from Mr. Cruise's *Digest of the Law of Real Property*.[3]

'Before the Council of Lateran, which was held A.D. 1180, every person was at liberty to pay his tithes to whatever church or monastery he pleased ; or he might pay them into the hands of the Bishop, who distributed the revenues of his Church among his diocesan clergy.[4] But when dioceses were divided into parishes, the tithes of each parish were allotted to its own particular minister ; first by common consent, or appointment of the lord of the manor ; and afterwards by law.'

On a view of the authorities upon which this doctrine is founded, the first observation necessary to be made is, that the persons who are said to have had the liberty of thus appropriating at their pleasure their tithes, were the lords of

---

[1] Coke's *Reports*, part ii. p. 44 (*b*); Hobart's *Reports*, p. 295, etc.; also Lyndwode's *Provinciale*, cap. *de locato et conducto*, fol. 117.

[2] *Commentaries*, vol. i. p. 112. [3] *Tit.*, 22; *Tithes*, sect. 53.

[4] Blackstone adds : 'And for other pious purposes, according to his own discretion' (vol. i. p. 112).

the soil, not the occupiers who cultivated it as their 'villeins' or tenants, and by whom the render of tithe was directly to be made. The earliest judicial authority is that of King Edward the Third's Chief Justice (afterwards Lord Treasurer and Lord Chancellor), Sir Robert Parnynge. His words are;[1] that, 'of ancient time, before a new Constitution made by the Pope, the patron of one church might grant his tithes in that parish to another parish.' The 'patron' here meant was the lord of the manor or lordship; and in the case supposed he could not have already granted the tithes of his land for the perpetual endowment of the church of which he was patron; but (according to Parnynge) was at liberty to do so to a parish as well as to a religious house, and to any parish, not only that within which the tithes arose. And though a later jurist of the same reign (Ludlow, A.D. 1371) said[2]—in terms repeated by most of the great lawyers of the seventeenth century—that 'anciently every man could grant the tithes of his land to any church that he chose,' it is plain, that the lord or land-owner, who alone could make a grant of the land, or of any charge upon it, was meant.

As to the 'Council of Lateran,' mentioned in so many books as having in some way put an end to that liberty, there has been controversy among the learned. There were four 'Lateran' Councils, held between A.D. 1119 and A.D. 1216; of which the third was held A.D. 1179-80, under Pope Alexander the Third, and the fourth A.D. 1215, under Innocent the Third. Sir Edward Coke,[3] not finding in the Acts of any of them exactly what he

---

[1] *Year-Book*, 7 Edw. III., fol. 5, pl. 8.
[2] *Year-Book*, 44 Edw. III.-VI., pl. 22.
[3] *Second Institute*, p. 641.

looked for, thought that he had discovered it in a letter of Pope Innocent the Third to Walter, Archbishop of Canterbury, dated from the Lateran Palace at Rome in A.D. 1200;—not a document likely to have been confounded by lawyers with a canon or decree of a General Council. Selden thought[1] that the reference commonly made to the Third Lateran Council, of A.D. 1179-80, might be correct, although some perplexity arose from the glosses of later Canonists upon it—and this appears to be a reasonable view. 'So far' (it was said in the Acts of that Council) 'has the boldness of laymen been carried, that they collate clerks to churches without institution from the Bishops, and remove them at their will; and, besides this, they commonly dispose as they please of the possessions and goods of churches.' Orders were then made against the continuance of these practices; which may have caused all the ecclesiastical authorities, from that time forward, to oppose themselves to what Selden calls 'arbitrary consecrations' of tithe; that is, to appropriations by landowners, at their own will and pleasure, of the tithes arising within their lordships and estates.

The proof, that lords of manors and other great landowners did make perpetual grants of tithes (not only as incident to 'appropriated' Rectories of churches, but also separately) is abundant: and if they had power to do this, as they certainly did, to Capitular bodies and monasteries, it seems to follow (as Sir Robert Parnynge expressly stated) that they could do so, and did, to parish churches also; and that Selden is right in regarding this as the true origin of the general endowment of parish churches with tithes. This would naturally be the result of the power of the

[1] Seld., *Hist. Tithes*, chap. ix. (*Works*, vol. iii. p. 1226).

Bishops to make proper conditions before consenting to the constitution of parishes, or the consecration of churches for them. The practice could not have become so nearly universal and uniform as it did, unless it had grown into a custom under the support and influence of ecclesiastical authority.

It is true (as Dean Prideaux[1] observes) that the examples of lay grants of tithes, apart from Churches, which the industry of Selden collected,[2] were all to religious houses, and not to parish Churches, and that they were all of Norman times. So also are all such as have fallen under my own observation; as, for instance, the extensive grants of tithes made to the Abbey of Chester by Hugh Lupus and his barons before A.D. 1100;[3] and the grant by King Henry the Second[4] to the Bishopric and Chapter of Salisbury of all the tithes of the New Forest, and of the King's other Forests in Wiltshire, Berkshire, and Dorsetshire, and of four parishes expressly named in that charter. But as has been already said, written documents of this kind were much more likely to exist, and to be preserved, in the case of Religious houses than in that of parish churches; which were in all probability endowed (after as well as before the Conquest) simultaneously with and as part of the solemnities of consecration. On the same principle on which the Bishop insisted upon the provision of a proper manse and glebe, he might require an endowment of the parish church by the lord or patron with the local tithes, unless some valid and permanent appropriation had been already made of them; and that endowment, as well as the other, might take place without writing.

[1] Prideaux, pp. 192, 195.
[2] *Hist. Tithes*, chap. xi. (*Works*, vol. iii. pp. 1228-53).
[3] Dugd., *Monast.*, vol. ii. p. 371.   [4] *Ibid.*, vol. vi. p. 1296.

Dean Prideaux acknowledged that, until the disuse of the practice of lay investiture (which was not disused till the time of Henry the First),—

'Patrons had such an arbitrary disposition of their Churches, and the tithes and other endowments belonging to them, that on all occasions they could dispose of them as they thought fit, to any that were by law capable of holding them; and this in parcels, as well as whole;' and that 'so long as patrons had this power they granted the Churches and tithes of their advowsons in charters of appropriation in very absolute terms, as if they had been their own inheritance, calling them "my Churches" and "my tithes."'[1]

To what extent some laymen proceeded in the exercise of these powers of 'arbitrary disposition' appears from Selden's statements, that 'sometimes laymen *sold*[2] the tithes to the Church' (not always of the same place); and that 'these grants were not always free consecrations, but oft-times were made for valuable consideration given by the Church;'[3] and from the Canon of the Council of Westminster, held under Anselm, A.D. 1102, 'that tithes be not paid but to the Church only.'[4]

Of the English writers who have investigated this subject there has been none more learned, and none more impartial, than Selden. He was free from ecclesiastical prepossessions; and it is chiefly by those who had such prepossessions[5] that his views have been controverted. The best of our later common law authorities have followed him; I shall not scruple, generally, to do the same.

[1] Prideaux, pp. 192, 193.
[2] *Hist. Tithes*, chap. vi. (*Works*, vol. iii. p. 1114).
[3] *Ibid.* (p. 1119).
[4] Johnson, *Laws and Canons*, vol. ii. p. 1102 (Canon 13).
[5] Dean Comber, Dean Prideaux, Bishop Stillingfleet, etc.

CHAPTER VIII

PAROCHIAL TITHES

1. *The Parish System.*

THE parochial system, like other things in England, grew up gradually. For the statement of Camden, that England was divided into parishes by Honorius, Archbishop of Canterbury, about A.D. 630, there is no foundation;[1] nor is there much more cause to believe that this was done by Theodore (who was Primate from A.D. 668 to 690), as others[2] have supposed. Archbishop Theodore did indeed labour, not without success, for the subdivision of the English dioceses,[3] then much too large; and the word 'parish' was at first applied to a diocese, which may have led in after times to a misconception of his work. Bede, writing about the end of the seventh century, mentioned two noblemen in the kingdom of Northumberland as having built churches in their manors; but Bede, who held Archbishop Theodore in great reverence, says nothing about any such institution

---

[1] Seld., chap. ix. (vol. iii. p. 1208); Blackstone's *Comm.*, vol. i. p. 113.

[2] *E.g.* Soames (*Anglo-Saxon Church*, 2d edition, 1838, p. 119), and Bishop Harold Browne, in his paper read at the Carlisle Congress. But I know no evidence to be set against the silence of Bede.

[3] Haddan and Stubbs, vol. iii. pp. 125, 127; Bede, *Hist.*, lib. 4, cap. 12.

as that of parishes.¹ Between Bede's time and the beginning of the ninth century many such churches, in many parts of the country, were built and endowed with tithes by the lords of the soil. Of this fact there is evidence in the appropriation of some of those churches by the lords, their patrons, to religious houses.

'About the year 800' (says Selden) 'many churches founded by laymen are recorded to have been appropriated to the Abbey of Crowland, as you see in the charters of confirmation made by Bertulph, king of Mercland, and of others to the same Abbey reported by Ingulphus. Whence it may be observed that by this time lay foundations were grown very common, and parochial limits also of the parishioners' devotions.'[2]

He mentions, as evidence to the same effect, two of the Canons made in a Council held at Chalchyth[3] (A.D. 816) under Wulfred, Archbishop of Canterbury; one of which provided for the consecration of churches, wherever built, by the Bishop of the diocese; and the other for special services to be held in all the churches of every 'parochia' (which there plainly means diocese) upon the death of the Bishop, for which the people were to be called together by the beating or tolling of a bell[4] in each church.

His account of the practice between A.D. 800 and A.D. 1200 (speaking, as I understand him, not of England particularly) is this, that it consisted—

'in some ordinary payments of tithes, as in the former ages; in more frequent consecrations of a perpetual gift of them alone

---

[1] Bede, *Hist.*, lib. 4, cap. 2, 12; and lib. 5, cap. 4, 5, 8.
[2] Seld., *Hist. Tithes*, chap. ix. (vol. iii. p. 1210).
[3] *Ibid.*; and see Johnson, *Laws and Canons*, vol. i. p. 301, 306 (Canons 2 and 10).
[4] *Pulsato signo.*

to any church or monastery at the owner's choice; in appropriations of them, with the churches in which they were by custom or consecration established; in infeudations of them into lay hands; and in exemptions for discharge of payment.'[1]

With regard to England, he says:—

'When devotion grew firmer, and most laymen of fair estate desired the country residence of some chaplains that might be always ready for Christian instruction among them, their families, and adjoining tenants, oratories and churches began to be built by their order; and, being hallowed by the Bishops, were endowed with peculiar maintenance from the founders for the incumbents that should there only reside. Which, nevertheless, with all other ecclesiastical profits that came to the hands of every such several incumbent (in regard that now the lay-founder had, according to the territory of his demesnes, tenancies, or neighbouring possessions, made and assigned both the limits within which the holy function was to be exercised, and appointed the persons that should repair to the church and offer there, as also provided a special salary for the performance), was afterward also restrained from the common treasury of the diocese, and made the only revenue which became perpetually annexed to the church of that clerk who received it. Neither was it wonder that the Bishops should give way to such restraint; for, had they denied that to lay-founders, they had given no small cause also of restraining their devotion. Every man, questionless, would have been the unwillinger to have specially endowed the church founded chiefly for the holy use of him, his family, and tenants, if withal he might not have had the liberty to have given his incumbent there resident a special and several maintenance, which could not have been had the former community of the clergy's revenue still remained. Out of these lay-foundations chiefly (doubtless), came those kind of parishes which, at this day, are in every diocese; their differences in quantity being originally out of the difference of the several circuits of the demesnes or territories possessed by the founders. And after such time as,

---

[1] *Hist. Tithes*, chap. vi. (vol. iii. p. 1114).

upon lay-foundations, churches had their profits so limited to their incumbents, no doubt can be but that the Bishops, in their prebends or advowsons of parishes, both in cities and in the country (formerly limited only in regard of the minister's function) restrained also the profits of their several churches to the incumbents, that an uniformity might be received in that innovation of parochial right.'[1]

There are, in particular places, special customs, which must necessarily have had their origin in express grants from the lords of the soil, for the payment of tithes in respect of matters not generally titheable. By one[2] of the charters of Hugh Lupus to the Abbey of Chester, not only the tithe of corn and of other titheable produce in fifteen of that Earl's manors, but also the tithes of four several fisheries, and of all the fish taken in the river Dee, were granted to that monastery. By the ancient custom of London, there was a house-tithe; now regulated under Acts[3] passed in Henry the Eighth's reign. By the custom of the parish of Stanhope in Durham (I believe there are also like customs in other places), a tithe of lead-ore and other minerals was payable. For perpetual grants of tithes, no license in mortmain, or other temporal confirmation, was ever necessary. They were deemed in law to be things 'merely spiritual;'[4] and were held by no feudal tenure. If the ecclesiastical authorities were consenting parties to their appropriation by way of endowment, that was sufficient.

[1] Seld., *Tithes*, chap. ix. (vol. iii. p. 1209).
[2] Dugd., *Monast.*, vol. ii. pp. 385, 386.
[3] 27 Hen. VIII., cap. 21; 37 Hen. VIII., cap. 12.
[4] Coke, *Second Inst.*, p. 640: citing the 'Prior of Worcester's Case,' in which it was so determined by the Chancellor and all the Judges and Barons.

2. *King Edgar's Laws.*

King Edgar's laws[1] (afterwards repeated by Canute), alone among English legislative Acts of times anterior to the thirteenth century, contain provisions which seem to refer to the parochial system, not perhaps in its final, but in an earlier stage. They distinguish between three kinds of churches:[2]—(1) the 'older,' or 'principal,' church; (2) churches with burial-grounds, which the lords of manors or other seignories might have in their lordships; and (3) churches of the latter sort, without burial-grounds. They recognise the title of the 'older,' or 'principal' church to the tithes arising within the 'adjacent parish,' except when there might be within that parish any church of the second class; in which case, one-third of the tithes was to be paid to that church, the 'older' or 'principal' church taking the rest.

Sir William Blackstone[3] concluded, from these laws of King Edgar, that England was then generally divided into parishes, such as now exist. That conclusion depends upon the word 'parish,' which is equivocal; and in part, perhaps, upon the meaning of 'older' or 'principal' Church. Mr. Johnson[4] translated it 'minster:' and it might mean the Cathedral[5] of the diocese. Selden[6] considered it to mean here 'the ancientest church or monastery, to which a land-owner, having no church of his

---

[1] Johnson, *Laws and Canons*, vol. i. p. 409 (Canons 1 and 2).
[2] Seld., *Tithes*, chap. ix. (vol. iii. p. 1211).
[3] *Comm.*, vol. i. p. 113.
[4] Johnson, *Laws and Canons*, vol. i. p. 409.
[5] Seld., *Tithes*, chap. ix. (vol. iii. p. 1211); Dugd., *Antiq. Warw.*, p. 14.
[6] Seld., *Tithes*, chap. ix. (vol. iii. pp. 1211, 1212).

own, would usually, by reason of the situation of his farms, houses, and lands, repair to hear God's service.' And he thought that all churches of King Edgar's second class became, in process of time, separate and independent, with parishes of their own, endowed with all the tithes arising within their limits, and not with one-third only;—while those of the third class, as long as they were without burial-grounds, remained chapels of ease.

3. *Subdivision of Parishes.*

The process of subdivision of parishes has been going on from the time of their first formation to the present day. An early example is given by Selden, from a decretal epistle of Pope Alexander the Third[1] (A.D. 1159-1181) to the then Archbishop of York, enjoining such a subdivision. It recites the distance of a certain town from the parish-church; and that 'the church-revenue of the parish, although that town were separated, was not insufficient for the minister of the mother-church.' It then proceeds to enjoin the Archbishop 'to build in that town a church, and, with the assent of the founder of the mother-church, to institute, at the presentation of the Rector, an incumbent there, that ought to have for his own use all ecclesiastical profits increasing within the limits of the same town.' This was to be done, whether the Rector of the mother-church consented or not.

4. *Later History of Tithes.*

The parochial organisation had become universal, or nearly so, in England, before the end of the twelfth cen-

[1] Seld., *Tithes*, chap. ix. (vol. iii. p. 1213).

tury; and ever since that time the legal presumption (in the absence of proof to the contrary) has been that the tithes of all titheable produce within each parish belong of common right to the Rector. It was so understood in the time of the Pope just named, Alexander the Third; an epistle [1] from whom to the Bishops of Worcester and Winchester is quoted by Selden, as 'reciting the general institution' or custom 'of the Church of England to be, that every parishioner should pay his tithe-corn to his own parish.' And in that letter of Pope Innocent the Third [2] (A.D. 1200) to Walter, Archbishop of Canterbury, which Sir Edward Coke thought might have been confounded by earlier lawyers with a decree of a Lateran Council, the exercise of some power of arbitrary choice by the tithe-payer as to the recipient of his tithes (which had been represented to the Pope as still continuing in the diocese of Canterbury) was treated as an abuse to be corrected, without regard to custom, by canonical censures. The Provincial Constitutions of Archbishop Winchelsey [3] (A.D. 1305), which regulated various matters as to tithe, were founded throughout upon the presumption of the right to 'prædial' tithes being in the Rector of the parish where they arose.

When the Rectory of any parish was 'appropriated' to a monastery or other non-parochial corporation (of which appropriations there were too many, both before and after the Conquest), the 'appropriators' performed the spiritual duties by a 'Vicar,' whose office soon became permanent. The practice which gradually followed, and which in course of time, by the aid of episcopal authority, grew

---

[1] Seld., *Tithes*, chap. x. (vol. iii. p. 1221).

[2] *Ibid.*, chap. viii. (vol. iii. p. 1197). Coke, *Second Inst.*, p. 641.

[3] Johnson's *Laws and Canons*, vol. ii. p. 315.

into a legal right, was for the tithes, in those cases, to be apportioned between the Rector and the Vicar; the Vicar receiving for his maintenance what were called the 'small' tithes, and the 'appropriators' taking the 'great.' To prevent abuses, beyond the original evil of the 'appropriation' of the Rectory, one of Archbishop Stratford's Constitutions,[1] made A.D. 1342 in a Council at London, ordained, that Religious houses, 'having ecclesiastical benefices appropriate,' should be 'compelled by the Bishops every year to distribute to the poor parishioners a certain portion of their benefices in alms, to be moderated at the discretion of the Bishops in proportion to the value of such benefices.' This was made Statute law by an Act of Parliament passed in A.D. 1391;[2] which also required the Bishops, upon any new 'appropriations' being made, to assign to the Vicar a sufficient endowment, according to the value of the Churches. Another Statute[3] was passed in A.D. 1402, annulling all appropriations of Vicarages.

Nothing else of importance affecting tithes was done before the Reformation, except that there was an Act[4] (A.D. 1400) prohibiting the purchase of Papal Bulls for discharge of tithes. Henry the Eighth's legislation gave to the lay tithe-owners who then came into existence remedies for the recovery of tithes, both in the temporal and in the ecclesiastical courts;[5] but, as to prædial tithes in ecclesiastical hands, it made no change, either in the right or in the remedy. On the dissolution of the monasteries, those Rectorial tithes which had belonged to the dissolved corporations passed, with their other possessions, to the

[1] Johnson's *Laws and Canons*, vol. ii. p. 364 ('Extravagants,' 4).
[2] 15 Rich. II., cap. 6. [3] 4 Hen. IV., cap. 12.
[4] 2 Hen. IV., cap. 4. [5] 32 Hen. VIII., cap. 7.

Crown, and the greater part of them were granted away to lay proprietors, under titles derived from whom tithes have ever since been largely held by laymen, as ordinary heritable property. The rent of tithe-free land is always greater than that of land subject to tithe: if there were no tithe, the landowner, and not the occupier, would have the benefit.

Many Inclosure, and some other local Acts, passed during the last and the present century, have contained provisions for allotting to tithe-owners, lay and ecclesiastical, lands instead of tithes; and under some of those Acts the tithes of whole parishes were commuted for fixed money payments,—not, however, to any considerable amount in the whole. In 1836 the general Act for the commutation of tithes in England was passed, under which all tithes, lay and ecclesiastical, have been commuted into rent-charges, settled originally according to the average values of grain produce for the seven years preceding the commutation, and variable in amount from year to year, according to the averages of the last seven years.

All these Acts, and these forms of commutation, have proceeded, equally and indifferently as to lay and ecclesiastical tithe-owners, upon the footing of the existing titles; altering only (in what was considered to be the common interest of tithe-owner and tithe-payer) the legal form and quality of the subject-matter of the right, and the manner of its perception and enjoyment; and giving remedies for its infringement, appropriate to its altered forms.

5. *Tithes and the Poor.*

Here I might have concluded this chapter, but for a passage[1] in the *Case for Disestablishment*, in which it

[1] *C. D.*, p. 57.

is suggested (though with a degree of caution rather unusual in the writer, and indicating some consciousness that he was treading on insecure ground) that the same fourfold division of tithe which prevailed in parts of the Continent, and was enjoined by several of the 'Capitulars'[1] of Charlemagne and his successors, ought of right to have been made in England: for which purpose Southey's *Book of the Church*,[2] and a recent contribution to periodical literature of an Oxford clergyman,[3] are quoted: and there the matter is left.

But, if the matter is so left in the *Case for Disestablishment*, it has been very differently treated in a leaflet scattered far and wide over the land (I suppose to influence the minds of candidates and electors who knew nothing about these things), by the 'Liberation Society,' during the two last general elections. That production is entitled, 'Tithes and the Poor;' and it is difficult to read it without remembering that there was once a man[4] who asked why certain 'very precious ointment' was not 'sold for three hundred pence, and given to the poor':—which he said, 'not that he cared for the poor,'—but for other reasons.

The author of that tract—evidently speaking throughout of England—says (1) that 'in all the early laws about tithes, it is clearly laid down that the poor were to have a share of the tithes, and as good a share as the clergy;' (2) that 'at first' the division into four parts, and 'after a while,'

---

[1] Baluze's *Capitularia regum Francorum*, vol. i. p. 356 (Lombard law of A.D. 801); *ibid.*, p. 428 (A.D. 845); *ibid.* in lib. vii. p. 1104 (date uncertain); *ibid.* in '4th Addition,' p. 1205 (date uncertain).
[2] Southey speaks of the quadripartite (not the tripartite) division, vol. i. p. 80, 1st ed. He probably relied upon Kennett.
[3] The Rev. Dr. Hatch. [4] John xii. 4, 5.

when 'the Bishops had land allotted to them,' the division into three parts—one for the poor—prevailed here ; (3) that 'later on, when the tithes were not offered freely enough to satisfy the priests,' and 'a law was therefore passed to compel people to give them, the same plan was insisted upon, and the poor still had their share ;' (4) that this was 'before the time of Parliaments ; but, when Parliament made laws upon the subject, the right of the poor to their share was preserved ;' (5) that 'nobody seems to know exactly how, or when, the poor lost their legal claim to a share of the tithes ;'—that 'it is sometimes put down to the Reformation ;' 'but this can hardly be the reason ; for in Queen Elizabeth's time the old law still held good.'

His conclusion is—

'It is quite clear, then, that the poor were meant to have a share of the tithe ; and, when they come into the hands of the nation, the poor will be right in claiming that the tithes shall be employed in part for their benefit. But the clergy have the tithes now ; and, so long as the Church remains Established, they will keep them. The first step, therefore, towards getting back the tithes for the benefit of the poor, is disestablishment and disendowment.'

Of these statements, there is but one to which that degree of respect is due, which may be accorded to all opinions which have been the subject of honest controversy among learned men. I mean that which relates to the division of tithes in a remote age, before parishes were endowed with them, into parts (four, or three), of which one was for the poor. What is said about this is nearly in the words of Blackstone ;[1] who, however,

---

[1] *Comm.*, vol. i. pp. 384, 385 (book i. chap. xi.) Blackstone, of course, does not talk about Bishops having 'land *allotted* to them.'

probably was not,[1] in that passage of his Commentaries, referring to any supposed custom of *England*. But it is certainly true that some respectable writers[2] have thought that such a division of tithes was, during some part of the Anglo-Saxon period, more or less customary in England. Other writers,[3] of greater weight and authority, have thought and still think otherwise. But it is necessary for those who maintain that opinion to show, by historical evidence, that at some time or other, in all or some part of England, any such custom or practice did, in fact, prevail: and this has never been, and never can be, done. There is no ground for the opinion, except the existence, in manuscripts later than the Conquest, of three miscellaneous Collections of Canons, and one set of 'Constitutions,' ascribed to King Ethelred the Unready, and supposed to have been made at the end of his troubled reign. In all these, a threefold (not in any case a fourfold) division of tithes is mentioned. Of the three Collections of Canons, the first[4] is by an unknown hand, though with a venerable name

---

[1] Compare the passage just cited with *Comm.*, vol. ii. p. 25, in which he refers to Charlemagne as the author of the fourfold division; *i.e.* (I suppose), as the author of the earliest temporal laws upon that subject.

[2] *E.g.*, Bishop Kennett (*Case of Appropriations*, 1704, pp. 14-17), and, lately, Mr. Brewer (*Endowments and Establishment of the Church of England*, 1885, p. 135), who thought there could be 'no question' but that 'the quadripartite' (he does not say the tripartite) 'division prevailed in England.' The reasons for dissenting from that opinion, and also for rejecting the supposed authorities for a tripartite division, are succinctly stated by the learned editor of Mr. Brewer's work, Mr. Dibdin, in a note at p. 156.

[3] *E.g.* Mr. Soames, Archdeacon Hale, Bishop Stubbs; and Professor Freeman, quoted in Mr. Morris Fuller's *Tract*, pp. 5, 25, 34. As to Bishop Stubbs, see *post*, p. 158.

[4] See Johnson, *Laws and Canons*, vol. i. pp. 180-235 (the particular Canon is the fifth, p. 185). The tendency of Mr. Johnson and of other

prefixed to it, that of Egbert (or Ecgbright), Archbishop of York in the eighth century. It does not purport to represent that the Canons contained in it were ever received as law in England; they had plainly no original force here; some of them are Oriental, some African, some Irish, and some from various other foreign sources. Some are mere texts extracted from Scripture or from the Fathers. No English Council or Synod adopted them. Many of them are copied (as Selden[1] and others have shown) from the Capitulars of Charlemagne and his successors; some are plainly inapplicable to England; and the particular Canon relating to the threefold division of tithes refers to 'witnesses,' as to whom the first Imperial legislation[2] was later than Charlemagne. These 'Excerpts' (for that is their title), in their actual form, and with this canon as to tithes in them, could not possibly have been collected by Archbishop Egbert, who died[3] before Charlemagne succeeded to his father's throne.—The second Collection of Canons is contained in a manuscript in one of the Libraries at Cambridge,[4] under the name of Archbishop

---

ecclesiastical writers of the seventeenth century (see Spelman on *Tithes*, p. 132, and Stillingfleet, *Eccl. Cases*, etc., p. 89) was to accept ancient documents of this kind, not as to tithes only, but on other subjects also, with little discrimination.

[1] Seld., *Tithes*, chap. viii. (*Works*, vol. iii. pp. 1178, 1179); Arch. Hale, *Essay on the Supposed Existence of a Quadripartite and Tripartite Division of Tithes*, 1842, p. 25; Soames, *Hist. of Anglo-Saxon Church*, 2d ed., p. 105; Haddan and Stubbs, *Councils*, etc., preface to vol. i., p. xvi.

[2] See Baluze's *Capitularia*, vol. ii. p. 339 (Lombard Laws of (?) Lothair, Law 37). The same reference occurs in the corresponding 'Canon,' ascribed to Archbishop Theodore.

[3] Archbishop Egbert died A.D. 767. Charlemagne became king of the Franks A.D. 768.

[4] In the library of Corpus Christi College. See Wanley's *Catalogue*

Theodore; but these (which are copied, so far as relates to the threefold division of titles, from Egbert's 'Excerpts') are clearly not the work of Theodore, nor of his time. The most competent critics regard them as containing some rule on the Benedictine model (Theodore was not a Benedictine), put together by an unknown author.—The third Collection[1] bears the name of Aelfric, and appears to have been written at the request of a Bishop named Wulfin, to whom it is addressed, being put into the form of a charge, or pastoral epistle, from that Bishop to his clergy. Who Aelfric and Wulfin were, has been a subject of doubt and controversy. The most probable opinion identifies the one with Wulfsin, Bishop of Sherborne in the time of Ethelred the Unready, to whom a charter (printed in Wharton's *Anglia Sacra*[2]) was granted by that King; the other with a learned monk,—not to be confounded with another Aelfric, who was Archbishop of Canterbury about the same time. Neither Aelfric nor Wulfin could have any power to legislate for the Church of England. The monk seems to have wished the Bishop to adopt or promulgate these 'Canons,' as rules for his own diocese. There is no evidence that Bishop Wulfin, or any other Bishop, ever did so, or that they were received or acted upon as laws in any diocese.—As for the alleged 'Constitutions' of King Ethelred,[3] they have no satis-

of Anglo-Saxon MSS., p. 131; Soames, *Anglo-Saxon Church*, p. 105; and a Tract on the Tripartite Division, by the Rev. Morris Fuller (London, 1885), pp. 23, 25.

[1] Johnson, *Laws and Canons*, vol. i. pp. 383-407 (Canon 24, p. 398). As to the questions, who Aelfric and Wulfin were, see Wharton's *Anglia Sacra* (*de duobus Aelfricis*); also Soames, *Anglo-Saxon Church*, pp. 212, 217; and Mr. Johnson's Preface (*ibid.*, p. 382), and the note of his editor of 1851, *ibid.*, p. 387.   [2] Vol. i. p. 170.

[3] They are combined by Wilkins, who first printed them (*Leges*

factory authentication. Mr. Thorpe supposed them to have been made in the year of that King's restoration, after his temporary dispossession by Sweyn, two years before his death; and it is clear, from internal evidence, that they could not have been earlier. Their ecclesiastical origin is evident: there is nothing to show that they were ever acted upon: and the portion of them material to the present question has no counterpart in any later (or earlier) Anglo-Saxon or Danish laws upon the same subject. It would be too long a digression if I were to say more about these documents: they constitute the whole and sole evidence in support of the opinion, that either a fourfold or a threefold division of tithes was ever the law or custom of this kingdom, or of any part of it. Well might Mr. Soames[1] say : ' To build arguments affecting the characters of past clergymen, and the interests of present, upon obscure compilations by unknown authors, is hardly reasonable.'

Putting these aside, the fact is, that no law of any kind was ever made in England, or can be shown to have been accepted as of force in England, in which it was laid down, 'clearly,' or otherwise, that the poor were to have any share in the 'tithes.' Consequently, the three first assertions made in the tract on which I am commenting are without foundation. That there was such a division as would have thrown the burden of the repair of Churches upon the tithes, is at variance with the well-known ecclesi-

Anglo-Saxonicæ, 1721, p. 106; and see p. 113) with others, from which they are separated by Mr. Thorpe (*Ancient Laws*, p. 343). The (supposed) law in question is that numbered 6 by Mr. Thorpe. As to this, see Soames, *Anglo-Saxon Church*, p. 212, note; and Mr. Fuller's Tract, pp. 28-33, particularly his extract from Professor Freeman, at p. 34.   [1] Soames, *Anglo-Saxon Church*, p. 105.

astical and Common law of England[1] as to the repair of parish churches; and could hardly be reconciled with the twenty-ninth article[2] of the laws of Canute (Ethelred's immediate successor) of A.D. 1018, that 'all people ought of right to assist in repairing the church.'

The statements that, by any Acts or Act made after the era of Parliaments, 'the right of the poor to their (supposed) share was preserved,' and that 'the old law still held good in Queen Elizabeth's time,' exceed the limits of excusable error. All that can be suggested in extenuation of them is, that the writer's researches into the history and law of tithes may not have been extensive; perhaps they did not go beyond Blackstone's *Commentaries*, and Degge's *Parson's Counsellor:* and what was found in those books may have been misunderstood.

Sir Simon Degge was a (not particularly distinguished) lawyer of Charles the Second's time. After speaking of King Henry the Eighth's Statute against non-residence as a 'good law,' one end of which was 'to maintain hospitality,' he uttered the sentiment which has made him an oracle to this tract-writer. 'And I would wish every clergyman to remember, that the poor have a share in the tithes with him.'[3] In explanation, he quoted a supposed decree of Pope Sylvester in the fourth century, taking for genuine (apparently) all that was in Isidore's forged decretals; the twenty-fourth of Aelfric's (so-called) 'Canons,' which he took for 'a Canon of our own, made in the time of King Alfred;' and Archbishop Stratford's Provincial Canon of A.D. 1342,[4] which I

---

[1] Coke, *Second Inst.*, p. 653.
[2] Johnson, *Laws and Canons*, vol. i. p. 518.
[3] Degge's *Parson's Counsellor* (7th ed., 1820), p. 79.
[4] Stratford's *Extravagants* (Johnson, *Laws and Canons*, vol. ii. p. 364).

have mentioned in its proper place, and as to which he does not appear to have perceived that it related to monasteries only, having churches appropriated to them, and not to the parochial clergy: and that, even as to monasteries, what it did was to impose a new charge, and not to enforce or recognise any previously existing law or practice for a partition of tithes; to which, indeed, it did not refer, more than to other profits of appropriated benefices. Having made these references, the *Parson's Counsellor* thus closed his admonition:[1] 'By all which it appears, that *originally* the poor had a share of the tithe.' His object was to impress upon his clerical readers (by authorities not greatly to the purpose) the moral obligation of beneficence towards the poor, as one of the things contemplated and intended by the parochial system and its endowments. He could not have meant to assert that in his own time, as well as 'originally,' the poor 'had a share in the tithes' by law: every lawyer's apprentice, and every clergyman, must have known that not to be true.

For his citation of *Pope Sylvester*, etc., he was called to account in his own day; and, in a later edition,[2] he defended it, lamely enough: maintaining, on the authority of some Roman Canonists, the genuineness of the Extracts from the Synodical Acts of Pope Sylvester, published by Isidore:[3] and, it must therefore be supposed, of the other forgeries in the same collection also.

Of Sir Simon Degge's authorities (such as they were) Archbishop Stratford's Canon alone related to the law of England after the commencement of Parliaments.

---

[1] Degge (7th ed., 1820), pp. 80, 81.   [2] *Ibid.* (7th ed.), p. 86.
[3] See Van Espen, *Comm. in Jus novum Canonicum*, part ii. pp. 451-475. As to the supposed Synod of Rome, under Pope Sylvester: *ibid.*, p. 470.

The tract-writer, however, refers to four Statutes (all irrelevant to the propositions which they are cited to prove); to which his attention may perhaps have been drawn by references to them, which he had found elsewhere in the *Parson's Counsellor*.

'A law (he says) of the time of Richard the Second requires the bishops to set aside a part of the fruits and profits of certain parish churches for the poor parishioners, in aid of their living and sustenance for ever:' meaning the Statute of A.D. 1391,[1] to which I have already adverted. It might have been more candid if, instead of saying 'certain parish churches,' he had explained, that this law had nothing to do with tithes in particular, or with the fruits and profits of any churches not appropriated to monasteries. Its object was the same as that of Archbishop Stratford's Canon, made about half a century earlier. That Statute is, indeed, more than irrelevant; for, if there had been then a law for a partition of tithes, as against all Rectors, giving the poor one-third or any other definite share, no such legislation could have been necessary: nothing would have been wanted, except simply to enforce that existing law.

All the other Statutes referred to had for their object (or for one of their objects) to compel, under penalties, the residence of the parochial clergy. They were passed in the twenty-first year of Henry the Eighth, and in the thirteenth and eighteenth years of Elizabeth. That of Henry the Eighth[2] punished non-residence, beyond a certain term, with a fine of £10 for each offence; of which half was to go to the King, and half to the informer. That of the thirteenth year of Elizabeth[3] punished it by forfeiture of a whole year's

---

[1] 15 Rich. II., cap. 6.   [2] 21 Hen. VIII., cap. 13.
[3] 13 Eliz., cap. 20.

profit of the living; which the Bishop was to 'distribute among the poor of the parish.' That of the eighteenth year of Elizabeth[1] provided further means of enforcing the same penalty:—the Bishop was to sequester the living; and, if he omitted to do so, it was to be lawful for every parishioner, during the interval while there was no sequestration, to 'retain and keep his tithes;' and 'likewise for the churchwardens of the parish to enter and take the profits of the glebe lands and other rents and duties of every such benefice, to be employed to the use of the poor, as aforesaid.'

What was to be forfeited for non-residence, under these Statutes, and (when forfeited) distributed among the poor, was not anything which already belonged, either wholly or in part, to the poor: it was that which, until forfeiture, belonged to the incumbent. The object expressed in the earlier of Queen Elizabeth's two Statutes was, 'that the livings appointed for ecclesiastical ministers might not, by corrupt and indirect dealings, be transferred to other uses.' The object expressed in that of Henry the Eighth was, to secure the use of parochial endowments for their proper purposes, which without the residence of the clergy could not be accomplished; those purposes (as specified in the preamble) being:

'The more quiet and virtuous increase and maintenance of Divine service; the preaching and teaching the Word of God, with godly and good example-giving: the better discharge of curates; the maintenance of hospitality; the relief of poor people; the increase of devotion, and good opinion of the lay-fee towards the spiritual persons.'

The tract-writer says; 'here we have the relief of the

[1] 18 Eliz., cap. 11, sect. 7.

poor.' Certainly: but, as certainly, not any partition of tithes between the clergyman and the poor. What could residence or non-residence, clerical farming or trading, pluralities or dispensations (all which are struck at by the same means, under the same Statute), have to do with that? If the poor had by law a right to a share of the tithes, they would get it, although the clergyman might be non-resident, or a pluralist, or a farmer, or trader.

This Statute of Henry the Eighth was the first which prohibited non-residence under temporal penalties. But the evil had been felt before; and modes of repression had been suggested, in which there was no trace of the notion that any one except the parson had a legal right to a share of the tithes, or of any other fruits of a benefice. The *Parson's Counsellor* mentions[1] (the tract on which I am commenting does not) the legislation which the Commons had asked for in the reigns of Henry the Fourth and Henry the Sixth;—in the former reign, that 'the King might have a moiety of the profits of all benefices where the incumbent was non-resident;' in the latter, 'that all Parsons and Vicars, and all others having cures, and not being resident thereon, should forfeit their benefices, one half to the King, and the other half to the patron.'

One thing more. In the fifth and eighteenth years of Queen Elizabeth, the two earliest Acts[2] for the relief of the poor in England were passed. If one-third, or any other share of the tithe, had been then applicable by law for relief of the poor, that must certainly have been the first fund to which the legislature would have resorted; instead of which, a poor-rate was to be levied, under those Acts, from the

---

[1] Degge (7th ed. 1820), p. 76.
[2] 5 Eliz., cap. 3; and 18 Eliz., cap. 3.

parishioners—just as the repair of the church was provided for by church-rates, and not by the application for that purpose of one-third or any other portion of the tithes.

It is, therefore, not at all wonderful, that 'nobody seems exactly to know how, or when, the poor lost their legal claim to a share of the tithes.' It would have been extremely wonderful indeed, if they ever had any such legal claim, that it should have disappeared without observation. Rights of that kind could not have been barred by neglect, or prescription, or under any Statute of Limitation; and the supposition of the loss of such a right by unperceived, uniform, and universal oversight, all over England, without complaint, objection, or interference in any place by any public authority or any private person, is extravagant and fantastic indeed. But that nobody should know how or when that was lost, which never existed, is intelligible enough.

That the poor have now, and have always had, a real and substantial interest in the ministrations of the parochial clergy, and in the provision made for their maintenance, is most true; but it is an interest of a different kind from a right to a share in the tithes. I may here adopt the words of Bishop Stubbs[1]:—'The claim of the poor on the tithe was a part of the claim of the Church; and, although this claim was never made the subject of an apportionment, tripartite or quadripartite, except in unauthoritative or tentative recommendations, it has never been ignored or disregarded by the Church or Clergy.' The end and object of the parochial system, and of all its endowments, is that there may be in every parish a

[1] Printed letter to a Rural Dean of the diocese of Chester (12th December 1885).

resident clergyman, with such suitable provision for his maintenance as may enable him to do as much good as possible, in all sorts of ways, among his people, and especially to the poor: the permanent beneficiaries, for whose sake the system and the endowments exist, are the general body of Churchmen in every parish, and especially the poor. It is not by a legal partition of tithes, or of other fruits of a benefice, that this object could be accomplished. In point of fact, the parochial clergy of the Church of England, without legal constraint,—and although their endowments are too often insufficient for the decent maintenance of themselves and their families, unless supplemented by private means,—are, throughout the country, the main dispensers of most of the charities of life; ministering generously and liberally, not so much of their abundance as of their poverty, to the temporal as well as spiritual necessities of their poor. Where others can and will help, they bear their full share; and in many places, if the good were not done by them, it would not be done at all, but everything would be left to the poor law. If there is any class in the country who beyond all others would suffer by the disendowment of the parochial clergy, it is most surely the poor. Those are not their true friends who endeavour to persuade them to the contrary.

CHAPTER IX

AUGMENTATION FUNDS AND MODERN GIFTS

1. *Queen Anne's Bounty.*

IN the year 1704, the fund since known as Queen Anne's Bounty was formed, with a view to the augmentation or improvement of benefices insufficiently endowed, of which there were ascertained to be at that time a great number. The Queen sent a message to Parliament, expressing her desire to grant to a Corporation to be chartered for that purpose the 'first-fruits' and 'tenths,' then part of the Royal Revenue; and Parliament willingly passed the necessary Act.

These 'first-fruits' and 'tenths' were imposts upon the clergy (calculated, not on the improved value of their revenues, but as they stood in what are called 'the King's Books,' according to a valuation made in Henry the Eighth's time), which were Papal exactions before the Reformation, and were then taken from the Pope, and given by Act of Parliament to the King. 'First-fruits' were one year's profit, levied originally (about A.D. 1316) from the successors to vacant Bishoprics, and afterwards extended to other ecclesiastical benefices. 'Tenths' were an annual tax upon the rateable value of all benefices.

The original pretext for these imposts was to support the Crusades; but after that occasion for them had ceased they were still continued. Their total amount is said by Bishop Burnet[1] (who claims the credit of having nearly persuaded King William the Third and Queen Mary to do what Queen Anne did, and of having prevailed by his advice with Queen Anne) to have been, in Charles the Second's time, about £16,000 a year; which exceeds their present net value; for in 1885 the net amount received from them by the Bounty Board, after deducting expenses, was only £14,409 : 8 : 8.[2] 'This' (says Burnet) 'was not brought into the treasury : but the Bishops, who had been the Pope's Collectors, were now the King's; so persons in favour obtained assignations on them for life, or for a term of years :— this had never been applied to any good use, but was still obtained by favourites, for themselves and their friends.' Queen Anne's grant therefore was, in substance, an act of restitution, rather than donation; the revenue so granted had never been used for any national or public purpose.

The funds derived from this source have been largely employed in loans (repayable out of the incomes of benefices by instalments extending over a series of years), to enable the parochial clergy to build, rebuild, or improve their residence-houses, or buildings necessary for the cultivation of their glebes. The amount outstanding and due to the Board for such loans in March 1886 was £1,051,167 : 12 : 9.[3] The 'Bounty' funds have also been applied towards the augmentation of the incomes of poor livings; and in aid of that object, a sum of £100,000 per annum was, in each of the eleven years from 1809 to 1820, granted

---

[1] *Hist. of his own Time* (ed. 1883 in one volume, p. 744).
[2] Annual Report of Governors, 1886.
[3] Report, 1886.

by Parliament to the Bounty Board, making altogether £1,100,000. The augmentations so made by the Governors of Queen Anne's Bounty have not been gratuitous. They have been conditional upon an equal or larger amount being found for the same purpose by private gift or contribution, which would not otherwise have been given. In the six years from 1880 to 1885 (both inclusive) 492 poor benefices were augmented by grants from Queen Anne's Bounty, amounting altogether to £135,800 sterling, in consideration of private benefactions to the total value of £166,851.[1]

In the *Case for Disestablishment*, evidence given by the Secretary of the Bounty Board is quoted in a manner which might easily be misunderstood. It is there stated[2] that 'private gifts from time to time have greatly increased the amount *at the disposal of the Governors;*' and then (after mentioning the £1,100,000 granted by Parliament) Mr. Aston's authority is given for the statement, that 'in 1878 the gross annual income' (of the Board) 'was £150,000.'

It is not the fact that private gifts have greatly or at all increased the amount 'at the disposal of the Governors.' All those private gifts were appropriated, absolutely and permanently, when they were given, to particular churches, being met at the same time by grants of greater or less amount out of the funds of the Governors. And the gross annual income 'of £150,000' in 1878 (increased in 1885 to £167,147 : 8 : 3) consists chiefly of the dividends and interest of funds held in trust by the Bounty Board for the several augmented benefices; *i.e.* of the income of investments, representing partly those private gifts, and partly the

[1] Report, 1886; and *Official Year-Book* (1886), pp. 498-99.
[2] Page 62.

corresponding grants out of the first-fruits and tenths, and the £1,100,000 voted by Parliament.

2. *Ecclesiastical Commissioners.*

During the short administration of Sir Robert Peel in 1834, a Royal Commission was appointed to inquire into Ecclesiastical duties and revenues, with the concurrence of the heads of the Church, several of whom were members of the Commission; and it reported (without, as far as I know, any substantial difference of opinion) in favour of an improved management of Episcopal and Capitular estates, and a better distribution of the revenues arising from them, with a view to the application of the ultimate surplus funds which might be so obtained towards the augmentation of poor benefices, and the endowment of new parishes and ecclesiastical districts. Under the Acts which were passed to carry into effect its Reports, and the amendments which they afterwards from time to time received, the body now known by the name of the Ecclesiastical Commissioners was incorporated, and the Episcopal and Capitular estates, generally, were vested in them, with a view to their better and more economical management, and to carry into effect the other provisions of the Acts. Under those provisions, the incomes of all the Archbishops and Bishops of the Sees then existing were regulated and fixed at their present amounts, some of them having been excessive, while others were small and inadequate. The large demands for general Church purposes falling upon the two Archbishops and the Bishop of London caused their stipends to be fixed considerably above the rest; for the other Bishops, the scale fixed was not absolutely equal; Durham,

Winchester, and Ely were thought to require a larger provision than others; the rest (except Sodor and Man) were more nearly equalised, their present stipends in five cases not exceeding, and in all other cases falling below the salaries of the Ordinary Judges of the Supreme Court of Justice. (Of the Sees more recently founded, and of Sodor and Man, the incomes are much less than the rest.) Two new Bishoprics (those of Manchester and Ripon), created in 1836, were endowed out of surplus funds obtained from the estates of the other Sees. What was thought superfluous in the establishments of the several Capitular Bodies was retrenched; the numbers and the stipends of their Canons and assistant ministers were regulated by law. By these arrangements, after providing for all the fixed incomes of the Bishops and other dignitaries, a 'common fund' was created, and was increased from time to time as vested interests fell in, and as improvements took place in the value of the estates under the charge of the Commissioners. Out of this 'common fund' much has been done towards the endowment of new and the augmentation of poor benefices (chiefly in populous places) from 1840 to the present day. As in the case of Queen Anne's Bounty, the grants of the Commissioners (except when there were special local claims, or when the population was four thousand or more) have been, as a rule, conditional upon, and made in consideration of, an equal or greater amount of private gifts or contributions towards the same objects.

In their 38th Report (February 1886) the Ecclesiastical Commissioners have given a summary of the whole work accomplished by them in the augmentation and endowment of benefices during the forty-five years from 1840, when the 'common fund' was first created, to the 31st

October 1885. The total number of benefices augmented or endowed by them during that period is above 5300; the total yearly value of their grants for those purposes, consisting partly of annual payments charged upon the 'common fund,' partly of capital sums expended in the provision or improvement of parsonage-houses, or in the purchase of property, and partly of land or tithes annexed to the benefices, is about £739,000 per annum in perpetuity. The benefactions of private donors, consisting of stock, cash, land, tithes, and other property, received by and conveyed to the Commissioners or to the incumbents of benefices, to meet grants made by the Commissioners, amount in capital value to £4,530,000, and are equivalent to a permanent increase in the endowments of those benefices of about £151,000 per annum.

During the five years ending in 1884, the total amounts of the Commissioners' grants were (in capital sums) £171,738, and (in annual sums) £15,475 per annum, in consideration of private benefactions, amounting altogether to £738,473.[1] In addition to these grants there were others (out of the Commissioners' funds only, without aid from other sources) in respect of local claims, and populations exceeding 4000; the places in which tithes or other funds under the charge of the Commissioners arise being recognised by the Acts as entitled to special consideration. The grants of this class during the same five years, in capital sums, amounted to £283,881; those in annual sums to £82,583 per annum.[2] During the same period of time the Commissioners also granted towards the maintenance of assistant curates in parishes with mining populations

---

[1] *Official Year-Book* (1886), pp. 494, 495.
[2] *Ibid.*, pp. 496, 497.

£137,260, to meet private benefactions of £137,960; those grants being for one year only, and renewable year by year.[1]

In the Report just referred to, the Commissioners state that their funds 'have been very seriously affected by the continuance of agricultural and commercial depression,' and that 'there is reason to believe that the income of the Commissioners has for the present ceased to expand, and that any improvement in this respect must be very gradual.' The balance of their 'common fund account' for the year preceding the 1st November 1885 shows an excess of the year's expenditure over the year's receipts amounting to £73,791 : 16 : 9; but, having still in hand a balance of £643,583 : 17 : 4 from accumulations of former years, they contemplated making, during the present year, an appropriation to an amount equivalent to a capital sum of £450,000, or a permanent annual charge of £15,000, partly to meet benefactions in favour of poor benefices, partly to endow new parishes having a population of more than 4000 persons, and partly to meet local claims.

It is needless to add, that the funds under the management of the Ecclesiastical Commissioners have arisen wholly from what was already Church property; *i.e.* from estates which had been given for the endowment of Bishoprics and Capitular Bodies, in the manner mentioned in a former chapter; without any addition to those funds by any public grant.

3. *Parliamentary Grants.*

The erection, rebuilding, and completion of certain Churches out of coal duties, after the Fire of London, and

[1] *Official Year-Book* (1886), p. 493.

the annual grants made in aid of Queen Anne's Bounty from 1809 to 1820 (making altogether £1,100,000) have been already mentioned.

In 1818, £1,000,000 was granted by Parliament to Commissioners for the erection of new Churches in populous places, and to this £500,000 more was added in 1824, making altogether £1,500,000. From the terms of the Acts of 1818 and 1824 it might have been understood that these grants were made for the benefit of the Church of England only; and it has been, therefore, commonly assumed that the whole £1,500,000 was so expended. But this does not seem to have been the case; part appears to have been applied for the benefit of the Established Church of Scotland. The Churches and Chapels built or enlarged out of these funds, were not, generally, at the sole cost of the Commissioners; in most cases grants by them were met by private contributions. During the ten years from 1830 to 1840, 127 Churches and Chapels were built and consecrated by assistance from these funds; but the whole cost was provided by the Commissioners in only 22 of those cases.[1]

In the *Case for Disestablishment* it is stated,[2] that to the £1,500,000 granted in 1818 and 1824 (and there assumed to have been employed for the benefit of the Church of England alone) 'a further sum of £89,406 was added.' This is a mistake, arising out of the inclusion of that sum (which was *not* the subject of any Parliamentary vote or grant, but represents interest and accretions on the £1,500,000 before it was expended) in a return[3]

[1] *Parliamentary Return*, No. 620 (10th August 1840).
[2] *C. D.*, p. 62.   [3] No. 572 (14th August 1843).

made to the House of Commons in 1843. The £1,500,000 (neither more nor less) was issued to the Church Building Commissioners in Exchequer Bills;—the £89,406 arose from the 'sale, exchange, and interest' of those Exchequer Bills, and from 'interest on loans due from parishes.'

In the same publication it is also (in effect) stated,[1] that between 1817 and 1845 a further sum of £336,340 : 13 : 8 was granted by Parliament to the Church in the shape of drawbacks or remissions of duties chargeable upon materials used in Church building during that period. Exemptions of duty allowed by the State, when it is desired for reasons of public policy to encourage particular works or industries, may be good or bad in principle, and may perhaps be regarded, from an economical point of view, as equivalent to money grants. But, from the point of view of the receiver, they are not the same thing.

Under a Statute passed in 1819,[2] the drawbacks in question were allowed, not on all materials used for Church building generally, but on those which might be used for Churches and Chapels built or enlarged under the Act of 1818; and that allowance was extended to materials used in like manner under the Act of 1824. The total sum of £336,340 : 13 : 8, debited against the Church of England on this account by the *Case for Disestablishment*, includes a considerable amount which, if the principle were admissible, ought to be debited to the Church of Scotland, and not to the Church of England. For by the returns,[3] from which that sum of £336,340 : 13 : 8 was obtained, it appears that it includes drawbacks to the total amount of £49,829 : 1 : 6 on materials used for not less than 259

---

[1] *C. D.*, pp. 62, 63. [2] 59 Geo. III., cap. 134, sect. 21.
[3] No. 325 (26th April 1838), and No. 322 (26th May 1845).

Churches (including two Cathedrals), and 27 Chapels, in Scotland. This ought not to have escaped the observation of the industrious author of the *Case for Disestablishment*, and it might perhaps have been expected that he would have taken some notice of the figures bearing upon the same point which are contained in another return,[1] the same from which he obtained his £89,406. The amount of 'drawback on materials used in building Churches' is there stated, in the part relating to the Church of England, at £244,196 : 9 : 6. In the part relating to the Church of Scotland, there is a corresponding item, amounting to £47,219, down to that date. The total amount, therefore, of drawbacks in favour of the Church of England was £286,511 : 12 : 2.

It was not only in reduction of the expenditure of the £1,500,000 granted by Parliament—it was on *all* materials used for churches or chapels to which the Church-building Commissioners, under the Acts of 1818 and 1824, contributed—that these drawbacks were allowed. They were inducements held out by the State to private persons to lay out their money (as they did to a large amount) on those churches and chapels.

In the *Case for Disestablishment*, mention is also made [2] of another drawback—that allowed on paper used in printing the Book of Common Prayer—(as it was on the paper used in the printing of Bibles too, though that is not mentioned). The immediate remission of duty was, in these cases, to the printers (the King's printers, and the Universities)—the ultimate benefit was to the individual purchasers of Prayer-Books and Bibles, in cheapness of price. This is gravely treated as an item of 'grants, rates, and remissions of duty' to the Church of England.

[1] No. 572 (14th August 1843).   [2] *C. D.*, p. 63.

I have now mentioned everything in the nature of public grants, or remissions of duty not shared by other religious bodies, for which the Church of England was ever indebted to the State or to Parliament. A few words must be added about Church rates.

4. *Church Rates.*

That the Common law, and also the law administered in the Ecclesiastical Courts, cast the burden of repairing the body of parish churches, and the fences, etc., of Churchyards, with some other incidental expenses, upon the parishioners, regarding them all as having an interest in the sacred buildings and in the burial grounds, by reason of those rights of 'seat and sepulture,' of which Lord Campbell spoke in the 'Ilminster School case,'[1] is undoubtedly true. And during the long ages when all Christians in this land were professedly Churchmen, the justice and reasonableness of such a burden for such a benefit was not matter of controversy. Like many other ancient laws, it had grown up, not by positive enactment, but out of a sense of duty first, and custom afterwards. Its continuance during the time when the State endeavoured to enforce conformity by law on the unwilling needs no explanation; nor does its survival afterwards till 1868, when compulsory Church rates were abolished.[2] During all that time the Church never shut her doors against any parishioner, nor does she now; during all that time Non-Conformists had always an equal right with Churchmen to have the remains of their relatives and friends laid in the Churchyard, and they made use of that right, as they

---

[1] Baker *v.* Lee (*House of Lords Cases*, vol. viii. p. 505).
[2] 31 & 32 Vict., cap. 109.

do now. It was within living memory that the agitation against Church rates as a grievance to Non-Conformists first arose. When it did arise, it was soon discovered that there were no means of compelling a Church rate to be made against the will of a majority of the parishioners in vestry assembled. All rateable property had been subject, long before existing titles to it were acquired, to this burden : its removal was rather a gain to those who resisted it than its continuance a loss. It was natural that, with such a history, Churchmen should but slowly come to see that those rates were really a survival of what was unfit rather than fit for these times; and that there was a difference in principle between an obligation upon each local community to levy a tax from time to time, by resolutions which it might pass or refuse, on all rateable property within its limits, and the proprietary title to endowments vested by law in Church corporations. The controversy ended in the abolition of compulsory Church rates, without taking from any man any right, either in the Church or in the Churchyard, which he before had. Since that time (eighteen years ago) all the parish churches in the kingdom have been repaired by the voluntary contributions of those parishioners who are Churchmen, or who care for the Church. To treat the repair of parish churches by rates, while that was law, as a matter of account against the Church, or as affecting in any way the title to churches or to endowments, would be very unreasonable.

5. *Recent Private Gifts.*

Of private gifts for Church-building, Church-restoration, and Church-endowment between the time of the Reformation and the year 1840 (though doubtless they were made,[1] and that to a large amount), there is no general public record, nor am I aware of any source of information from which the facts or figures relating to the greater part of them can be collected. But the returns[2] laid before Parliament on the motion of Lord Hampton in 1875-76 show what was done, in the building and restoration of churches only, during the thirty-four years ending in 1874. Those returns did not include any work on which the total amount expended was less than £500. The whole expenditure, of which they gave the particulars (excluding Cathedrals), was £24,453,361. In most dioceses the sources of that expenditure were accurately distinguished, so as to show the exact amount which arose from private voluntary gifts and contributions; but in some they were not. Taking the proportion to be generally the same, the total amount of the private voluntary gifts and contributions which enter into that sum of £24,453,361 is certainly not less than £23,000,000; and this, it must be remembered, does not include anything which was given in the shape of lands, buildings, rent-charges, invested funds, or money, for parsonage-houses, glebes, or endowments. The total value of gifts of those kinds during the same period of thirty-

---

[1] *E.g.*, Mr. Brewer (*Endowments*, etc., pp. 122, 123) mentions the augmentations, by Archbishop Juxon, of the incomes of 32 vicarages; the expenditure of £72,000, for the like purposes, by Archbishop Sheldon; and other gifts by Bishop Warner, Dr. Thorndike, Dr. Barrow, Bishop Gunning, Bishop Morley, Archbishop Sancroft, and others, in the seventeenth century. I have referred to the private contributions made between 1830 and 1840 towards 105 of the 127 churches and chapels built in those ten years by aid from the Church-building Commissioners.

[2] See a summary of those returns in the *Official Year-Book* (1886), p. 500.

four years must (beyond all doubt) have been of large amount.

With respect to what has been done since 1874, it has been ascertained, that, in 1884 only, the voluntary contributions of Churchmen for Church building and restoration (still excluding Cathedrals), amounted to £1,163,544;[1] which if multiplied by ten, would give for the whole time, from 1874 to the end of 1884, £11,635,440. There is no reason to suppose that the amount given in 1884 exceeded the average; rather, under the political circumstances of the day, it might have been expected to be less. The aggregate, therefore, of private contributions during the forty-four years from 1840 to 1884, for ordinary church-building and Church-restoration only, may be taken as not less than £34,635,440. The amount expended on Cathedral-restoration during the same period of time was £1,738,640;[2] of which, also, the greater part was found by private contributions, though some part was given by the Ecclesiastical Commissioners.

The total amount of private gifts for parsonage-houses and endowment of benefices, met by grants from the Ecclesiastical Commissioners and Queen Anne's Bounty, during the twenty-four years from 1860 to 1884 inclusive, was £3,951,381.[3] Assuming the same annual average to be applicable to the preceding twenty years, the whole amount of such gifts, from the commencement of the period covered by Lord Hampton's returns to 1884, would be £7,250,871. To that sum may be added £322,764, for private gifts of burial-grounds; an estimate obtained by multiplying £7381, the value of such gifts for burial-grounds in 1884,[4] by forty-four years. Deducting from the sum expended in Cathedral-

---

[1] *Official Year-Book* (1886), pp. 501-510 ('Summary,' p. 511).
[2] *Ibid.*, pp. 500, 512.   [3] *Ibid.*, p. 513.   [4] *Ibid.*, p. 511.

restoration the same proportion which, in Lord Hampton's returns, represents the ratio of contributions from other sources to that of private gifts for ordinary Church-building and Church-restoration, the total estimate, resulting from the figures which I have mentioned, of the amount of private gifts during the forty-four years ending in 1884 for the Church purposes above specified (in which the endowment of new Bishoprics is not included), is £44,841,275 :—all which would be swept away, and confiscated to the State, by a measure of general disendowment.

6. *New Bishoprics.*

The evidence of Church life, energy, and activity afforded by the increase of the English Episcopate during the last fifty years, is too remarkable not to deserve separate notice. The facts as to the foundation during that period of seven new sees have been already stated; and also, that subscriptions are now in progress for the formation of an eighth new Bishopric at Wakefield, and for the re-endowment of Bristol as a separate See from Gloucester. The total amount contributed by private donations towards the endowment of the five Sees of St. Albans, Truro, Liverpool, Newcastle, and Southwell is £375,399.[1] The amount already subscribed towards the endowments of Wakefield and Bristol is, together, £107,362.[2] Those figures, added to the £44,841,275, make a total of £45,324,936.

What has happened, during the same period, as to the Bishoprics of Bangor and Bristol, is very significant of the violence which would be done to the natural feelings,

---

[1] *Official Year-Book* (1886), p. 272.
[2] The *Year-Book* (*ibid.*) gives the amount for Wakefield only.

not of Churchmen only, but of Englishmen generally, if the promoters of Disestablishment and Disendowment should have their way.

The Commission of inquiry into ecclesiastical duties and revenues, appointed in 1834, did not propose that there should be any permanent increase in the number of English Bishoprics. While recommending the creation of the new sees of Manchester and Ripon, they also recommended the union of the See of Bangor with St. Asaph, and of Bristol (then distinct) with Gloucester, as vacancies might occur. The Bishopric of Bristol became vacant in 1836, and, by order in Council made under the first Act for carrying into effect the recommendations of the Commissioners, it was united to Gloucester; which union still continues.

The Bishopric of Bangor did not become vacant for many years afterwards: but an order in Council was made in 1838 for uniting it to St. Asaph, whenever that event should happen. Bangor is a Welsh Bishopric; the Non-Conformists are strong in Wales; and it might be supposed, from what is often said about the unpopularity of the Church in Wales, that the Welsh people would have been glad to see one of their old Welsh Bishoprics suppressed. But it was not so. The proposed suppression of the See of Bangor was then decidedly unacceptable to the Welsh people; the expression of opinion against it was strong and general; and, in deference to that opinion, the Act of Parliament and Order in Council for the union of that See to St. Asaph were repealed in 1847; and Bangor continues a separate Bishopric to this day.

As to Bristol, now united for fifty years to Gloucester, a desire for its restoration as a separate See has been of late years manifested in that great commercial city; and an Act of Parliament was passed, so recently as 1884, for that purpose. As soon as the subscription now in progress shall be sufficient (with part of the present income of the united Sees, given up by the Bishop of Gloucester) to provide the endowment deemed necessary by Parliament, that See will be restored.

CHAPTER X

THE NATIONAL PROPERTY ARGUMENT

1. *What is National?*

ALL the endowments of the Church are constantly represented as 'National property,' and the Clergy supported by them as 'State paid.' The *Case for Disestablishment* (in a passage already cited)[1] speaks of the Church of England as 'annually subsidised out of public property,' to the extent of the whole yearly value of all its possessions, churches included, whatever that value may be; and in another place[2] speaks of the claim of the Welsh people 'to be relieved from the needless burden of a costly establishment.' There is no such 'subsidy :'—there is no such 'burden.' The Church of England is self-supporting; it receives no pecuniary aid from the State at the present time, directly or indirectly; and in past times it has never received any such aid from the State which (having regard to the magnitude of the general question) is worth mentioning, unless the compulsory rates formerly levied for the repairs of churches ought to be so considered. When the question was recently put in a letter to Mr. Gladstone, he answered, shortly, but emphatically :—'The Clergy of the Church of England are *not* State-paid.'

[1] *C. D.*, p. 65.   [2] *Ibid.*, p. 117.

It is, nevertheless, upon the idea expressed or insinuated in such phrases as these, 'national property,' 'subsidised,' 'State-paid,' and the like, that the conclusion is sought to be reached, that the property of the Church ought to be diverted from its present uses, and applied in some other way for the benefit of the nation.

The truth is, as stated by Professor Freeman,[1] that

'Church property is not national property, except in the same sense in which all property is national property. It is not *folkland*, *ager publicus*, property of which the nation is not only sovereign, but landlord. It ceased to be so whenever it passed into the hands of the ecclesiastical corporations, or into the hands of those who founded the ecclesiastical corporations.'

To this quotation from Professor Freeman, I may add another, from Burke:[2]—

'From the united considerations of religion and constitutional policy—from the opinion of a duty to make a sure provision for the consolation of the feeble and the instruction of the ignorant, they [the people of England] have incorporated the estate of the Church with the mass of private property, of which the State is not the proprietor, either for use or dominion, but the guardian only, and the regulator.'

The word 'National' may be fitly applied to many subjects, in a sense on which no reasonable man would think of founding a claim by the State to a proprietary right. Hospitals, and other charitable institutions supported by voluntary donations and subscriptions, are often called National. The Bank of England is generally so called; and its agency is employed by the State for many public purposes, as to some of which its duties are prescribed by

---

[1] Freeman, p. 16.
[2] *French Revolution* (*Works*, ed. 1826, vol. v. p. 191).

Acts of Parliament;—it has also special privileges, by Charter and Statute. We speak, too, of the aggregate of all the property in the country, as National wealth. But nobody, I suppose, would contend that the State is the owner of all the property of the Bank of England, or of all the property of all the individual citizens whose fortunes go to make up the national wealth.

There is, no doubt, a true sense, in which the Church of England may be called a National Institution. It has filled a great space, and has been a great power, in the national history; and, both as representing in various public ways the religion of the country, and as being connected with the State by those relations which are summed up in the word 'Establishment,' it has a just title to be spoken of as the National Church. But this does not make its property National property.

The argument which I am controverting assumes the revenues derived from Church endowments to be funds at present belonging, in point of right and title, to the public treasury, and their appropriation to Church purposes to be the same thing in substance as if they were monies voted by Parliament. Both assumptions are legally, historically, practically, absolutely, in every sense, untrue.

2. *The Word 'Public.'*

What has been said of 'National' is equally true of another word, 'public.' It is a common, but an obvious fallacy, to reason from one sense to another of a word which has various applications. Between private property, belonging directly by lawful titles to individual men for their personal benefit, and public property belonging directly to the State for the benefit of the nation as a whole, there is a large intermediate category of property which is neither private in the former sense, nor public in the latter. Such is the property of all municipal and Academical corporations; of all religious bodies, whether 'established' by law or not; and of all permanent trusts for purposes of the kind which our law calls 'charitable.' In some respects, property in this middle category may be justly (as it often is) called 'public.' It is not only held (as all private property is) under the general sanctions and guarantees of law, but it has some special qualities of a public nature, especially those of inalienability, and of public guardianship; and its proper use, for the benefit of those local or other communities or classes of people who are directly benefited by it, is a matter of public interest. But it is not in the nature of things possible, that the real use and enjoyment of any property can be in the legal abstraction called a corporation, as distinguished from its members and those whom they represent, or in trustees whose title is merely fiduciary. We must, therefore, look behind the form to discover the substance, the real persons who have and enjoy the beneficial interest in the right use of property of this description, for the purposes to which it is devoted; and we find them in the members of that class for whose benefit the property is, in each case, held. Every such class is an aggregate of the individuals answering to a certain description. The property partakes, as to its use and enjoyment by them (for the purposes and in the manner fixed by the terms of the endowment or trust) of some of the characters of private property. It is held upon a trust, from which they obtain advantages (often capable of estimation in money, but the full value of which cannot, generally, be measured by any such standard) which they would not otherwise have enjoyed. Churchmen as to Church-property, Dissenters as to property held on perpetual trusts for their religious purposes, are in this respect exactly alike.

An illustration may be derived from a case decided by the House of Lords in 1857,[1] upon the Statute of Limitations. The question was, whether a charitable trust for the poor inhabitants of a metropolitan parish was barred by adverse possession for more than twenty years. The Statute was a bar to a suit, not only by an individual or a Corporation, but also by a 'class of persons;' not, however, expressly to a suit by the Attorney-General. The suit, in that case, was by the Attorney-General, as the public officer authorised to sue on behalf of charities. But it was held by the House of Lords that this was in reality and substance a suit by the poor inhabitants entitled to the benefit of the charity; and that they, as a 'class of persons' (and the trust for their benefit), were barred by the Statute.

3. *The Test of Law and History.*

I do not understand that the opponents of the Church of England put their case upon any principle which would extend to all corporate property, or to all perpetual charitable trusts. The questions, therefore, to be considered and answered, are these. First, were the endowments of the Church of England originally, and have they always been, State property? Or, secondly, if not originally and always State property, did they ever, and when, and how, become so?

[1] Magdalen College *v.* Attorney-General (*House of Lords Cases*, vol. vi. p. 189).

It may be well to consider separately, with a view to these questions: (1) gifts by private persons; (2) gifts by kings; (3) tithes; and (4) parliamentary grants; applying to each and all of them the ordinary tests of law and history.

4. *Gifts by Private Persons.*

As to those endowments of the Church, whether ancient or modern, which came from the gifts of private persons, it is certain that they were not, before those gifts were made, State property; and that, unless those gifts made them so, they have never become so: because they are held, to this day, upon the titles created by those gifts. It is equally certain, that it was neither the intention of the givers, nor the effect in law of any of those gifts, to make them State property. The donors did, indeed, divest themselves absolutely of their own former rights over the property given; but the new title which they created, and which the law enabled and encouraged them to create, was for a definite lawful purpose of their own choosing; a purpose of which they contemplated and intended the permanence, and which is still a living purpose at the present day. From the seventh century of the Christian Era, when the earliest of such gifts were made, until now, there has never been any question, in law or in practice, as to their validity and efficacy for the purposes intended by the donors. The definite object of every one of them was to endow with the property given, not the State but the Church, by its permanent appropriation to one or more of the corporations or organised institutions of the Church, for the benefit of its members, and of all others whom the ministrations so provided for might in the ordinary course of things reach;

it being an essential part of the objects of the Church to extend itself, and to endeavour to do good to those beyond its pale. It would be a mockery and an affront to the reason and common sense of mankind, and as plainly against law as against reason, to treat a gift made yesterday —say, of land with a church built upon it, dedicated to the worship and service of Almighty God for ever through the ministry of the Church of England, by a solemn deed and solemn service of consecration—as vesting that land in the State for the general purposes of the nation, either directly, or through the medium of an implied trust for the State,—an absurd and ridiculous figment (as Professor Freeman[1] well points out), which the veriest *tyro* in equitable jurisprudence would laugh to scorn. Unless every man has an equal right to the enjoyment of every other man's property, this is not State-property—it was not so originally, it never has been so, it is not so now, in fact or in law. Nor can it, in that respect, make any difference, whether the land was given or the church built yesterday, or a thousand years ago; in both cases the origin and lawfulness of the gift, and the nature and continuity of the subsequent title and enjoyment, have been the same. What is true of land with a church built upon it is, of course, equally true of any other private endowment. If the longer period of enjoyment did make any difference, it could only be in favour of, and not against, the title. It is true that, if what was given yesterday were taken away, the donor might be living, to feel personally the wrong; which the donor of a thousand years ago would not be. But, in each case alike, the donor's personal and individual right of property ceased when he gave his land to the Church; in

[1] Freeman, p. 17.

each case alike, the primary beneficial interest passed to those for whom the ministrations of the Church, in that particular place, were provided—to a permanent undying class, which still continues and will hereafter continue, and who are as much interested in the gift at this day as their ancestors or predecessors may have been a thousand years ago. In all other cases, titles are fortified, not impaired, by length of possession :—to dissenting chapels, and other trusts for the religious purposes of dissenters, that principle was, not long since, applied by Parliament. Why should the Church of England only be deprived of her ancient endowments, for no other reason, than that she has been so long in possession of them?

5. *Gifts by Kings.*

There is no principle, on which gifts by kings, made not by public Acts of State, but as territorial land-owners, can be distinguished for this purpose from gifts by private persons. They were made in times when kings could hold and grant lands, or other property, as freely as their subjects. The lands, so granted in this country from the Heptarchy downwards, were never—most certainly they were not after those grants—the common property of the nation. What those kings granted, whether to ecclesiastical or to lay corporations, or to private individuals (in theory of law all private titles to land in the kingdom originated in some such grants)—ceased absolutely to be theirs when so granted away. Unless legally forfeited, it could never afterwards be resumed. The titles, so created, were the same in point of law, to all intents and purposes, as if made by private persons; and a possession of centuries has followed upon them.

6. *Tithes.*

As to tithes, whatever else may be doubtful, this is quite certain, that they never were the property of or payable to the State, either before or after their appropriation (or, in Mr. Selden's phrase, 'consecration'), as endowments, to the particular ecclesiastical corporations which became entitled to them; and also, that they were never so appropriated or 'consecrated' by any general public Act of the State. Originating (as has been shown) in an idea of moral obligation, which passed through the stage of custom into ecclesiastical law, and came to be recognised by the Civil Power, as other ecclesiastical customs and laws were—they never entered into, and were never granted out of, the general public revenue, and never became part of it under any law, ecclesiastical or temporal, which recognised either the obligation to pay or the right to receive them. If the State were to withdraw or abolish the civil sanctions and remedies for the recovery of tithes, which alone it granted or provided—if it were to do no more—they would not pass into the public treasury, from which they never came. The Church (as in France) would lose them, except where they might still be paid, as of old, upon the footing of voluntary offerings; but the State would not gain, nor would the cultivators of the soil, unless farming their own land. What the advocates of Disendowment mean is, to do as was done after the suppression of the monasteries, and in the recent case of the Irish Church—still to exact the full amount of the tithe from the tithe-payer; taking it from the Church, and converting it to secular uses.

7. *Parliamentary Grants.*

The fabrics, etc., on which monies granted by Parliament, from the reign of Charles the Second to the present day, were expended, did not and could not thereby become National property, unless they were so before. Those monies were granted without reservation of any charge or right of repayment. It has never been law, that the title to or tenure of any property should be altered or affected by the mere receipt of some public bounty; it has never been the practice of Parliament to treat any institution, religious or civil, to which it may have given such assistance, as its debtor on that account, unless the money was expressly advanced by way of loan. On the contrary, when the annual grant to Maynooth College ceased in 1869, a large debt then due for monies previously advanced was remitted; and, both in that case, and in the case of the 'Regium Donum' to the Irish Presbyterians, further allowances, on a liberal scale, were made for the disappointment of future expectations.

8. *Public Regulation.*

Proprietary rights are in their nature essentially different from regulative powers:—the exercise of the latter by the State is a necessary consequence of the special protection and guardianship extended by the law to all property the use and destination of which partakes, in any manner or degree, of a public character; without it, in the particular circumstances of an Established Church, such adjustments as changes of time may require could not lawfully be made. That regulative power is incident to, and arises out of, the uses to which the endowments are dedicated, and the duty and interest, in respect of those uses, of the public authority. The translation of Bishops' Sees from one Cathedral City to another; the increase and subdivision of Bishoprics or parishes; the change of Conventual Chapters into Deans and Canons; the revision of their Statutes, numbers, and stipends; the exchange of tithes for lands, and their commutation into fixed money payments or variable rent charges; provisions against the waste, or for the better management, of Church or other corporate property: —these, and the like, are examples of regulation, proceeding upon the footing of existing titles, and certainly not derogating from them. Such powers have been exercised from time to time as to all corporate and trust property under the special guardianship of public law. It is so with respect to Universities, Colleges, Schools, Municipal corporations; people's parks and recreation grounds; religious, denominational, and other charitable trusts. The State, sometimes by direct legislation, sometimes by delegation of power to public bodies (such as the Ecclesiastical or the Charity Commissioners), and at all times through the ordinary Courts of Equitable jurisdiction, has been accustomed to exercise over the property of such institutions and trusts, with a view to the better attainment of the objects for which they exist (not in subversion of those objects), a large superintending authority; and has frequently introduced such changes, great or small, as were deemed to be consistent with and conducive to those objects. And this has usually been done (except when any gross abuses may have required correction) at the instance and with the concurrence of the worthiest and most intelligent representatives of the communities or classes directly interested. It was in this manner (to mention one example) that the Institution called 'Manchester New College,' founded at Manchester by and for Non-Conformists, and vested in trustees or governors for their educational purposes, was in 1853 removed, by order of the Court of Chancery,[1] from Manchester to London;—no authority for that purpose was contained in any instrument of foundation.

When the 'Burials Bill' of 1880 was before the House of Lords, it was proposed in Committee to except from its operation all additions which might have been made to Churchyards by recent gifts; and it became my duty to oppose that proposal. In the Appendix to the *Case for Disestablishment*,[2] part of what I then said has been quoted without its context; I will not say with an intention, but certainly with a tendency, to mislead. I said[3] (in the part *not* quoted) that the Burials Bill 'did not propose either alienation or spoliation of recent endowments' (there was no question then as to any others):—

'It proposed merely a regulation by law, in a manner which, on every principle of reason, ought to be within the moral as well as the legal competency of Parliament. It proposed to regulate, not as to the right of burial itself, but as to certain accessories and incidents of that right, the manner in which those endowments should be used *for the purposes for which they were given*. That which was given to be part of the Churchyard would still remain part of the Churchyard. A more complete contrast and difference could not be imagined than between legislation such as that, and legislation which withdrew the gift altogether from the purposes for which it was given.'

---

[1] Case of 'The Manchester New College' (*Beavan's Reports*, vol. xvi. p. 610).

[2] *C. D.*, p. 197.

[3] Hansard's *Parliamentary Debates* (June 15, 1880).

I added more, to the same effect, and then (in the part which *is* quoted), I said that—

'It would be fatal to all sound principles of public legislation for their Lordships to sanction the doctrine, that those who had given out and out for public purposes land which was once private property ought to be treated as if they had reserved or could have reserved to themselves the right of dictating to Parliament, as to how *its use for such purposes* should, or should not be regulated or modified.'

The doctrine on which I then insisted is the same which I am stating now;—that regulation or modification of the manner in which property is to be used for the purposes for which it was given is one thing; spoliation, abstraction, diversion from those purposes, conversion to the general fiscal uses of the State, is quite another. Reasonable regulation assumes the continuance of the endowment; disendowment annuls it.

9. *Redistribution of Surplus Funds.*

But it is contended,[1] that a redistribution of Church property, such as was made with respect to Episcopal and Capitular revenues under the Acts vesting the lands of Bishops and Capitular bodies in the Ecclesiastical Commissioners, is at all events not within the principle of regulation; that it is equivalent to the destruction of all the old titles to those endowments, to the assumption of the absolute property in them by the State, and to a new grant, as if out of funds at the general disposal of Parliament, of the annual or other payments made through the Ecclesiastical Commissioners.

[1] *C. D.*, pp. 76, 77.

It would be strange if this were so; for it certainly was not with that intention that the Legislature passed those Acts. The intention, manifested upon the face of them, was not to secularise ecclesiastical funds, or to bring them into, or pass them through, the treasury of the State; but only to provide for their better management, and more advantageous application, for the purposes and uses of the Church.

To the formal argument, that not the Church of England generally, but particular ecclesiastical corporations were, until the passing of those Acts, entitled to the constituent parts of that mass of property, it might be a sufficient formal answer, that all those titles were preserved, and were collectively transferred to the Ecclesiastical Commissioners, as a board of trustees for the better administration and management of the estates. But I prefer to consider substance, not form.

It is agreeable to the best and most settled principles of our law of public and charitable trusts, that any surplus of funds given in trust for a religious or charitable purpose, which is not required for the useful and adequate fulfilment of that purpose, should be applied to other kindred uses. This is the well-known doctrine of '*cy-pres*,' constantly acted upon, in such cases, by our Courts of Equitable Jurisdiction. If, for example, property were held in trust for the maintenance of a Non-Conformist minister of a particular Chapel at Manchester or Liverpool, which increased so largely in value as to exceed all that could wisely and usefully be applied for that object, it would be a matter of course for the Equitable Jurisdiction, if properly applied to, to settle and bring into operation a scheme for the application of the surplus towards the extension, or otherwise for the benefit, of the same denomination, in other parts of those towns, or elsewhere. The case with which we have to deal did not fall within that jurisdiction; because Ecclesiastical Corporations are not technically trustees subject to the authority of the Court of Chancery, like the trustees of a Chapel, such as I have supposed. But in a true and higher sense, every such perpetual Corporation was and is a trustee; the permanent interest in the endowment is not in the Bishop, or Dean, or other dignitary or incumbent for the time being; his interest is only for his life, and with that the Legislature does not (unless he consents) interfere; he holds the fee, in his corporate capacity, for a perpetual purpose, on what is really and morally (though not technically), a trust; and if he were to deal with it (as in some recorded cases has happened) in a manner not consistent with that fiduciary character, he would be liable to be called to account, even in a Court of Equity. What the Court of Chancery cannot do, the Legislature can; and the Legislature, when it has acted upon the same principle on which that Court would have acted in a case of trust within its jurisdiction, has followed the analogy of law, and has done no more than what was a just consequence of, and corollary from, the regulative power. The revenues of certain Bishoprics and Chapters were found to be in excess of what was necessary for their immediate objects, and likely still further to increase. A large part of those revenues was derived, in the shape of tithes or otherwise, from poor and often populous parishes and places, the parochial ministry of which was insufficiently provided for. What was done was, first, to secure suitable residences and adequate stipends for the Bishops, Deans, and members of Chapters (upon what was thought a proper and sufficient scale of establishment), who had the immediate interest in the endowments; then, out of the surplus, to make a proper increase of the stipends of other Bishops, Deans, and members of other Chapters and Diocesan officers, whose incomes from their own endowments were insufficient; and, lastly, to apply the ultimate saving towards the augmentation or endowment of poor benefices where the population exceeded four thousand souls, and in aid of private benefactions towards similar objects in other cases; regard being had to the wants of those parishes from which the funds were derived. Nothing could be more conformable to that equitable principle of our law to which I have referred. All this was done with the assent and concurrence of the Church at large, and upon the advice and recommendation of the Primates and other leading Bishops of the day. The Church-property, so dealt with, never passed through any intermediate stage of secularisation or State-ownership; the former titles, though transferred, for the sake of a uniform system of management and an improved distribution of revenue, to the Commissioners, were preserved, not destroyed. The new distribution of revenues was not in derogation of the rights of the Church to Church-property; it was a just consequence of the interest of the Church, as a whole, in the endowments of the several corporations, of which its organisation consisted.

PART III

THE ADVERSARIES AND THEIR CASE

o

CHAPTER XI

NON-CONFORMITY

THE power, such as it is, of the movement for Disestablishment and Disendowment, proceeds from Non-Conformists; —not that all Non-Conformists are in this respect alike. There are some[1] (I hope many) who can be just, even generous, towards the Church of England; who understand the good work which the Church does and is doing; who are willing to do to others as, under like circumstances, they would be done by; and who place the common cause of Christianity before the rivalry of sects.

Useful light, both as to principles and for their application, may be derived from the history of Non-Conformity in this country. For this purpose it is not necessary to go back beyond the 'Toleration Act' of A.D. 1689,[2] which gave Non-Conformists, on certain conditions, religious liberty and legal recognition.

1. *Church Membership.*

It has sometimes been said, that every Englishman is, in the view of the law, a member of the Church of England.

---

[1] Such, *e.g.*, as the Rev. W. M. Statham of Islington, and the Rev. Urijah Thomas of Bristol, both Independent ministers, who, in 1885, publicly declared themselves against Disestablishment.

[2] 1 Will. and Mary, Sess. 1, cap. 18.

That notion is glanced at (not much insisted on) in the *Case for Disestablishment*,[1] where a late very eminent person [2] (to the peculiarity of some of whose ecclesiastical opinions I have elsewhere referred) is said to have been 'in the habit of speaking of Dissenters as Non-Conformist members of the Church of England.' I imagine that few Dissenters are in the habit of so describing themselves. Such a notion might, perhaps, have been a technical deduction from a former state of the law, which aimed at enforcing by penalties universal conformity to the Church; but it could not, and did not, survive the Toleration Acts.

It is true, now as much as ever, that the Church does not repel from the rights and privileges of Church membership any persons, baptized and not excommunicated, who honestly seek, or willingly accept them. It is also true, that the law does not, without proof of the fact, presume any man to be a Dissenter. But the question is one of fact. The law is not so unreasonable as to call the same man at the same time a Churchman and a Dissenter from the Church. When, either in Statutes or judicially, it speaks of members of the Church of England, it uses those words in that distinctive practical sense, with which (since 1689 at all events) all men have been familiar.

In the 'Ilminster School Case,'[3] which was before the House of Lords in 1860, opinions were divided upon the question, whether it was necessary for the trustees of a certain charity to be members of the Church of England. But the Lords unanimously rejected the proposition (which had been advanced at the bar) 'that Courts of Justice cannot recognise any distinction between members of the

---

[1] *C. D.*, p. 46. [2] Dean Stanley.
[3] Baker *v.* Lee (*House of Lords Cases*, vol. viii. pp. 504, 505).

Church of England and Dissenters, and that all the inhabitants of the parish are to be deemed members of the Church of England.'

'*Prima facie*' (said Lord Campbell), 'they have all a right to seat and sepulture in the church and churchyard; but Non-Conformists, as a class having serious disabilities [1] and some privileges, have long been recognised in Acts of Parliament and in judicial proceedings. The distinction is reasoned upon by both sides in this suit; and the three gentlemen, whose appointment as trustees of the charity is in controversy, are admitted not to be members of the Church of England.'

The title of the Toleration Act of 1689 [2] was, 'An Act exempting their Majesties' Protestant subjects dissenting from the Church of England from the penalties of certain laws.' The same language pervades its enactments, by which the persons so described were relieved from liability to be proceeded against for Non-Conformity in any Ecclesiastical Court, and from the penalties of all the Statutes relating to the ministers, doctrines, and worship of the Church of England. The language of later Acts, founded upon the same policy, is similar.

On the other hand, there are enactments (such, *e.g.*, as the Universities Act of 1871 [3]) as to members of the Church of England. By this Act, University and College offices were thrown open, generally, to all persons, whether belonging or not 'to any specified Church, sect, or denomination;' but, as to some particular offices, it was provided, that they should not be opened to 'any person not a member of the Church of England;' and the governing body of every College was required to 'provide sufficient religious

---

[1] They have now no disabilities that I am aware of.
[2] 1 Will. and Mary, Sess. 1, cap. 18.   [3] 34 Vict., cap. 26.

instruction for all the members thereof *in statu pupillari* belonging to the Established Church.'

2. *State Law as to Non-Conformists.*

We are told[1] (in effect) that there is something unchristian in principle in all State legislation concerning matters of religion, and in the acceptance by a Church of any *modus vivendi* with the Civil Power, on terms of acquiescence in that kind of legislation. If this were so, the principle must be equally good for established and unestablished Churches, whether the benefits accepted may be those of establishment, or of legal recognition and toleration only. That cannot have been the opinion of the dissenting ministers and schoolmasters in England, who from 1689 to 1779 were content to take the benefit of the Toleration Act, upon the terms which it prescribed (though terms not agreeable to them), viz., of subscribing, with certain exceptions, the Thirty-Nine Articles of the Church of England. It cannot have been the opinion of those, who afterwards made the declaration, substituted for that subscription by the Act of 1779:[2]—

'That I am a Christian and a Protestant, and, as such, I believe that the Scriptures of the Old and New Testaments, as commonly received among Protestant Churches, do contain the revealed will of God; and that I do receive the same as the rule of my doctrine and practice.'

3. *Royal Supremacy.*

To the general Supremacy of the Crown, Non-Conformists are as much subject as Churchmen. Neither as to the

[1] *C. D.*, pp. 2 and 5, etc.   [2] 19 Geo. III., cap. 44.

Church, nor as to Dissenters, is that Supremacy hierarchical, or one of personal government by the reigning Sovereign; it is the Supremacy of law, represented by the Sovereign as Head of the State, 'over all persons, and in all causes,' within this realm. It is exercised, as to matters concerning the Church of England, in the manner prescribed by the laws relating to that Church. As to other religious bodies, it is exercised according to such Statutes as may be in force affecting them, and in other cases according to the general law of the land. The difference is, not that Non-Conformists are exempt from State authority and control, either as to the terms of their denominational union and connection, or as to the voluntary tribunals by which they enforce those terms upon their ministers and members; but that, whenever the authority and control of the State comes in, it does so under the ordinary forms and in the ordinary manner of civil justice, and not through Courts specially constituted for the purpose. The voluntary tribunals of Non-Conformists stand, in point of law, on the footing of mutual agreement among their members, and are not public Courts. They are not, therefore, subject to 'prohibition,' nor to any direct appeal to a Royal Court. But, if the validity of any of their sentences affecting pulpits, chapels, or the interest of any minister or other person in any of their endowments, is disputed, they can only be enforced by the public authority of the State; and they are so enforced, when found lawful. Any person who thinks himself aggrieved by any such sentence may seek redress in the Queen's Courts. In any such case, it is for the Queen's Court to decide, whether, in the procedure which has led to the disputed sentence, there has been a departure from the due observance of any essential principle of justice; and, if not, whether the tribunal which pronounced the sentence had authority to do so, consistently with the laws of the realm, and also with the rules, doctrines, and discipline of the religious body concerned, and with the terms of any particular deed of trust which may affect the case. If (as I believe is the case with some of the more numerous and important Non-Conformist denominations) no binding provision has been made for referring questions of this nature to voluntary tribunals, they may be litigated in the first instance in the Queen's Courts. In these ways, the doctrine, as well as the discipline, of voluntary religious bodies may be, and from time to time has been, brought within the cognisance of the Civil Courts, just as that of the Church of England is within the cognisance of the Ecclesiastical Courts. And it is material to observe, that in both cases the Courts proceed upon the same principles.

4. *Principles of Judicature in religious Questions.*

This seems to have been misunderstood, or lost sight of, in a passage[1] which occurs in the opening chapter of the *Case for Disestablishment*, under the heading, 'State-Churches inconsistent with the nature of religion;' which, notwithstanding its length, I extract:—

'Religion being divine in its origin and sanctions, and essentially spiritual in its nature, State-establishments of religion necessarily do violence to its principles. When the Legislature interferes with religion, it substitutes human Statutes for the divine will. Parliament brooks no rival, allows no superior authority. The civil ruler permits no

---

[1] *C. D.*, pp. 5, 6.

appeal from his decisions to the Word of God. It must necessarily be so. Otherwise there could not be either certainty or uniformity in the administration of the law. The terms of the judgment of the Privy Council, in *Heath* v. *Burder*, delivered on June 6, 1862, by Lord Cranworth, are explicit on this point :—

'" The offence charged against Mr. Heath, though of an ecclesiastical nature, is one strictly defined by Statute. He is accused of having, in violation of an Act of Parliament, propounded doctrine contrary to that laid down in certain of the Articles of religion. In investigating the justice of such a charge, we are bound to look *solely* to the Statute and the Articles. *It would be a departure from our duty, if we were to permit any discussion as to the conformity or non-conformity of the Articles of religion or any of them with the Holy Scriptures.* The Statute forbids the promulgation of any doctrine contradicting the Articles. It leaves no discretion."

'The State can insist on obedience only to human laws. And, to the extent to which it legislates about religion, the State supersedes divine authority, sets aside divine sanctions, and enforces its own Statutes; refusing to allow any appeal to the Word of God. The very constitution of an Established Church, therefore, compels it, when the law of the realm differs from the divine law, to accept the former as its rule.'

The *italics*, in the extract from Lord Cranworth's judgment, are not his, or mine; they are those of the *Case for Disestablishment*. I need hardly say, that the Statute to which Lord Cranworth referred did not formulate the Thirty-Nine Articles; that had been done synodically by the Church of England eight years before. It only added Civil consent and Civil sanctions to what the Church had done. There is not one word in the Statute affecting, directly or indirectly, the matter, or the construction, of the Articles, which were themselves a series of declarations by the Church concerning its own doctrines, required to be taught (or at least not to be contravened) by its ministers. In that respect they do not differ from any other confessions, formularies of faith, catechisms, or authoritative declarations on doctrinal subjects, in which the received doctrines of any voluntary Church or religious community may have been at any time set forth, so as to constitute, in that Church or community, terms of communion, or of ministerial obligation—such, *e.g.*, as the Westminster Confession, or the Confession of Augsburg. These, and everything else of the same kind which now is, or ever has been, in use by any Non-Conformist denomination, or expressed in any of their trust-deeds, are as much 'human laws' as the Thirty-Nine Articles; and would be treated by our Courts as laws not less binding on those whom they were intended to bind, although the obligation may not be enforced by any Statute.

This being understood, it will be useful to add, to the quotation from Lord Cranworth's judgment in *Heath* v. *Burder*, a few words from another more celebrated judgment of the same tribunal (in the case of *Gorham* v. *The Bishop of Exeter*), elucidating the same principle; and then to compare them with another judgment, delivered in a case where (as in that of Mr. Gorham) questions were raised about the doctrine of Baptism, but where the religious body concerned was, not the Church of England, but the denomination of Congregationalist dissenters, called 'Particular Baptists.'

In Mr. Gorham's case,[1] Lord Langdale, delivering the opinion of the Judicial Committee of the Privy Council, said:—

'This Court, constituted for the purpose of advising Her Majesty in matters which come within its competency, has no

---

[1] Brodrick and Fremantle's *Eccl. Cases*, p. 102.

jurisdiction or authority to settle matters of faith, or to determine what ought, in any particular, to be the doctrine of the Church of England. Its duty extends only to the consideration of that which is by law established to be the doctrine of the Church of England, upon the true and legal construction of her Articles and Formularies.'

In the case of the 'Particular Baptists' (*Attorney-General v. Gould*),[1] the Master of the Rolls, Lord Romilly, said :—

'The question brought before me is, whether, having regard to the trusts of a deed establishing for the use of Particular Baptists the chapel in the city of Norwich, that building may be opened and employed for the reception of communicants who have not been baptized by immersion upon a profession of faith, although in all other essential particulars they concur with those who are the full members of that Church. . . . It does not lie within my province (nor have I any desire) to look beyond the law of the case, or to consider what may be the consequence of my decision to the large and influential class of dissenters comprised within this denomination. . . . Neither am I at liberty to speculate upon, or to examine, the various passages of Scripture which relate to this subject, for the purpose of ascertaining what might be, in my opinion, if the matter were *res integra*, the practice most in accordance with divine writ. I am simply to determine a legal question, which is, whether, having regard to the terms of the deed founding this chapel, free communion is to be henceforth interdicted in the practice of its members.'

The Courts, therefore, decline, in all cases arising under Non-Conformist trust-deeds, as much as in cases under the Articles of the Church of England, to entertain an appeal from the 'human law,' which governs the rights of the parties, to the text of Holy Scripture; and, in both classes of cases, they do so on the same principle. There is nothing in the 'constitution of an Established Church,'

[1] Beavan's *Reports*, vol. xxviii. p. 493.

which 'compels it, when the law of the realm differs from the divine law, to accept the former as its rule,' any more than there is in the constitution of the denomination of Particular Baptists. All that, in either case, the Judge does, is to inquire into, and to determine in accordance with, the law of the particular Church or denomination; not taking upon himself the office of a spiritual legislator, or of an authoritative interpreter of Holy Scripture. The law accepted as his rule of judgment is that which, according to its declared tenets, is held by that Church or denomination to be agreeable to, and not different from, the divine law. For a Court to say that it 'differs from the divine law,' and on that account to absolve members or ministers of that Church or denomination from obedience to its laws, would be to assume the functions of a Pope, not to discharge the duty of a Judge.

The passage which I have extracted is followed, in the same book, by another, in which the writer lays down and expatiates rhetorically upon the proposition that—

'Violence is done to the nature of religion by the coercion which the State employs in securing conformity to the prescribed standards of faith and worship. . . . The penalties which [the Judge] inflicts are worldly in their character; loss of office or emoluments, fine or imprisonment, follows an adverse judgment. This is wholly unlike the method adopted by Christ and His Apostles.'[1]

It cannot be meant, that if a Non-Conformist minister violates the terms of his trust-deed, and insists nevertheless on retaining his chapel and pulpit, and resists adverse judgments of the Queen's Courts when appealed to, and all the means provided by law for giving effect to them, he

[1] *C. D.*, p. 6.

ought not to be deprived, 'by the coercion which the State employs,' of his office and emoluments; or that, if he is pertinacious and obstructive enough to drive the Queen's Courts to that imprisonment, by which alone obedience to any of their lawful orders can be enforced in the last resort, 'violence will be done to the nature of religion,' unless he is allowed to have his way. If that is not meant, what is? There cannot be one divine law in such matters for Non-Conformist bodies and another for the Church of England.

5. '*State-Courts.*'

I am unwilling (although what has been said might be sufficient) to leave unnoticed another passage of the same book, in the chapter which professes to describe the '*historical and legal position of the English Establishment.*'[1]

'The Arches Court is now (whatever was its character in former times) a State-Court, and its President is one of her Majesty's Judges. An Appeal lies from the judgment of this Court to the Queen; that is, to the Judicial Committee of the Privy Council, whose duty it is to advise the Crown as to all questions thus submitted to it. In effect, therefore, the State controls the clergy of the Established Church, by declaring what they must believe and teach, and how they must conduct their religious services; by appointing Courts for the purpose of hearing complaints against them; and by prescribing the penalties which are to be imposed upon them for any violation of the laws.'

It is not true that the Arches Court is now a State-Court, or its President one of Her Majesty's Judges, more than at any former time. All legal and coercive jurisdiction has always been derived from the Crown, and always must be;

[1] *C. D.*, p. 51.

and every Court, having such jurisdiction, must in that sense be a State-Court, and its Judge one of the Queen's Judges, whatever ecclesiastical character it may also possess. The Statute of 1874,[1] which is supposed in this passage (adopting so far the ideas of some partisans in the Church of England) to have altered the character of the Arches Court, only required that the same person should fill the two offices, of Judge of the Arches Court, and Official Principal of the Archbishop of York (an arrangement manifestly convenient with a view to uniformity of judgment in the two provinces);—it left the selection and appointment of the Judge still in Ecclesiastical hands, viz. those of the two Archbishops; providing only for the improbable case (which has not occurred) of neglect or disagreement on their part. I have never been able to understand (nor can I now persuade myself that, apart from certain passing controversies in the Church, it would have been suggested) that such legislation did or could involve any principle, which was not involved in, *e.g.*, the laws of Edgar and Canute requiring the Bishop, as Ecclesiastical Judge, to sit in the Hundred-Court with the Sheriff; or the law of William the Conqueror, separating those jurisdictions; or the law of Henry the Eighth, enabling married doctors of law to be ecclesiastical Judges.[2] Nor have I ever been able to see how any such Acts can reasonably be held to exceed the legitimate province of the Civil legislature in an Established Church.

For the present purpose, however, it is superfluous to examine these matters from the point of view of controversies internal to the Church of England. It is begging the question to argue, that such incidents as these prove an Established Church to be wrong. And the absurdity of

---

[1] 37 and 38 Vict., cap. 85.   [2] 37 Hen. VIII., cap. 17.

such a contention is the more apparent, when it is remembered, that if the Church were disestablished, all judicial questions whatever as to the due observance of its laws concerning ritual, doctrine, or anything else upon which temporal rights depend, might (and, unless provision were made by mutual agreement to the contrary, necessarily must) come before the ordinary State-Courts, and the Judges presiding in them; over the whole constitution of and procedure in which the State has absolute control. So absolutely is this the case, at present, with respect to (at least) some of the largest and most important of the Non-Conformist bodies, as to leave them without any remedy except secession (a remedy always open to Churchmen also, when their consciences are offended), if they should be dissatisfied with the way in which such questions as, *e.g.*, that of the necessity of baptism for communion among 'Particular Baptists,' may be decided by those State-Courts. I am not aware that Congregationalists acknowledge any common or central authority, either as a domestic tribunal for the decision of such controversies, or as a denominational legislature, capable of settling them for the future for the whole denomination by new rules; nor could any particular congregation or its trustees exercise any such functions, without special provisions expressly made beforehand for that purpose in its trust-deeds. I believe the case to be the same with more than one other Non-Conformist body: and although some (as the Wesleyans) have Conferences or General Assemblies, with larger powers, there is always some limit to those powers under the deeds or agreements which constitute or contain the fundamental laws of the denomination; the construction and legal effect of which, in case of dispute, the Courts of law only can determine.

Under the 'Dissenters' Chapels Act' (an Act of Parliament applicable to all denominations of Dissenters), a certain length of usage (unless contrary to the express terms of some instrument in writing) is to prevail, without reference to any question of truth or falsehood, or variance from the tenets of the original founders. If there should be controversy as to that usage, the State-Courts only can decide it. The State, therefore, no more 'controls the clergy, by declaring what they must believe and teach,' or 'how they must conduct their religious services,' than it controls Non-Conformists. It has already been shown, that the office of Judicature, when any such questions arise, is the same, whether they arise in the Ecclesiastical or in the Temporal Courts. It is not legislative, nor dogmatic; it prescribes no new rule for belief, for doctrine, or for worship: it simply finds out, as well as it can, by ordinary judicial methods, what the existing rule is; and it enforces that rule, and that only, by its decisions. Human judgment is fallible; some people may think such decisions wrong; but that must be equally liable to happen, whether the litigants are Churchmen in Ecclesiastical, or Non-Conformists in Temporal Courts. And as to penalties, if in any such case as that of the Particular Baptists an injunction were granted by the Court, and disobeyed, it must be enforced by 'State-penalties,' as much as the sentence of an Ecclesiastical Court, if disobeyed by a clergyman of the Church of England.

CHAPTER XII

DISSENTERS' ENDOWMENTS

1. *Non-Conformist Places of Worship, etc.*

DISSENTERS have their churches, chapels, and endowments, the permanence of which is secured to them by the public law of the State, and which are in some respects under special regulation, and in others enjoy privileges, by Act of Parliament. The aggregate value of their places of meeting for religious worship must be large. They are required by law to be certified to, and registered in the office of, the Registrar-General. The number of places of worship so certified and registered in December 1884[1] (including those of Roman Catholics and Jews, and including such as are not, as well as those which are, of a permanent character) was 23,438:—of which 9377 were registered for the solemnisation of marriage, and may be taken as having been of a permanent character. Of endowments productive of income, belonging to the various Non-Conformist bodies, those officially recorded in the office of the Charity Commissioners under the head of 'Non-Conformist chapels and ministers' (which in 1877[2] produced a total income of £38,832 per annum) cannot be more than

[1] Reg.-Gen. Forty-seventh Annual Report.
[2] Twenty-fourth Report of Charity Commissioners, 1877.

a small part. I have before me a statement made in a public address[1] by a clergyman of ability and character, that 'the Wesleyan connection is said to have ten millions of capital invested, besides the value of their chapels and schools, and ministers' houses.' I have no means of testing that statement, nor do I understand the clergyman who made it to have done so; I refer to it, therefore, not as of authority, but for the reputation, in which there is nothing improbable.

The churches, chapels, and places of worship of Dissenters, as well as those of the Established Church, are by law[2] exempted from rates and taxes. If drawbacks of duties on materials for church-building ought to be reckoned as grants of public money, it is not easy to see why exemptions from rates and taxes, to which other kinds of property are subject, should be regarded in a different light.

By an Act passed in 1850,[3] provision was made (not expressly, but practically, for the benefit of Non-Conformists only) for simplifying the titles to all lands acquired by any congregation or society or body of persons associated for religious purposes, 'for chapels, meeting-houses, or other places of religious worship, or for dwelling-houses, offices, gardens, or lands in the nature of glebe, for the ministers of any such congregations, or for educational purposes connected with them,' by vesting the property in their successive trustees, without conveyance, as if they were incorporated. In all these respects Non-Conformists, though not 'established' in the same sense that the Church of England is, are recognised and made the subject of special legislation by the State.

---

[1] Rev. Joseph Foxley, Address, in 1885, to his parishioners at Market Weighton.
[2] 3 and 4 Will. IV., cap. 30.   [3] 13 and 14 Vict., cap. 28.

2. *State-Grants to Non-Conformists.*

'There is an opinion sometimes held' (said Mr. Gladstone[1] in 1838) 'that the consecration of funds by States to the support of religion does not promote religion. Such an opinion is the very essence of paradox, and is contradicted by the nearly universal practice of mankind.' That paradox appears to have entered into the 'basis of association' of the founders of the (so-called) 'Liberation Society' in 1844;[2] in which the proposition that 'all legislation by secular governments in affairs of religion is an encroachment upon the rights of man, and an invasion of the prerogatives of God,' is coupled with another: 'that the application by law of the revenues of the State to the maintenance of any form of religious worship and instruction is contrary to reason, hostile to liberty, and directly opposed to the Word of God.' Which is right? Mr. Gladstone in 1838, or the 'Liberation Society' in 1844? They are wide as the poles asunder: unless it be possible, that religion can be promoted by that which is 'contrary to reason, hostile to liberty, and directly opposed to the Word of God.'

If the denunciation of the 'Liberation Society' were right, it would not practically touch the case of the Church of England; because (as has been shown in preceding chapters) the 'resources of the State' have not been applied to, or in aid of, the maintenance of the ministry or worship of the Church of England, except to an extent so small, in comparison with the whole endowments of the Church, that it may practically be laid out of sight. Those endowments are as much the accumulated results of the voluntary

---

[1] *The State in its Relations with the Church* (1st ed. 1838), p. 44.
[2] *C. D.*, p. 2.

liberality and munificence of men whom the law enabled to dispose of their own property as they pleased, without touching any 'resources of the State,' as are any of the Non-Conformist places of worship, or any of the trust-estates for Non-Conformist 'chapels and ministers,' recorded, or not recorded, in the office of the Charity Commissioners. But when did Non-Conformists first discover that doctrine? How long have they acted upon it? How do they stand with respect to it, even at this day?

3. *Regium Donum in England.*

Down to the formation of the 'Liberation Society' (it is convenient to use the name which it finally assumed) this doctrine remained undiscovered; Non-Conformists received, without scruple, the 'Regium Donum,' of which the *Case for Disestablishment*[1] says, that 'It was originated in 1722 by Sir Robert Walpole, whose maxim is well known, that "every man has his price."' It may, perhaps, be a comfort to some Churchmen to find, that the reckless evil-speaking of this publication can, upon occasion, be extended to all generations of Non-Conformists which preceded 1844, as well as to the Church of England; and nothing less, probably, would have satisfied the exigencies of the argument. It is, happily, not so necessary for Churchmen to believe that the acceptance of this Royal bounty, which Calamy,[2] when it was first granted, 'elaborately justified,' and which Dr. Pye-Smith[3] also justified after it had been denounced by the 'Liberation Society,' 'had all the demoralising effects of a bribe,' or 'destroyed the self-respect of those who received it.'[4] The

---

[1] *C. D.*, p. 198.
[2] *Ibid.*, p. 198.
[3] *Ibid.*, p. 200.
[4] *Ibid.*, pp. 198, 199.

Non-Conformists of the days of Calamy, Doddridge, Watts, Price, Robert Hall, and others hardly less famous, were at least as incorruptible, and as little wanting in self-respect, as any of those who have succeeded them. Appeals to sectarian animosity may have the 'demoralising effects of a bribe' quite as much as the acceptance of a small public provision for the widows of dissenting ministers, or for necessitous ministers themselves. It was to them only that the 'Regium Donum' in England was given. And, in truth, this imputation upon the whole English Non-Conformist community from 1722 to 1844 is as irrational as it is scandalous; because there was no return to the State which, during the greater part of that time, they could possibly have been expected to make for what they received, unless it were loyalty to the Crown, and to the established system of constitutional government; which (I presume) the authors of the manifesto of 1844 would not pronounce to be 'contrary to reason,' 'hostile to liberty,' or 'opposed to the Word of God.' It could not be that they were to abstain from attacking the Established Church, at a time when they had neither numbers nor political influence sufficient for that purpose. The true explanation of their acceptance of the Royal bounty, under the actual circumstances, is the simple one, that it presented no difficulty at all to their consciences, and was acceptable, for the sake of those among them who were in need.

Before 1840 more than £197,000 in the whole had been received from this 'Regium Donum' by the English Non-Conformists. It was continued till 1852: I have not ascertained how much was received from it during the twelve years from 1840 to 1852. Its relinquishment was a consequence of the opening of the attack upon the Church of England in 1844. 'One of the earliest acts' (says the *Case for Disestablishment*) 'of the Executive Committee of the Society, was to present an earnest address (in July 1845) to the "Distributors and Recipients" of the grant, urging them to refuse any longer to receive it.' In that address it was described as a 'flagrant violation' of what the Society had laid down as its 'fundamental principle': and, speaking avowedly as 'the standing representatives of the British Anti-State-Church Association,' they said :—

'We complain that we are suffering an injustice from which we cannot escape, unless we can prevail upon you to abandon your position. . . . What weight can be due to our remonstrances against ecclesiastical exactions, so long as the body to which we in common belong can be charged with accepting any share in the division of the spoil?'[1]

Dr. Pye-Smith's reply in defence of the grant did not long avail. The amount was small: none but necessitous ministers and their widows had any interest in its continuance. Its sacrifice, which conscience had never been felt to require, was demanded in the interest of an aggressive political movement against the Church of England. It was, after seven years, sacrificed accordingly.

4. *Regium Donum in Ireland.*

But England was not the only part of the United Kingdom in which there was a 'Regium Donum.' There were Protestant Non-Conformists in Ireland too, friends and brethren of the English Non-Conformists. 'Reason,' also, and 'the Word of God,' were the same in Ireland as in England. The Presbyterian body in Ireland received from

[1] *C. D.*, p. 199.

the State, in aid of the maintenance of the Presbyterian 'form of religious worship and instruction,' for 180 years, from 1690 to 1870, an annual public grant, under the same name of 'Regium Donum.' The sums paid on that account from 1690 to 1803 were, as I calculate them, altogether £168,480. After 1803 the grant was increased and put upon a new footing, viz., that of a yearly payment to every minister, upon a scale regulated by the number of families in his congregation and the amount of his voluntary stipend. In 1831 the system of classification was altered; and in 1870 there were 35 ministers of the first class receiving £92:6:2 per annum each, and 512 of the second class receiving £69:4:10 each, making altogether £38,682:10:6. The total sum voted by Parliament for those purposes, for the year ending 31st March 1862, was £39,746:10:10.[1] I have not been able to obtain the exact total amount of all the sums voted on account of this Irish 'Regium Donum' from 1803 to 1870; but they may be taken as not less than £1,700,000.

When the Irish Church Act of 1869[2] was passed, provision was made, on favourable terms of allowances and compensations, for the discontinuance of all annual grants, both to the Presbyterians and to the Roman Catholic College of Maynooth. By clauses in that and another Act[3] (passed in 1871), Parliament authorised the appropriation of part of the funds of the disestablished Church for (1) the payment of annuities to those Presbyterian ministers who had expectations in the nature of vested interests; (2) the voluntary commutation of those annuities into capital sums, as the basis of a 'Sustentation Fund' for the Presbyterian

---

[1] See *Thom's Almanack* for 1870, pp. 670, 671.
[2] 32 and 33 Vict., cap. 42.   [3] 34 and 35 Vict., cap. 24.

ministry; (3) the addition of a bonus of twelve per cent, for the benefit of that Sustentation Fund, if more than three-fourths of the ministers should commute; and (4) the payment of a further capital sum (by way of compensation for the loss of grants to ministers' widows) to the Ministers' Widows' Fund Associations.

More than three-fourths of the ministers did commute; and the total payments made by the Irish Church Commissioners, under these Acts, to the Presbyterian body or bodies in Ireland, from the 26th July 1869 to the 31st March 1885, were as follows:[1]—

	£	s.	d.
Life Annuities	57,177	4	3
Commutation Money	555,897	9	7
Bonus of 12 per cent	65,766	10	2
Widow and Orphan Fund (Synod of Ulster)	5,124	0	0
Other widows' funds	19,955	18	3
Ministers' payments to widows' funds	18,900	8	2
Clerks of the Synod	2,131	19	4
General Assembly College at Belfast	39,775	19	2
Non-subscribing Associations of Presbyterians	4,200	0	0
	£768,929	8	11

The figures which I have given, added together, viz.,

£168,480
1,700,000
768,929

make a total of . . £2,637,409

---

[1] Report of Comptroller and Auditor-General, 27th January 1886, p. 17 (*Parl. Paper*, H. C., No. 53, 1886).

The Irish Presbyterians, therefore, alone (without taking into account the Regium Donum in England) have received more out of public revenue than the aggregate amount of the £1,500,000 granted for Church-building in England in 1818 and 1824, and the £1,100,000 granted in aid of Queen Anne's Bounty, put together.

5. *Irish Presbyterian Church Act*, 1871.

The 'Irish Presbyterian Church Act' of 1871[1] (besides the provisions to which reference has already been made) incorporated a general body of 'Trustees of the Presbyterian Church in Ireland' to receive the commutation monies and bonus; and it also vested in them (with detailed regulations for their proceedings and management) all colleges, property, and trust-funds held under any gifts or bequests for the education of ministers of that Church, and all churches, manses, and property connected therewith, held by any trustees for congregations of the same Church; and also all trust-funds and monies given and bequeathed by members of that Church for its missions and other charities. And it provided, that the monies arising from the commutation fund and bonus should be held (subject to the annuities charged upon it) 'upon such trusts, *by way of permanent endowment*, for the benefit of the ministers for the time being of congregations of the Presbyterian Church in Ireland, in connection with and under the jurisdiction of its General Assembly,' as the Assembly should direct. And the Statutes against mortmain were, by the same Act, dispensed with, in favour of gifts for the religious or charitable purposes of the Irish Presbyterian Church.

[1] 34 and 35 Vict., cap. 24.

To object that these Statutes, and all that has been done under them, relate to Ireland and not to England, would be to no purpose. The question is one of principle, not of the local application of principles. The principles (that is, the real principles, as distinguished from those formulated for the purpose of attack upon Established Churches) of voluntary Protestant bodies, in England and in Ireland, are the same. All that has been so done in Ireland was done from seventeen to nineteen years after the English Non-Conformists had been induced, at the instance of the 'Liberation Society,' to relinquish the 'Regium Donum' in England: it was done without remonstrance or objection (that I am aware of) from the 'Liberation Society,' or from those who then represented its views in Parliament.

6. *Dissenters' Chapels Act.*

The Dissenters' Chapels Act of 1844[1] has an important bearing upon some of the principles which enter into this controversy. Its title is, 'An Act for the regulation of suits relating to meeting-houses and other property, held for religious purposes by persons dissenting from the United Church of England and Ireland.' It applies to, and it operates in favour of, Non-Conformists of every denomination. Its effect is to exclude, by a special law of limitation made for that express purpose, all inquiry into the conformity or otherwise of the doctrines taught, or ritual practised, in any chapel or meeting-house of any Non-Conformist Body, with the intentions of the Founders by whom the building or its accessories or endowments were given, when such

---

[1] 7 and 8 Vict., cap. 45 (the very year in which the 'Liberation Society' was founded).

doctrines have been taught there, or such ritual practised, for the last twenty-five years; unless they are, in express terms, prohibited or excluded by some written instrument governing the foundation. The words are these :—

'Be it enacted, that, so far as no particular religious doctrines or opinions, or mode of regulating worship, shall on the face of the will, deed, or other instrument declaring the trusts of any meeting-house for the worship of God by persons dissenting as aforesaid, either in express terms, or by reference to some book or other document as containing such doctrines or opinions, or mode of regulating worship, be required to be taught or observed therein, the usage for twenty-five years immediately preceding any suit relating to such meeting-house of the congregation frequenting the same shall be taken as conclusive evidence that such religious doctrines or opinions or mode of worship as have for such period been taught or observed in such meeting-house may properly be taught or observed in such meeting-house; and the right or title of the congregation to hold such meeting-house, together with any burial-ground, Sunday or day school, or minister's house, attached thereto, and any fund for the benefit of such congregation, or of the minister or other officer of such congregation, or of the widow of any such minister, shall not be called in question on account of the doctrines or opinions or mode of worship so taught or observed in such meeting-house.' [A proviso follows, saving express declarations in any deeds of trust, etc., as to ministers' houses, schools, and funds, in the same way as in the case of a meeting-house.]

I will now state under what circumstances that Act was passed, and will refer to some of the reasons and principles on which it was defended by the lawyers and statesmen of the day.

Towards the end of the seventeenth century, and early in the eighteenth, a large number of chapels were erected and endowed by charitable persons, members of the Presbyterian denomination, in England and Ireland; and trust-deeds were executed concerning them, in the manner usual in that denomination. The doctrine of the Holy Trinity was held by all the founders of those chapels and endowments; and was regarded by them (as it must be by all Christians who receive it) as a primary article of the Christian Faith. There had been controversies among the ministers of the denomination as to the use of religious tests, creeds, confessions, and formularies of faith; and the opinion of the majority was against requiring subscription to any documents of that kind: they were, therefore, not imposed, either by the general law of the whole Body, or by the common forms of those deeds of trust which were in use among them. But those deeds described the religious objects for which the trust-property was to be held, in terms which, when interpreted on legal principles, were found sufficient in law to confine them to Trinitarian Non-Conformists; though neither excluding the Church of England, nor requiring the profession of Trinitarian doctrine, by express words on the face of the deeds, or by reference to particular books or other documents. When those trusts were created there was no religious denomination in England which professed Unitarianism: the persons who may have privately held that opinion were few in number; there were none such within the Presbyterian pale: it was not till a century afterwards that the benefit of the Toleration Acts was extended to Unitarians.

It happened, nevertheless, that towards the year 1730 some of the Presbyterian ministers, both in England and in Ireland, and their congregations after them, began to decline from Trinitarian doctrine; and, by the end of the eighteenth century, all the ministers and congregations of the Presbyterian denomination in England, and a large section of them in Ireland, had become Unitarian, remaining in possession of their chapels and endowments.

The question of their legal right to retain those chapels and endowments, under that altered state of circumstances, came before the Court of Chancery in 1833, in a suit[1] commonly known as 'Lady Hewley's Case:' and the decision, (confirmed upon appeal by Lord Chancellor Lyndhurst, and finally, in 1842, by the House of Lords) was against them. The consequence (unless the Legislature had intervened) would have been to deprive them of all the property held under any of those trusts, of which they were then in possession. They applied to the Legislature for relief; and they obtained it, by the Dissenters' Chapels Act.

If it was right for Parliament to give to those Non-Conformists, on principles of public equity, what they were not held entitled to by law, how can it be possible that Parliament, at the instance of the same or other Non-Conformists, should now be induced to depart from the same principles, for the purpose of taking away from Churchmen what the Church of England is, and always has been, entitled to by law? Even those who refuse to recognise the identity, in a religious sense, of the Church of England after the Reformation with the Church of England before the Reformation, can hardly maintain that the difference is equal to that between Trinitarians and Unitarians. If, in the latter case, a title enjoyed without interruption, under the original trust-deeds, for more than twenty-five years, was to be made free from challenge on that account, why should not a title enjoyed, on the footing of ancient foundations, for above three hundred years since the Reformation, be free from challenge on

---

[1] Attorney-General v. Shore; Shore v. Wilson (*Clark and Finnelly's Reports*, vol. ix. p. 356).

account of the differences between the Reformed and the Unreformed Church?

What said Mr. Gladstone?[1]

'Although the original founders of those meeting-houses might have been, and were, persons entertaining Trinitarian opinions, yet, on principles of justice, the present holders of the property, being Unitarians, ought to be protected in the enjoyment of it. . . . You are dealing with a body which, if you examine its history, you will find was from generation to generation, almost from year to year, during the seventeenth and eighteenth centuries, in a state of perpetual change: and it affords no argument at all, and will only tend to bewilder and mislead the judgment, if you go back to the writings of the ancient Puritans, and ask what they thought upon these great questions of Christian doctrine. You must go on from year to year, and consider the direction which religious inquiry was taking, and the progress from time to time, as well as its position at a given time.'

True:—not less true, as to the Church of England, in which mediæval opinions and practices succeeded for a time to primitive; and by the Reformation the more primitive were (at least in intention and endeavour) restored instead of the mediæval. Upon what principle is the power and the process of internal change, even from opposite to opposite, to be recognised in favour of Presbyterians, as a reason for holding it unjust to treat the state of religious opinion among them at a former time as a test of their present titles to the chapels and endowments in their possession, and not also recognised for the same purpose in the case of the Church of England, which has only come nearer to, and not departed farther from, its original state? If the English Presbyterians, whose tenets are now Unitarian,

[1] *Parliamentary Debates on the Dissenters' Chapels Bill* (London, 1844), p. 171.

were to return to Trinitarian doctrine, and then to remain in possession as Trinitarians for twenty-five years, would their moral right to retain their chapels and endowments be less than it is now?

I have quoted Mr. Gladstone's words on that occasion, who looked at the question from (what may be called) an ecclesiastical, certainly a historical, point of view. I turn to those of Lord Lyndhurst.[1]

'It is a principle known to our law, that uniform possession, during a long series of years, establishes a title. . . . That principle we apply to our estates and to our civil rights: why should we not apply it to a case of this description? Parties value the rights of property of this nature perhaps more highly than their property of any other description. The place, with respect to which the question arises, may have been the place of religious worship frequented by their forefathers for a long period of years. The burial-ground attached to it may contain the ashes of their dearest relatives and nearest friends.'

Lord Cottenham[2] said—

'The petitions all state, that from time to time large sums of money have been laid out on these chapels; that ministers' houses have been rebuilt, and that schools have been rebuilt, out of the money subscribed by the congregation professing Unitarian opinions. Now, my lords, are we to take away from these congregations property created by their own subscriptions? Because, beyond all doubt, the persons who have supported them and who have contributed their money to build them, and to establish schools and so on, must be entitled to the property in which their money is so invested.'

Last, not least, Thomas Babington Macaulay[3]—

'The real truth is, that the property of the Unitarians is so mixed up in this case with the property which they have

---

[1] *Parliamentary Debates on the Dissenters' Chapels Bill*, pp. 11, 12.
[2] *Ibid.*, p. 58.   [3] *Ibid.*, pp. 134-136.

acquired under these trust-deeds, that I believe it would be impossible in almost every case to take from them the original soil without taking also something of greater value and which is indisputably their own. This is not the case of ordinary property where a man gets rents and profits, and expends nothing which increases the value of the ground.'

After stating some particulars as to the expenditure of the Unitarians upon some of the chapels in question :— £4000 in Leeds, £2000 in Exeter, £700 in Maidstone, other sums in other places—he continued—

'Now, are these places which the British Legislature will consent to *rob*—for I can use no other word? How should we feel if such a proposition were made with respect to any other property? Would it be borne for a single moment? And now, what are those who oppose this Bill to get in comparison with what those who are injuriously affected by the present law are to lose? . . . To them these places are most valuable, from the old and dear associations connected with them. To those who seek to intrude into them they are of no value beyond that which belongs to any place where men can have a roof over their heads. If we throw out this Bill we shall rob one party of that which they consider to be invaluable, to bestow it in a quarter where it can have no other value but as a trophy of a most inglorious war, and as an evidence of the humiliation of those from whom this property has been wrested.'

7. *Practical Conclusions.*

These passages, which I have cited from the speeches on that occasion of some famous men of this century, are more to the present purpose (unless a great Church is to have less justice done her than a small sect) than all the quotations in the *Case for Disestablishment* put together. Why is the Church of England not to have the same benefit as Non-Conformists from the principle, that 'uniform possession during a long series of years establishes a title'? If the Unitarians had built and rebuilt these chapels and ministers' houses, and otherwise improved them, expending for those purposes, over a series of years, many thousand pounds of their own money, and had so mixed inseparably their own funds with those of the original trusts—have not the members of the Church of England, during the last fifty years only, expended upon the fabrics of their churches (on the lowest computation) more than thirty-six millions sterling, and upon other Church endowments above eight millions more? If to take away property on which expenditure of this kind had been made from the Unitarians, when the law itself would have done so, would have been *robbery* in the view of that higher equity which guided the Legislature, what else than robbery can it be to take away by legislation property of vastly greater value from the Church of England, when the only other difference is that the law is upon the side of the Church, and not against her? Are the associations of members of the Church of England with the houses of God, in which for so many long centuries their forefathers have worshipped, and the burial-grounds which 'contain the ashes of their dearest relatives and nearest friends,' less old or less dear than those of Unitarians? Do not they also 'value the rights of property of this nature, perhaps more highly than their property of any other description?' And what, in comparison with the loss to the Church of England and her members, would be the gain to those who advocate her spoliation? What but 'a trophy of a most inglorious war; an evidence of the humiliation of those from whom the property had been wrested'?

Some people talk as if the Church of England ought to be ashamed of caring about her endowments, as if it might be better for her to be stripped of them, as if the desire to keep what is her own, what has been given to her for the better and more effectual performance of her appointed work, implied want of faith in her spiritual mission. Doubtless, it is not for any other reason, but for the sake of her work and of her spiritual mission, and of the people for whom and among whom she labours, that she ought to care for these temporal things: but for their sakes she is intrusted with them; for their sakes she does and ought to care for them. It cannot be out of place to refer, on that point, to what Burke[1] said, as to similar doctrines, advanced by Revolutionists in France.

'The ears of the people of England are distinguishing. They hear these men speak broad. Their tongue betrays them. Their language is in the *patois* of fraud, in the cant and gibberish of hypocrisy. The people of England must think so when these praters affect to carry back the clergy to that primitive evangelic poverty, which in the spirit ought always to exist in them (and in us too, however we may like it); but the thing must be varied when the relation of that body to the State is altered, when manners, when modes of life, when indeed the whole order of human affairs, has undergone a total revolution.'

To those with whom I am contending I decline to apply Burke's strong words of honest indignation. But it is difficult to think such talk honest and sincere, now more than in 1790, in England more than in France. Some persons I know there are, who repeat it without perceiving how unreasonable it is. But is there any man who really

[1] *Reflections on French Revolution* (*Works*, ed. 1826, vol. v. pp. 196, 197).

supposes that the work of a Church, any more than other kinds of work, can be carried on all over England, or anywhere, without the use of temporal means? It may be the general practice of Non-Conformists, and (notwithstanding the dangers of popularity on the one hand, and penury on the other) a majority of them may perhaps prefer, that their ministers should be dependent on their congregations. But that is not, and never has been, the system of the Church of England; nor can it be the system, willingly adopted, of any Church which aims at the nearest practicable approach to universality of well-doing, by means of a settled ministry present everywhere, even in the poorest places and those most remote from large centres of population. That Non-Conformists do not always reject or despise endowments; that, when they have them, they wish to retain them, and would think it wrong and robbery if they were taken from them,—the history of the Dissenters' Chapels Act is enough to show.

CHAPTER XIII

POWER AND JUSTICE—PRECEDENTS

1. *Power of the State.*

THE power of the State to change by law the ownership or use of any kind of property is, of course, unquestionable. The controversy is as to the principles and grounds on which that power may be rightfully exercised. All agree that it may be rightfully exercised to correct serious public mischief; to enforce, by forfeiture for crime or for failure in duty, the express or the fairly implied terms and conditions on which property is held; to promote, on terms of reasonable compensation, public improvements; and to provide by taxation for the necessary expenses of government. But it is not less certain that States and Kings and Parliaments may so use their powers as to do injustice and wrong. There is such a thing as public as well as private robbery. If it were not so, there would be no meaning in the words 'oppression' and 'tyranny,' or in arguments from equity and justice, as applied to the acts of any Supreme Government in the world. And this does not depend upon the particular form of government. A Republic is as capable of tyranny as a monarchy; the majority of a representative assembly, as much as a single despot.

Professor Freeman (a writer who joins sincerity to clear thought, and generally accurate knowledge) says:[1]—

'An Act of Parliament may be unjust, but it cannot be *unlawful*. ... In this sense the State may do anything and deal with anything; and, as it may deal with anything, so it may deal with Churches, and with all that belongs to them. Disestablishment and Disendowment are therefore acts which may be either just or unjust. If they cannot be shown to be for the common good of the nation, they are unjust acts; but they are acts which, if done by the Supreme Power, are perfectly *lawful*. They are acts which it is open to King, Lords, and Commons to do whenever they think good. It is necessary to lay down this principle, truism as it may sound, because it is practically set aside by the disputants on both sides whenever the question of Disestablishment and Disendowment is argued. ... One side says, that the State may meddle with Church property because it is "national property." The other side says, that the State may not meddle with Church property because it is something too sacred to meddle with. Yet it is perfectly certain, on the one hand, that Church property is *not* national property, in the sense which the disputants mean; and it is equally certain, on the other hand, that no power can so tie up or dedicate anything as to bar the right of the Supreme Power to deal with it. Both these misconceptions, on opposite sides, must be got rid of before the question can be fairly argued. The true way of looking at the matter is simply this. The State has the same power to deal with Church property that it has with any other property; neither more nor less. ... The one sound principle is, that the State may, when it sees good reason for doing so, take or confiscate any property, of any kind. From this rule property given to ecclesiastical purposes can claim no exemption. It is liable, on just and sufficient cause, to be taken and applied to some other purpose; and of such just and sufficient cause the State itself is the only judge. The power of the State to deal with Church property is nothing special with regard to that kind of property; it is simply one branch of its right to deal with property of

---

[1] Freeman, pp. 11-15.

every kind. The cases where it is just and expedient to meddle with corporate property, temporal or ecclesiastical, come much oftener [than those in which it is just and expedient to meddle with private property]. But the inherent right is the same in both cases; and of the justice and expediency of the act, in either case, the State itself is the only judge.'

Summing up the practical question, he says :[1]—

'Are there as good reasons for disendowing the Church of England,—that is, for confiscating the property of all the ecclesiastical corporations in England,—as there were for confiscating the property of the alien Priories under Henry the Fifth, or for confiscating the property of all the ecclesiastical corporations in Ireland? The supporters and the enemies of Disendowment must be content to meet on this single issue. The question must not be confused by talk about "National property" on the one hand, or about "sacrilege" on the other. It is simply a question whether a great and violent change, but a change which the Supreme Power has a perfect right to make, is or is not called for in the general interest of the country?'

Under those reservations only, which the width and indefiniteness of such expressions as 'the common good of the nation,' the 'general interest of the country,' a 'perfect right,' 'the State is the only judge,' renders necessary to exclude misunderstanding, I have no difficulty in assenting to this doctrine. As to 'sacrilege,' it is certainly true, that no human consecration can so change the nature of any earthly things, as to displace, for that reason alone, what otherwise might be the rightful authority over them of the Temporal Power. If the word 'sacrilege' has any meaning (St. Paul[2] evidently thought that its Greek equivalent had), the *unjust* desecration or despoiling of Churches would seem to come within it; and Mr. Freeman thinks, in common with all reasonable men, that such an act, though

[1] Freeman, p. 25.   [2] Romans ii. 22.

done by the Supreme Power of a State, *may* be unjust. But I agree, that the secularisation of Church property by the Supreme Power of the State, if there were really just and sufficient cause for it, would not be sacrilege.

It is equally certain, that Mr. Freeman (not a man to contradict himself, and no disciple of Hobbes) does not mean, that the judgment of the Supreme Power of every State is conclusive, not only upon the question whether the thing shall be done or not, but as to its moral quality of justice or injustice. Nor is it possible, that he could intend to exclude considerations of political ethics from the questions of 'general interest,' and 'common good.' It is not because the public revenue might be increased by bringing four or five millions a year, from private property or from Church property, into the receipt of the Exchequer, that it can be right to confiscate so much property, whether held by some particular individuals for their own sole benefit, or by the Church to which they belong for the maintenance of the ministry and services of their religion. To be justified on the ground of general interest or common good, such an act must have for its foundation some public necessity, or the prevention of some grave mischief, or some offence against the State or other good cause of forfeiture on the part of those from whom the property is taken. Religion is the chief moral, and property is the chief material, bond of civilisation, and of union among the members of a nation. To take away from (let us say) half or more than half the people property dedicated for centuries to the religious uses of the Church to which they belong,—property which has continually received, from the private gifts and expenditure of members of that Church, renovation and augmentation upon an enormous scale, under the sanction and guarantee of law,—would disturb at once, by a very 'great and violent change,' both those bonds of national union and concord. Such violence, unless justified on grounds such as I have mentioned, is unjust; it is a breach of public faith, and the infliction, by superior force only, of loss and suffering upon those who have done nothing to deserve it. In proportion to the magnitude of the spoliation, is the extent of the loss and suffering, the shock to public security, the disturbance of civil and social unity; which, if political ethics are at all to be regarded, cannot be for the general interest, or the common good. If it is due to party warfare, political persecution, sectarian or social envy or jealousy, hostility of class to class, the very notion of just and equitable regard to the common good is, by such causes, excluded.

In all this, I am confident (though I am not entitled to speak for him) that Professor Freeman would not differ from me. At all events, it expresses my own unhesitating sense of what is just, and righteous, and true. We live in times which make adherence to sound principles, on such subjects as these, more than usually important. If public morality is corrupted about them, the taint may spread very far; and social disorganisation, of which there are already preachers not a few, may rapidly follow.

2. *The Irish Precedent.*

Of the precedents referred to, the most recent, and in some respects the most important, is that of the Irish Church. I shall not here argue whether (as I thought) disendowment was, in that case, carried farther than was consistent with justice and true policy, or whether (as the adversaries of the Church of England insist) it was not carried far enough. It will be sufficient to show, that between the circumstances of the Irish and those of the English Church there is no real parallel.

In the *Case for Disestablishment*[1] it is said, that 'the Disestablishment of the Irish Church created a precedent, and initiated a policy;'—and that

> 'The question as to the right of the State to what is called Church property was for all practical purposes finally settled by the passing of the Act to put an end to the Establishment of the Church of Ireland. Not that law and moral right are necessarily one and the same. But Church Establishments, as such, are simply the creations of law, and have neither rights nor property, excepting such as the law confers. And all the objections which are raised now to the claim of the nation to the ownership of Church property were urged against the Irish Church Bill, and urged in vain. The nation deliberately set them aside as invalid, and the Legislature ratified the decision. In such matters there is no going back,' etc.

The recklessness of statement and confusion of thought, characteristic of the publication from which these words are taken, are conspicuous in this passage. There is no property at all, which the law has conferred upon 'Church *Establishments, as such:*' it is difficult even to imagine what was meant by those words. It is as true of all other property whatever, as of Church property, that it is 'the creation of law;' and that nobody has 'either rights or property, excepting such as the law confers.' The law, and the law only, gives form, definition, and sanction, to all civil rights, and especially to all rights of property; though the principles out of which the necessity for government and law, and for property-rights in one form or another, arise, are moral and natural. It was impossible that an Act of Parliament to take away the property of the

[1] *C. D.*, pp. 67 and 163.

Irish Church could settle any question as to the right of the State to that property before it was taken away, much less as to the right of the State to the property of another Church. All that it did, or could do, was to prove (what nobody ever doubted) that the State had power to take it away; and also, that, under the particular circumstances of the Irish Church, the nation and Parliament thought fit to exercise that power, as it was exercised. It is not true, as a matter of fact, that 'all the objections which are raised now to the claim of the nation to the ownership of Church property were urged against the Irish Church Bill, and urged in vain.' The objections then urged were overruled, not on abstract grounds founded on any supposed claim of the nation to the ownership of Church property, but on practical grounds; not because the case of the Irish Church was the same as that of the English Church, but because it was different. Nothing was more strongly insisted upon by the authors of the measure than that difference; and (to do them justice) they insist on it still. Mr. Gladstone at Edinburgh, on the 11th November 1885, did so. After referring to some of the leading facts as to the Irish Church, he contrasted them with those relating to the Church of England, in this manner :—

'The case of the English Church, instead of being a case in which there is nothing to say, is a case in which there is a great deal to say. Instead of its being the mockery of a National Church, it is a Church with regard to which its defenders say, that it has the adhesion and support of a very large majority of the people; and I confess I am very doubtful whether the allegation can be refuted. It is a Church which works very hard. It is a Church that is endeavouring to do its business; a Church that has infinite ramifications through the whole fabric and structure of society; a Church which has laid a deep hold upon many hearts, as well as many minds.'

To these words of Mr. Gladstone, I may add those with which Professor Freeman concludes [1] his useful and impartial contribution towards the information of the public mind on the subject of Disestablishment and Disendowment.

'An argument which was formerly used one way seems now to be turned about, and used the other way. When the question of Disestablishment in Ireland was under debate, the defenders of the Established Church argued on its behalf that, if it were disestablished, we ought to disestablish the English Church also. Now, we are sometimes told, from quite the opposite side, that the disestablishment which has happened in Ireland is a precedent which we ought in consistency to follow in England. But in truth consistency has nothing to do with the matter. Many, perhaps most, of those who supported disestablishment in Ireland did so, not because they had any theory against Established Churches in general, but because they held that the Established Church in Ireland was a great practical evil. There is no inconsistency in holding that the Established Church in Ireland was a great practical evil, and yet holding that the Established Church in England is a great practical good. We are not now going to argue the point; all that we say is, that the circumstances of England and Ireland are so manifestly unlike, that there is no inconsistency in holding that an institution which was an evil in the one country may be a good in the other. In a word, it is for the advocates of Disestablishment to make out their case. They must show, that the Established Church is the cause of evils to the country, so great as not only to outweigh any advantages of which it may be the cause, but also to outweigh the evils inherent in so great a change, a change affecting so many interests, and rooting up so many associations. They are entitled to a fair hearing on this ground, and their adversaries are entitled to a fair hearing equally. All that we ask is, that the question may not be clouded over by prejudices and misconceptions on either side, by talk about "sacrilege" on one side, or about "national property" on the other.'

---

[1] Freeman, pp. 61, 62.

3. *Contrast between English and Irish Church.*

I shall now refer to some of the facts themselves, which prove that the case of the Irish Church is no precedent.

As to numbers, the Protestants in Ireland were about one-fifth of the whole population of Ireland; and, except in one province, Ulster, the proportion was very much smaller. Of the Protestants, the members of the Established Church were little more than one-half; or one-tenth of the whole population. The mass of the people were Roman Catholics; and, of all countries, Ireland was that in which the opposition between Popery and Protestantism was most intense. It had been aggravated by historical circumstances; and it obscured, in sentiment and in practice, the sense of a common Christianity. It was the fruitful parent of civil strife, disorder, and violence.

In England, on the contrary,—although I am far from thinking lightly of the differences, turning chiefly on questions of ecclesiastical organisation and sacramental doctrine, which lie at the root of the separation of Non-Conformists from the Church,—still it is true, that the field of religious agreement is large and wide, with a tendency, notwithstanding political agitation against the Church, to become larger and wider. This is due to two causes: to the great and necessary distinction between the general attitude of the Church of England towards Non-Conformists, and that of the Church of Rome towards Protestants; and to the effect of time upon the religious position and temper of Non-Conformists themselves. The Church of England, within her own borders, is liberal and comprehensive; she does not exclude those, willing to conform to her terms of communion, between whom and others outside her pale, in whatever direction, there is religious sympathy, and some approximation of opinion. Not claiming herself, and not acknowledging elsewhere, any infallible earthly authority over individual reason and conscience, she respects (though she laments), deviations from her pale, which are due to honest conviction; and she does not account as of no value service done to her Divine Master by any who love Him in sincerity, and really care for the souls of men. It is out of the abundance of the zeal of those who were her own children, as well as from that mixture of impatience and infirmity, and intolerance of restraints and imperfections and disturbing forces, by which ardent zeal is so often accompanied, that most of the Non-Conformist bodies have arisen. They have been (if I may be pardoned by my fellow-Churchmen, and also by Non-Conformists, for suggesting the comparison) our modern English Dominicans and Franciscans; and if (from causes into which I need not enter) we have not been able, as the Church of Rome was,—whether for good on the whole or not,—to retain within our ecclesiastical organisation those irregular forces, we may yet recognise the fact, that in some things they have been and are our allies, not our adversaries. Thorns they may often be in the sides of the parochial clergy, as the preaching friars were of old: but they are helpers, so far as they are really preachers of righteousness, temperance, and judgment to come, and of other essential truths of the Gospel, in any dark places of the land, and kindle or keep alive faith and love, and endeavours after purity of life, among those to whom irregular may have more facility of access than regular ministrations.

With respect, again, to the effect of time upon the Non-Conformist bodies. The chief cause of their original separation has probably been, in most cases, a longing (natural to earnest Christians) after a perfection not humanly attainable,—after a return to that first beginning, when 'the multitude of them that believed were of one heart and one soul,'[1]—after an earthly Church 'without spot or wrinkle or any such thing,'[2]—after some sensible realisation of the glorious visions of ancient prophets. From the days of George Fox to those of the Plymouth Brethren, this history has been repeating itself. But there is no escape, even in religion, from natural laws. It is a natural law, that in all cases beginnings such as these should be succeeded by systems, no longer representing the spontaneous energy and enthusiasm which forced through all barriers new courses for itself, but inherited, derivative, traditionary. As age succeeds age, the bond of association may be strengthened, and the separation caused by the first centrifugal force so far confirmed: but the power of the original differences, which were the historical causes of separation, decreases; and the attractions of mutual sympathy and charity, if not towards the organic system from which the departure was made, yet towards as much of its principles and methods and good work as the traditions of the separated Body do not proscribe, are more and more felt. It is impossible not to perceive, that this has been the case with the older and more powerful Non-Conformist Bodies in England at the present day. Concurrently with the political agitations which have been going on, there has been in constant operation a tendency, visible in the style and architecture of their churches, and in their worship and ritual, not towards greater divergence from, but rather towards a greater approximation to, the Church of England. Notwithstanding their separation, the influ-

[1] Acts iv. 32.   [2] Ephesians v. 27.

ence of the Church of England has been and is felt by them; I do not doubt that it has been felt by them for good.

I cannot but think, that these facts, well considered, ought to and may detach from the ranks of the advocates of Disestablishment many of the best and most Christian-minded members of the Non-Conformist Bodies. At all events, they show that there is not in England, as there was in Ireland, a condition of things resulting from religious antagonism, hostile to the interests of public order, and dangerous to the State. If such a state of things is to be created here (a calamity which I trust it may please God to avert), it would be very far more likely to be produced by means of Disestablishment and Disendowment, than in any other way which I can conceive.

4. *History of Irish Endowments.*

Those who may wish to compare the facts relative to Church endowments in England, of which an account has been given in former chapters, with the facts in Ireland, would do well to study Mr. Shirley's Historical Sketch, in the Appendix to the Report of the Commissioners of Inquiry into the revenues of the Irish Church, and the Tables of Royal and Parliamentary grants of lands and tithes, extracted from the Patent Rolls of the Irish Chancery, which follow, in the same Appendix.[1]

Very little is known about the condition of the Irish Church between the Norman invasion and the Reformation, except that it had fallen into great degradation and decay. The greater part of such endowments as it possessed were

[1] *Report* (Dublin, 1868), see pp. 163, 169-203.

in the hands of the monasteries which Henry the Eighth suppressed; they had not less than half the tithes of the whole kingdom: and there seems to be some uncertainty, how far tithes (the payment of which had been first enjoined by Irish Synods in the twelfth century) were then paid at all, except in the four counties to which the English pale had been reduced. The Reformation never reached the people: the language in which it was offered to them was no better understood than the old Latin, and was less familiar. Things went from bad to worse, till the latter part of the first Stuart reign. The Bishops' lands were granted away to, or usurped by, lay proprietors, either through ignorance, or by design: the Church was denuded of almost all that it had formerly possessed.

The property which was taken from it by the Act of 1869 had been mainly acquired by public or Royal grants made under the Stuart princes; some of them made by Statutes and Acts of State. A detailed account of these is given in the Tables[1] to which I have referred. The most important of them were the grants connected with the settlement of Ulster, an Act of 1634, and the Acts of Settlement after the Restoration. These gave to the Irish Church, as parochial endowments, all appropriated tithes forfeited to or vested in the Crown, and a glebe for every parish, at the rate of two in every hundred acres, out of lands forfeited to the King, and not already otherwise distributed.

The general mass, therefore, of that Irish Church property of which possession was taken by the State in 1869 was a result and monument of the civil wars and confiscations of the sixteenth and seventeenth centuries. I did not in 1869, and I do not now, think this a good reason

[1] Report of 1868, pp. 169-203.

for taking it all away. But it had a history of its own, quite unlike that of the endowments of the Church of England.

5. *The Precedents of Monasteries, etc.*

If the case of the Irish Church is so different from that of the English, still more is that of the religious houses, etc., which were suppressed under Henry the Fifth, Henry the Eighth, and Edward the Sixth.

The Alien Priories, which Henry the Fifth suppressed, (110 in number), were dependencies of certain great Abbeys in Normandy, to which they had been granted when that Province was governed by Kings of England. The severance of Normandy from the British Crown made that foreign destination of the revenues of religious houses in England injurious to the State; and the English clergy were parties to their suppression. Of the alien Priories no more need be said.

Nor is it necessary to observe upon the irrelevance, as a precedent, of the Chantries, etc., suppressed by Edward the Sixth, when the Reformation had deprived them of their practical use, and numbered them among things merely superstitious.

The monasteries (some at least of them) had done, in their time, good service to the cause of humanity and piety, learning and civilisation; but they were not original or essential parts of the Church system; to the parochial organisation they were antagonistic, rather than otherwise. They had survived those conditions of society to which they owed their existence, and to the circumstances and wants of which they were adapted. Popes, and prelates such as Wolsey, led the way in the suppression of many of them: the rest were judged by the King and Parliament (not without the form of a public inquiry into their state and condition) to have become so corrupt, as to make their continued existence not only unprofitable, but mischievous to the country. They were, therefore, not only deprived of their endowments, but entirely abolished. Their corporations were dissolved; and, when the individual persons who were then monks and nuns died out, there was an end of them altogether: the institutions and their functions were both gone; nobody was left, nobody could come into existence, who would have been entitled to any benefit from their property, or who had suffered loss by its being taken away. But it cannot be imagined, even by the most bitter enemies of the Church of England, that, if Disestablishment and Disendowment should take place, the Church itself, as a permanent organised Institution, with (generally) the same members, the same functions and duties, and the same wants as before, would or could be suppressed or abolished. If its endowments were taken away, its members, a permanently continuing class, must necessarily lose what was so taken away, and must suffer permanently by that loss.

6. *How would Disendowment work?*

What would happen if the members of the Church of England were, in this wholesale way, deprived of the means already provided by the munificence and piety of the present and former generations of Churchmen for the maintenance of their ministry throughout the land? What was taken away would be in round numbers (if we accept the figures of the *Clergy List*) £4,800,000 a year, without reckoning parsonage-houses or churches. The parochial system would either still be maintained, or it would not. It could not be properly maintained at a much less average cost than £300 a year (which would be subject to rates, taxes, and curates' stipends) for each of the 13,739 parishes. This would come to a total cost of £4,121,700 a year. If parsonage houses were taken away, that want also must be supplied: if churches, that also. Unless the work were to suffer, those Churchmen of the living generation who might have the will and the means must find out of their own pockets that sum of £4,121,700 a year, or something very like it; besides parsonages and churches, if taken away, and so much more as might be necessary to maintain upon a proper footing the Episcopal government and diocesan organisation of their Church. In other words, the practical effect (I must suppose the design, for reason as well as law presumes men to mean the necessary or natural consequences of their actions),—the practical effect of a general disendowment of the Church would be, to inflict a fine or penalty of considerably more than four millions a year upon the members of the Church of England, who are certainly as loyal subjects and useful citizens as any of those who seek to do them this wrong. Can it be supposed that a burden of that kind, and of that magnitude, could be thrown upon the Churchmen of one generation who might be willing to make the needful sacrifices, without crippling their means of doing good, and of meeting the public, charitable, social, and private demands upon them, in a multitude of ways; or that it could be endured by them without an acute and lasting sense of oppression and injury?

The other alternative is, that the want would not be adequately supplied; that, for a considerable time at all events, large gaps and breaches would be made in the parochial system of the Church of England. And this, it may most reasonably be thought, is the probable alternative. Mr. Gladstone [1] has, indeed, expressed 'a strong conviction, that, if this great modification of our inherited institutions should hereafter be accomplished, the vitality of the Church of England will be found equal to all the needs of the occasion.' This is a very high tribute to the Church. But the adjustments, and the sacrifices, which so violent a revolution—likely enough to bring other revolutionary changes in its train—must render necessary, could hardly be made universally over the whole kingdom, all at once; and the pressure of the times in which we live upon most men's resources is even now severe. In this alternative, both the richer and the poorer Churchmen would, in varying degrees, be sufferers: the richer, in so far as they might actually bear the burden, and contribute to supply the want; the poorer, from any share of it which might fall upon themselves, as a similar burden now falls upon the Roman Catholic peasantry of Ireland; and still more, from the deprivation or diminution of the benefits of a settled ministry, in those places where they might for the time be altogether lost, or materially reduced; which would usually be the poorest places, where there might be nothing else to make up for the loss.

It would be impossible to put the true state of the case better or more forcibly than has been done by one of the present Bishops of the Church of England, my own diocesan;[2]—a man of great moderation, justly and universally respected and esteemed.

---

[1] Midlothian Address, September 1885.
[2] The Bishop of Winchester, Dr. Harold Browne. (Paper read at the Carlisle Church Congress, 3d October 1884.)

'I suppose it is sometimes said that the Church is expensive to the nation, and that its support involves an undue strain on the revenues and on the industry of the people. Let us look this question in the face. First of all, it is patent that no one really pays anything (except voluntarily) to the Church. The revenues of the Church are an ancient property, much of it given or bequeathed by private benefactors, and handed down through many centuries, like other property, from generation to generation. The whole amount is about £5,000,000 a year; and it is very doubtful if so much work was ever done for so small a sum. A few considerations will show this. The number of clergy, more or less, working for the Church and people, may be put in round numbers at 20,000. Five millions divided equally among 20,000 would give £250 a year to each. Is this an excessive sum for a man whose education may have cost £1000 or £2000, and who gives all his work for it? Is it nearly equal to that which would accrue to the average country surgeon, or country solicitor? I do not name the higher branches of professions, or the more lucrative callings in life. Then, to talk about cost to the nation;—at present it costs the nation nothing, nor does it cost any individual anything; though, of course, the nation could seize on the property, and so add something to its own revenue. . . . And suppose the revenues of the Church confiscated, the relief in the way of taxes to the rich would be very small—to the poor, nothing whatever. But both rich and poor, if they wished to have religious privileges preserved to them, must pay for them. Churches, clergy, Christian schools, every form of Christian privilege, must be subscribed for by those who needed them. The devout would, no doubt, give liberally, and so would be heavily taxed; the careless and indifferent would escape, as they do now; but they would have none of the privileges which, however unworthy of them, they now possess. I am sure that the country would be a great deal poorer if it disendowed the Church to-morrow. I do not think so ill of my countrymen as that they would let all the Churches fall to ruin, and all the clergy first starve and then fade away. But if not, then they would have to pay, and to pay heavily, and that for a less efficient ministry; less efficient, because the greatest private contributions can never equal long-established hereditary endowments. So the number of the clergy would be less; their wealth—and therefore their education and social status—much less; and, what is most important to remember, the large private incomes of the clergy would all, or almost all, be lost. At present a large proportion of the clergy bring into their parishes quite as much money as they draw from them. A not insignificant number spend all that they receive from Church endowments on the parish and the Church, and maintain themselves and their families on their own private means. You will lose all this when you lower the social status of your clergy by confiscation of their revenues. There are many who hope that the voluntary system, well worked, would supply all need—need of our despoiled clergy, need of the still more fatally despoiled towns and villages. Well, it is not impossible that in the wealthier parishes in our towns the clergy would be better provided for than they are at present. But how of our country villages, with no inhabitants but farmers and day-labourers? How of the dense regions in our crowded cities, where no one richer than very small tradesmen or successful operatives live? How of those which are filled almost by paupers only, and much worse than paupers—thieves and lost women? The voluntary system, at present, reaches none of these. Many Non-Conformist ministers work hard, and Non-Conformist laymen give freely; but statistics prove that these quarters, whether in town or country, would but for the labour, often almost incredibly great, of the national clergy, be left out in the cold and in the dark.'

The State, it must be admitted, has the power to bring about all this evil. But can it do so consistently with right or justice, or with a reasonable and sincere regard for the general interest, or the common good? This is not one of those things, which would be 'done, if 'twere done;'—of which the doing could 'trammel up the consequence.'[1] It would be a disturbance of the social and political system, widely felt, of long continuance, and far-reaching in its effects.

[1] *Macbeth*, Act I. Scene vii.

CHAPTER XIV

CHURCH WORK, AND THE CHARGE OF FAILURE

1. *The Parochial System.*

IF morals are of more importance than laws, if religion is concerned with the foundations and sanctions of morality, if the peaceable support of the authority of government by the people is to be preferred to penalties and coercion, then, from a political point of view, the clergyman is more useful than the soldier, the policeman, or the magistrate. We pay annually out of the public revenue, for our Army above seventeen, for our Navy above twelve, and for prisons and police (when county and borough rates are taken into account), above five, millions of money. The Church of England is maintained (as the Bishop of Winchester truly said) out of its own endowments, without any cost to the State.

When I speak of 'the clergyman,' I mean (of course) a minister who believes in the faith which he professes, and in his mission and vocation to teach its doctrines, and administer its ordinances, according to the order of his Church. That faith, that mission and vocation, are not from the State: they constitute, however, the firmest of the pillars upon which civil society rests.

What has been said is true, in an especial degree, of the ministry of a great and ancient Church, the oldest and most venerable of all our Institutions, older by centuries than the Monarchy or Parliament, identified with the whole course of our national history, planted everywhere throughout the country, rooted in the affections and the habits of multitudes of men,—on principle as well as by habit and tradition representing social union, and free from the disturbing influence of foreign connection. To have called such a power into existence by mere State policy would have been impossible; to despoil, degrade, and debase it, when it exists, may serve the ends of revolution, but cannot possibly be conducive to social order.

The Church is enabled to do this service to the State, not because that is the aim or object of her mission, but because it is the natural and necessary effect of faithfulness in the performance of her higher duties, which contribute, more directly still, to the good of the people of whom the nation is composed.

Laws and political changes may shift burdens from man to man, from class to class, and may, in a greater or less degree, affect the accumulation and the distribution of wealth. But they cannot produce, among men generally, equality of outward condition or fortune, any more than they can produce equality of bodily strength, or intellectual gifts, or moral qualities and characters. Poor, absolutely or by comparison, the greater number always and everywhere will be, dependent for no small part of their happiness and well-being upon their relations to other men;—most of them will unavoidably fall below the higher, large numbers will fall below the average, level of intellectual power and attainment, and also of moral strength. If a law-giver were devising ideal institutions for a nation, I do not think he could imagine one more beneficial, than that, in every place where any considerable number of people have settled habitations,—in every such place as our parishes are,—there should be at least one man, educated, intelligent, and religious, whose life should be dedicated to the especial business and duty of doing to all the people of that place all the good he can,—ministering to their souls, and ready always to be their friend and counsellor; setting before rich and poor a higher standard of good and evil, happiness and misery, than that of the world; helping them to understand the value of those best gifts which are open to all, Divine and human love, and true elevation of character; organising around him all practicable instrumental means of self-improvement and mutual help; instructing the young and ignorant; alleviating the necessities of the aged, infirm, sick, and needy; comforting, strengthening, and encouraging the unhappy and the weak; warning against evil example, corruption, and crime; and (as far as may be without impairing the force of those lessons) showing mercy and extending succour to the fallen.

Such, in idea, in principle, and in general intention, is the institution of the parochial ministry of the Church of England. Such, in that degree which is compatible with human weakness, and with the necessity of working on so large a scale by a great number and variety of instruments, it is in practice. It is not, of course, possible to ascertain, by any definite external tests, the spiritual results of this work of the Church; that requires a higher than human insight. But those who know and have observed the pastoral work of the Church from within are very much better entitled to speak of it than censors from without; and the testimony of most of these is, that it is of the greatest possible value. On such a subject, every man must draw, to some extent, upon his own experience. I have, in the course of my life, had opportunities of knowing much of the pastoral work of the Church in a good many parishes, some town, some country; and also of knowing well many others of the parochial clergy, besides those who laboured in the parishes which I knew best. Not a few of the parochial clergy whom I have known, and especially of those whom I knew most thoroughly, have been among the most excellent of men, the very salt of the earth, devoting their whole lives to their duties, and realising to the full the idea of the system;—men of different shades of opinion, and of varying intellectual gifts; but in these respects alike. Among the whole number, the general standard has been high; the differences (with few exceptions) being of degree, and not of kind. What I say, from personal knowledge and observation, as to these men, I believe to be true of the great body of the class of which they were members and examples.

2. *Admissions of the Adversary.*

If this be so, we have the confession of our opponents that our case must prevail. I quote from the *Case for Disestablishment*:[1]—

'In some respects, no doubt, the idea of the parochial system is admirable. It is an arrangement by which the blessings of the Gospel are assumed to be brought to every man's door; and which, professedly, gives to all the inhabitants of a certain district, whether they be rich or poor, a legally appointed spiritual guide, whose duty it is to minister the consolations of religion, and generally to care for the welfare of the whole community over which he is placed. It is beautiful as a theory; and it is not surprising that it has won the admiration of men of very different orders of mind.'

---

[1] *C. D.*, p. 97.

Again : [1]—

'It is acknowledged that, if the Church of England, notwithstanding theoretical and scriptural objections to the patronage and control of the Church by the State, had been fairly successful in its mission; had given sound and helpful instruction to the common people; had prevented the spread of vice and crime among the poor; had brought the rich under the influence of Christian truth, and had accomplished its avowed objects, the case for the Church Establishment would have been a strong one.'

3. *The Charge of Failure.*

It is denied, however, that the Church of England can stand this test. A chapter is devoted to an attempt to prove 'the practical failure of the Establishment.' We are told that the Church system 'has broken down in practice, after centuries of trial;' that it is 'beyond dispute that, in town and country alike, the parochial system is practically a failure;' that it has 'broken down absolutely in the large towns;' and that in the country districts it is 'too often a source of evil, rather than of good.'[2]

This, then, is set before us as the main issue. As the State, in Henry the Eighth's time, found cause of forfeiture against the monasteries, because (as was then judged) they had ceased to do good, and rather did evil, so a like indictment is now brought against the Church of England.

In dealing with that issue, the question which first arises is, what is 'failure'? Men are called as witnesses to it, from very opposite poles of observation and sentiment; reformers within the Church, who love her and are zealous for her, and in their desire for her greater perfection are

---

[1] *C. D.*, p. 94. [2] *Ibid.*, pp. 97, 98.

intolerant of, and sometimes exaggerate, defects or abuses which they wish to see corrected: and, on the other hand, those who play the part of 'devil's advocate,' bearing her nothing but ill-will, and having no eyes to see in her anything which is good. There is no value, for the present purpose, in either of those kinds of testimony. That which is borne by the former class is wrested to a purpose foreign to its true intent and meaning; that of the latter is essentially worthless.

When failure is charged against the Church of England, because she has not done what no Church or religious society has ever been able to do, because she has not suppressed vice or crime—(what is meant by the 'spread' of those evils 'among the poor' I do not know—if increase or progress is meant, I deny the fact, and emphatically assert the truth to be the exact contrary),—because she has not prevented divisions, or because she 'leaves large sections of the community uninfluenced by the Christian faith,'[1]—it seems to be forgotten, that the adversaries of the Christian faith might, on the same grounds, urge the same charge against Christianity; most certainly, against all other Churches and denominations, as much as the Church of England. To fall short of the ideal and absolute aim, of the full desired measure of perfect success; to realise that success which is possible imperfectly and by degrees only, and under many discouragements and drawbacks; to find continually something to improve, correct, and amend; to labour, like Sisyphus or Tantalus in the fable, against ever-recurring disappointments and difficulties—this is not failure: this is the appointed lot of all great benefactors and reformers of men, of all human institutions, especially those nearest to

[1] *C. D.*, p. 94.

the divine. No Church ever has been, or ever will be, without shortcomings, defects, and blemishes. The 'treasure' is divine, but it is contained 'in earthen vessels.'[1] There are, and there always must be, some ministers less efficient than others; some, also, whose faults are of a graver kind. It may have been to prepare us for this, and to put us upon our guard against therefore charging Churches with failure, that even among the chosen company of the Twelve (the germ of the whole Christian Ministry), there was permitted to be a 'son of perdition.'[2] Cases of that kind are (I suppose) not altogether unknown among Non-Conformists: some such there doubtless are, and unavoidably must be, among the 20,000 clergy of the Church of England. No man with a spark, I do not say of candour, but of ordinary reason, will pronounce the Church of England guilty of failure, on grounds such as these.

What, then, are the tests of failure brought forward in the *Case for Disestablishment?*

When examined, they come round to one point: the existence among the people of Non-Conformity, and diversities of opinion and practice with respect to religion. The Acts of Uniformity were meant to 'prevent diversities of opinion,' and to 'establish consent touching true religion': they have not done so. There are, outside, many sects and denominations: there are parties within, contending with each other. Every parishioner ought to be 'a member of the ecclesiastical fold': the mission of the Church is 'to bring all the people under the influence of the Christian religion': it has not done so. 'The Established Church is national, and ought to include the nation. Does it? The answer is, No!'[3]

---

[1] 2 Corinthians iv. 7. [2] John xvii. 12.
[3] *C. D.*, pp. 95, 96.

4. *Comparative Numbers.*

I have dealt by anticipation with the unreasonableness of the general principle of this argument. Those who advance it are evidently sensible that in so absolute a form it cannot hold good; because they appeal to figures. If completeness and universality of success were necessary to repel the imputation of failure, the appeal to figures would be superfluous. For my part, I do not deny that an extreme disparity between endowments and results, even as evidenced by numbers, might lay some foundation for a charge of practical failure,—as it was thought to do, for instance, in Ireland, where in 1868 the 683,000 members of the Established Church, standing side by side with a nearly equal number of Protestant Dissenters, were confronted by a solid body of 4,142,000 members of the opposing Roman Catholic Church, strictly united among themselves; and where, in all but one province, the disparity was very much greater than even those figures represent. But no such case can possibly be made out against the Church of England. Even among her assailants few, if any, are bold enough to dispute her numerical preponderance over all the other religious bodies put together. The assertion, that she has 'the adhesion and support of a very large majority of the people,' has (as Mr. Gladstone said[1]) 'not yet been refuted.'

Those who talk about bringing this question to the test of figures have themselves done everything which they could to prevent it: they object to such a census as would enable every man's form of religious profession to be stated on his own authority; they fall back upon argu-

---
[1] Speech at Edinburgh, November 11, 1885.

ments drawn from what they call 'the religious census of 1851,' which I reserve for another chapter. In the absence of the exact figures, which a census of the ordinary kind (such as has been taken in Ireland, and in all foreign countries where statistics are collected on such subjects) would alone enable any one to give, there are other facts, which I shall proceed to state—facts much more material to the question of the relative numbers, power, efficiency, usefulness, success, and acceptability to the people, of the Church of England, as compared with other Churches and religious bodies, than Mr. Horace Mann's Report of the inquiries made by him thirty-five years ago.

5. *Comparison of Local Ministrations.*

First, as to local ministrations. The County of Somerset, and the diocese of Bath and Wells, may be taken as a fair sample of all counties and dioceses in England (and they are many), of which the circumstances are generally similar. It has been lately ascertained, by a carefully-conducted and accurate investigation, that in that one county and diocese, out of 520 parishes, there are 195 which have no public religious worship or instruction, except that provided by the Church of England; and that in 400 (nearly four-fifths) of those 520 parishes there is no resident minister of religion, of any denomination, except the clergy of the Church of England.[1]

The total increase in the present[2] number of places of

[1] 'Some Comparative Aspects of the Work of the Church of England in the County of Somerset, and the Diocese of Bath and Wells' (Report of an inquiry made with the Bishop's sanction).

[2] $15,668 + 4248 = 19,916$ (see *ante*, pp. 111, 112). Deducting ten, from the 4248 for the Isle of Man, there remain 19,906.

worship of all kinds, 'customarily used' for religious services by the Church of England, within the last thirty-five years (as compared with that[1] returned to the Census Office by its enumerators in 1851), is 5829 (not including the Channel Islands or the Isle of Man). The total increase, during the same period, in the number[2] of the places of worship of all the other religious bodies put together (Roman Catholics and Jews included), certified to and registered in the office of the Registrar-General (as compared with that[3] returned by the 'enumerators' in 1851), is 3048. So far, therefore, as that test goes, the Church of England has been advancing at a rate exceeding that of all those other bodies put together in the ratio of nearly 29 to 15.[4]

But it is said,[5] that 'the parochial system has broken down absolutely in the large towns.' Such, at all events, was not the testimony of Mr. Horace Mann in 1851. He said :[6]—

'In thickly-peopled districts, where the rapid increase of population had rendered such additional accommodation most essential—in Cheshire, Lancashire, Middlesex, Surrey, and the West Riding of Yorkshire—the increase of Churches has been so much greater than the increase of the population, that the proportion between the accommodation and the number of inhabitants is now considerably more favourable than in 1831.'

If this was true in 1851, the subsequent progress, relatively to the increase of population, has certainly not been less

---

[1] 14,077 (Mann's *Report*, pp. xxxix, clxix, *et seq.*)

[2] 23,438 (47th *Report of Registrar-General*, p. viii).

[3] 20,390 (Mann's *Report, ubi supra*).

[4] The average capacity of places of worship of the Church of England is, it must be remembered, greater than that of the buildings used by other bodies.

[5] *C. D.*, p. 97. [6] *Report*, p. xxxix.

satisfactory. In the large towns there is a great want, which it is most difficult to overtake; but there can be no question, that the Church of England has done and is doing more to overtake it than all the other religious communities put together; and, if that work of the Church of England were seriously checked, much of the ground already gained might be lost, and whatever still remains of heathenism and barbarism would daily become worse and worse.

The sums raised for this purpose, in the metropolis, by the 'Bishop of London's Fund' (first established by Bishop Blomfield, and continued by all his successors),—the funds raised, and still raising, in the other metropolitan dioceses of Rochester and St. Albans, and by the Bishop of Bedford for the East of London,—the efforts of like character made in the dioceses of Winchester, Durham, and Newcastle, and elsewhere,—might alone be a sufficient answer to this imputation. I cannot go into the details of that work: those who desire to know the truth will find some particulars about it, with respect to such great towns as Portsmouth, Birmingham, Barrow, Bolton, Brighton, Rochdale, Leicester, Nottingham (which are but examples), in the *Official Year-Book of the Church of England.*[1] And of its vigour and vitality there can be no better proof, than the voluntary and zealous co-operation of lay agencies, such as the associations of Lay-helpers, Sisterhoods, and Parochial Mission-women; the 'Homes,' 'Houses,' and 'Missions,' to which many of our younger Churchmen from the universities and schools, and in almost all walks of active life, give much of their hearts and their time; and many other excellent Church Institutions, animated by the purest spirit of Christian philanthropy, and indefatigable in well-doing,

[1] *O. Y. B.* (1886), pp. 15, 21, 29-36.

whose work is carried on in the poorest districts of London, and other great cities.

6. *Marriages.*

I turn to the statistics of marriage. Nothing more is necessary[1] to enable any Non-Conformist place of worship to have marriages solemnised in it, than an application to the Registrar-General by any one of its proprietors or trustees, supported by any twenty householders, certifying that it has been, during one year, their usual place of worship, and that they wish it to be registered for the solemnisation of marriages. These conditions being easy of fulfilment in every case of a permanent Non-Conformist Church or chapel, and the convenience of having marriages solemnised in them being obvious, it may fairly be assumed that the number of such buildings certified and registered for that purpose represents, out of the total of 23,438 places of worship of other religious bodies than the Church of England entered on the general register in 1884, most, if not all, which were of a substantial and permanent character. That number was 9377; including 896 Roman Catholic Churches or Chapels, and some Jewish synagogues.[2] On the other hand, the total number of parish churches belonging to the Church in England[3] (in all which, as well as in some chapels of ease, marriages may be solemnised), is (as has been seen), 14,558.

So far as to buildings: next, as to the marriages solem-

---

[1] 6 and 7 Will. IV., cap. 85.
[2] 47th *Report of Registrar-General*, p. viii, and Table 11, p. xlii.
[3] Excluding the Channel Islands, and the Isle of Man, which are not included in the Registrar-General's report of marriages.

nised in them. The total number of marriages solemnised throughout England in the year 1884 was 204,301 : thus divided :[1]—

By ministers and in Churches of the Church of England	144,344
Roman Catholic	8,783
Jewish	601
In Registrars' offices	26,786
In places of worship of all the Protestant denominations put together	23,787
	204,301

The marriages, therefore, solemnised in Non-Conformist places of worship were fewer than those in Registrars' offices. Those solemnised in Churches, and according to the order of the Church of England, were 70·7 per cent of the whole year's marriages in England.

7. *Elementary Education.*

I come to education and schools: and here I must observe upon a charge made [2] against the Church, that her active efforts in the cause of elementary popular education date from the year 1811 (three-quarters of a century ago), and were then due to an apprehension that, by reason of the success of the 'Lancastrian' system, the children of the poor might, in the course of another generation, become alienated from the principles of the Church. The 'Lancastrian' system (now represented by the schools of the 'British and Foreign' Society), was, I do not say hostile to the religious element in school-teaching, but certainly

---

[1] *Registrar-General's Report*, pp. vi, vii, and Table 4, p. xxxv.
[2] *C. D.*, pp. 27-29.

opposed to the teaching of specific and definite religious doctrine. In the previous system of education (such as it was), the Church had taken a leading part: and if it was not within the Church that the earliest movement for the improvement of elementary schools took place, it well became her to perceive (as she did) its importance, and to do all that in her lay to promote it in such a manner and under such conditions, that sound religious teaching, according to the principles which she held to be true and necessary for the good of men's souls, and which it was her divine mission to maintain, should be combined with the communication of useful secular knowledge. If she had done otherwise, it would indeed have been matter of reproach to her: and if, from inability on her part to rise to the wants of the time in so great a matter, and to appropriate to the strengthening of her own work what was salutary and useful in that and other movements around her, the children of the poor had been drawn away from her influence, there might have been ground for the charge of failure, which there is not now. But, happily, she did not fall into that error; and it is her success, not her failure, in this matter, which has displeased her adversaries.

In 1870, when the Elementary Education Act was passed, the amount of accommodation, and the average attendance of scholars, in Church of England and other elementary schools, were as follows:[1]—

	Accommodation.	Attendance.
Church of England	1,365,080	844,334
'British,' Wesleyan, etc.	411,948	241,989
Roman Catholic	101,556	66,066

[1] *Official Year-Book* (1886), p. 171.

As compared with the aggregate of the 'British,' Wesleyan, and other Protestant Non-Conformist schools, the Church of England had a preponderance of considerably more than three to one in accommodation, and about seven to two in attendance.

The effect of the Elementary Education Act was gradual. It did not prevent a still progressive increase in every year down to 1884 (the last in which I have the materials for a comparison), both in the accommodation and in the attendance of Church Schools. In other denominational schools there was also an increase. The following table gives the figures for each class of elementary schools (Board schools included) in 1884:[1]—

	Accommodation.	Average Attendance.
Church of England	2,454,788	1,607,823
'British,' Wesleyan, etc.	597,262	381,628
Roman Catholic	284,514	167,841
Board Schools	1,490,174	1,115,832
	4,826,738	3,273,124

After fourteen years' experience of the working of the Elementary Schools Act, and when in many places Board schools had been established, into which large numbers of the children of parents belonging to the Church of England were absorbed, the number of children educated in Church of England schools, whether tried by the test of accommodation or by that of average attendance, still exceeded those in all other denominational schools, in a ratio of not much less than three to one; and it also very largely exceeded the whole number educated in Board schools. The accommodation in Church of England schools was more than half,

[1] *Official Year-Book* (1886), p. 171.

and the attendance was not far from half that in all the elementary schools of every kind in England put together. If two-fifths only of those educated in Board schools may be assumed to have been children of Church people, and if all the rest are attributed to Protestant Non-Conformists or persons belonging to no Christian denomination—an assumption so little favourable to the Church, as to supersede any question as to the numbers of children of Non-Conformists in Church schools, or of Churchmen in 'British' schools—the result would be to show an average attendance of (in round numbers) 2,000,000 Church children to 1,200,000 children of all other classes except Roman Catholics—a preponderance on the side of the Church in the ratio of five to three.

8. *Liberality.*

It is not willingly that I suggest any comparison, with respect to liberality in gifts and subscriptions for those purposes, which are, or ought to be, of common interest to all Christians. I am compelled to do so by the challenge as to numbers, and because one article of the impeachment against the Church of England (part of what is called 'the religious argument') is, that 'the Establishment discourages liberality.'

'This' (it is said [1]) 'is an almost inevitable result of the provision made for the maintenance of religion from public funds. It is not forgotten, that in recent years there has been a remarkable development of Christian willinghood within the Church of England. But this great liberality has been shown almost exclusively in connection with the endowment of new episcopal sees, and the erection of new churches, and gives evidence rather

---

[1] *C. D.*, p. 17.

of the wealth of the richer friends of the Establishment, than of the liberality of the general body of its adherents for the ordinary purposes of Christian work. It has, moreover, been in part necessitated by the cessation of all State aid for the purposes specified. The Legislature has ceased to make grants of public money for the building of churches; and it rigidly insists that the expense of founding new episcopal sees shall be met by voluntary contributions. In order, therefore, to extend its operations in these directions, the Church of England has been obliged, like other religious bodies, to appeal to the zeal and liberality of its own adherents; and the response has been such as to make it evident,—if it were otherwise possible to entertain a doubt upon the subject,—that the English Church is not likely to suffer from lack of funds, when it ceases to draw any portion of its revenues from public property.'

Upon the principles of the *Case for Disestablishment*, the Church can *never* 'cease to draw its revenues from public property'; because, upon those principles, the mere fact of property being given to the Church makes it 'public.' But I shall not be drawn aside from my immediate purpose by this illiberal passage. Enough has been said elsewhere about 'State aid' and 'public property;' and the suggestion that a Church, which is continually requiring extension by the addition of further means to those which she already possesses, would suffer no loss by being deprived of all the existing provision for her ministry, requires no comment. What I have now to notice is the attempt made to reconcile the admitted liberality of Churchmen with the statement that 'the Establishment discourages liberality, by the assertion, that it has been 'shown almost exclusively' in Church-building and in endowing new Bishoprics, and not 'for the ordinary purposes of Christian work.'

What has been done in Church-building, and in endowing new Bishoprics, is indeed (as has been seen) no small matter; and to account for it by the 'cessation of State aid' for such purposes (when no such aid was ever given before the Fire of London, or has been given since Queen Anne's reign, except the two grants made in 1818 and 1824), is simply absurd. But what are the facts, as to the liberality of Churchmen, 'for the ordinary purposes of Christian work'? To set them forth fully, in all their forms and ramifications, I should have to transcribe a great part of the *Official Year-Book of the Church of England*. It is enough to say, that in the year 1884 only (excluding altogether what was given for the building and improvement of churches and parsonage-houses, the endowment of benefices, and the extension of the Episcopate), the contributions of Churchmen for 'the ordinary purposes of Christian work' amounted to £2,412,610,[1]—exceeding by more than a million the whole amount given for Church-building and other kindred objects during the same time. And, during the twenty-five years from 1860 to 1884, the total sum given by Churchmen for those 'ordinary purposes' was £46,397,237; exceeding, by nearly eleven millions, the whole amount given during the same period for Church-building, etc., which was £35,175,000.[2]

The 'Hospital Sunday collections' (Metropolitan and Provincial) are included in these totals. If I repeat a comparison which has been made between the collections, for that purpose, of the Church of England and those of other religious bodies, it is by no means as calling in question the pecuniary liberality of any of those other bodies; their rich men (and they are not wanting in them) are often very generous givers. But the facts have a direct bearing upon the numerical question. The *Official Year-*

---

[1] *O. Y. B.* (1886), 'Short Summaries,' p. xviii.   [2] *Ibid.*

Book, to which I have frequently referred, thus exhibits [1] the results of those collections, during the thirteen years from 1873 to 1885, in the Metropolis, and in fifty-eight large Provincial centres of population :—

Church of England—	Collections.	Amount collected.		
Metropolitan	9,318	£272,476	4	4
Provincial	35,046	337,549	5	11
Total	44,364	£610,025	10	3
Other Bodies—				
Metropolitan	6,858	£92,627	18	11
Provincial	20,972	175,295	11	3
Total	27,830	£267,923	10	2

The amount so collected, for this one purpose, by the Church of England, has, therefore, been to that collected by all the other bodies put together, in a ratio considerably exceeding two to one; a proportion which has been maintained, within slight limits of variation, in every one of those thirteen years.

I have intentionally abstained from dwelling upon any evidences of the vigorous life of the Church of England which go beyond her own borders; such as the remarkable extension of the Colonial and Indian Episcopate during the last fifty years, and the work of her Missionary Societies in the colonies and among the heathen. Nor have I dwelt upon such signs of increased power in her organic and corporate life at home, as the successful restoration of the office of Rural Dean throughout the country, the renewed activity of the two Provincial Convocations, the meetings of Church Congresses and Diocesan Synods and Conferences, and

[1] *O. Y. B.* (1886), 'Short Summaries,' pp. 159, 540-546.

the organisation, lately begun at the instance of the Bishops and Convocation, of a general consultative body of Laymen. Of the value and usefulness of these forms of activity different estimates will be formed by different minds. Whatever may be in the future for them, their effect and their tendency has been, and is, to bring together Churchmen of various ways of thinking; to mitigate their differences; to organise and give free expression to opinion within the Church; to indicate wants to be supplied; and to prepare the way for practicable reforms.

The charge of failure has been, I think, sufficiently met; though on the point of numbers, and on some other topics connected with them, more remains to be said. The work represented by these facts and figures is not that of a failing Church. It is not at the call of a failing Church that such great sums have been, during so short a tract of time, so willingly given. Well might Mr. Gladstone[1] say:—

'Like all others, I have observed the vast and ever-increasing development, for the last fifty years, both at home and abroad, in the Church to which I belong, of the powers of voluntary support. Those abridgments of her prerogatives as an Establishment, which have been frequent of late years, have not brought about a decrease, and have at least been contemporaneous with an increase, of her spiritual and social strength. By devotedness of life, and by solidity of labour, the clergy are laying a good foundation for the time to come. The attachment of the laity improves, if I may so speak, both in quantity and in quality. The English Church also appears to be eminently suited, in many and weighty points, to the needs of the coming time.'

This is testimony, which may perhaps have weight in some quarters, where mine may not.

[1] Midlothian Address, September 1885.

CHAPTER XV

THE (SO-CALLED) RELIGIOUS CENSUS OF 1851

THE argument from figures of the *Case for Disestablishment*[1] depends, almost wholly, upon 'the official Report of the census of attendance at public worship, in 1851, by Mr. Horace Mann.'

1. *Mr. Horace Mann's Report.*

Against Mr. Horace Mann, and what he did, I have nothing to say. He was an Assistant Commissioner for taking the General Census of 1851, and his official superiors thought it desirable to take that opportunity of procuring 'correct intelligence on two important subjects, of much public interest and controversy; viz. the number and varieties and capabilities of, first, the religious and, secondly, the scholastic, institutions of the country.'[2] There was no legal authority for any such inquiries by the Census officers, and no obligation on any person to give the information desired: but Mr. Mann was directed to take the steps which, as far as religion was concerned, were thought proper for that purpose. This he did; and he stated the

---

[1] *C. D.*, p. 99.
[2] Mann's *Report*, p. i.

results in an elaborate Report[1] to the Registrar-General ; to which he prefixed a historical Essay, fairly enough described by Sir George Cornewall Lewis[2] as 'a work of considerable research and ability,' but 'going into matters foreign to the statistical precision and dryness suitable to those returns.'

If I had wished to multiply evidence in disproof of the charge of 'failure,' now brought against the Church of England, I should find some things very much to my purpose in that Report of Mr. Horace Mann. Even then, thirty-five years ago, he spoke[3] of 'the rapid progress in recent times, and conspicuously within the last twenty years, of the Church of England;' and of the 'wonderful and almost unparalleled achievements, in the way of self-extension, by which she has lately proved her inexhaustible vitality.'[4] He spoke of her, too, as 'unaltered in her doctrine, discipline, and polity, since 1688.' But my present business is to show (from materials contained in the Report itself, and from those only), what this 'religious census of 1851' really was; how it was conducted ; and what, for the purpose of any controversy as to the success or failure of the work of the Church of England, is the value of its results.

2. *The Method of Inquiry.*

It was decided, by those from whom Mr. Mann received his instructions, to ascertain, (1) the number of the buildings used for public worship ; (2) the number of 'sittings' provided in them ; and (3) the number of persons who

---

[1] Dated 8th December 1853.
[2] Hansard's *Debates*, vol. clix. p. 1707.
[3] Mann's *Report*, p. xxxix.
[4] *Ibid.*, p. xxxi.

were present at any of the services held for public worship in England on Sunday the 30th March 1851 : the day immediately preceding that appointed for taking the general Census. For the general purposes of the Census,[1] an 'enumerator' was appointed for every one of 30,610 districts, into which England was divided: and each of those enumerators was directed to prepare, in the course of the week preceding the 30th March, a list of the places in his district 'in which any religious services were customarily performed;' with the name of the minister, or other principal authority, of every such place. This being done, he was to send, during the same week, to the officiating minister of each place on his list, printed forms to be filled up; with columns for (1) the number of 'sittings;' (2) the 'estimated number attending divine service on Sunday, 30th March 1851;' and (3) the 'average number of attendants during [blank] months;' with other particulars not material for the present purpose. The enumerators did as they were ordered: and as it had all to be done within a few days before that Sunday, nobody who had not received beforehand some information upon the subject could know anything, either of the object of those inquiries, or of the fact that they were to be made.

The forms (filled up or not) were collected by the enumerators on the 31st of March, and were by them returned to the Census Office. In the enumerators' lists of the places 'in which religious services were customarily performed,' there were entered 14,077 such places belonging to the Church of England, and 20,390 belonging to other religious bodies. In the returns when first examined in the Census

[1] The whole population of England and Wales, according to the Census of 1851, was 17,927,609. In 1881, it had risen to 25,968,020.

Office, 'a considerable number of deficiencies were found;'—chiefly in those relating to places of worship of the Church of England, on account of scruples felt by many of the clergy as to making any such returns without episcopal authority. 'In all such cases, a second application' (it is not said after what lapse of time) 'was made direct from the Census Office:' and this (we are told) was, generally, followed by 'a courteous return of the particulars desired.' In the 'few remaining cases,' the defective papers were referred to one of the 2190 Registrars of Births, Deaths, and Marriages: under whose direction the 'enumerators' had been placed. The Registrar 'either got the necessary information from the secular officers of the church, or else supplied from his own knowledge, or from the most attainable and accurate sources, *an estimate of the number of sittings, and of the usual congregation.*'

By these means, 'a return was ultimately, and after very considerable time and labour, procured from every place of worship mentioned in the enumerators' lists.' But, even after this had been done, 'when the returns came to be tabulated in parochial order, it was again discovered, that many of them were defective, in not stating the number of sittings; and that others, which gave the sittings, omitted mention of the number of attendants.'

To supply the defects, so discovered in that last stage, requests were again made in every case, as to *sittings*, to rectify the return. But there remained at last 2524 cases in which no such information could be got, and in which the defects were supplied by estimates.

On the other point, as to attendance on Divine worship, Mr. Mann reported thus :—

'Where the number of attendants was not stated for the 30th March, and it appeared that there was, nevertheless, a service held on that day, the number specified as the usual average was assumed to have been the number present on the 30th, and was inserted in the columns for that day. Where neither in the column for the 30th March, nor yet in the column for the average congregation, was any number given, the deficiency was mentioned in the foot-notes, as in the case of the omitted "sittings"; and the number was supplied by estimate, the estimates being founded on averages derived, with reference to the number of known or estimated "sittings," from the actual returns.'

The returns, so finally found defective and not supplied by any sort of information, appear to have been, as to sittings, 2524 (as already mentioned, of which 1026 related to places of worship of the Church of England, and the rest, therefore, to other places of worship), and, as to attendance, 1004; of which 989—all but 15,—related to places of worship of the Church of England.[1] In how many cases the numbers had been filled up by the Registrars, from their 'own knowledge,' or from information given by 'the secular officers of the church,' or in any other way not explained, is not stated. It may safely be assumed that the number of cases in which the column for 'usual average attendance' was filled up at all were few; for there is nothing corresponding to that column in Mr. Mann's Tables. In those cases in which the numbers who were present at the different services of the 30th March were returned by the officiating minister, it would have been interesting to know how he obtained them. It may be taken for granted that he did not himself count his morning, afternoon, or evening congregations. Some persons must have been employed by somebody to stand at

[1] The facts, as stated, will all be found in Mr. Mann's *Report*, pp. i, xli, clxix, *et seq*.

all the doors of the church, or other place of worship, and count the persons going in, or coming out, at each service; and the minister must have adopted their figures. It would have been interesting to know how, and by whom, those persons were chosen, and what securities there were for their care or trustworthiness. Nor would a knowledge of the state and conditions of the weather on that 30th of March have been immaterial. I do not suppose it to be any fault of Mr. Mann that we are ignorant of these things; it is not probable that he had the means of stating them with sufficient accuracy, as to all the places of worship in all the 30,610 districts throughout the country.

3. *Mr. Mann's Tables and Calculations.*

The Tables appended to Mr. Mann's Report were compiled from these imperfect returns, supplemented in the manner which has been described. 'Table A'[1] represents the total number of persons included in the Returns (without any estimate for defective returns) as present at the different places of worship included in the 'Enumerators'' lists on that Sunday: their distribution between morning, afternoon, and evening services being immaterial for my present purpose. 'Supplement II.[2] to Table A' adds to the numbers in that Table the 'estimates for defective returns.' (The *Case for Disestablishment*,[3] characteristically, gives Table A only, *without* the Supplement, as 'the official enumeration of worshippers, according to the Report.')

[1] Mann's *Report*, p. clxxviii.
[2] *Ibid.*, p. clxxxii (and see p. xli).
[3] *C. D.*, p. 100.

	Table A.	Supplement II. to Table A.
Church of England services	4,939,514	5,292,551
Other services	5,479,876	5,603,515
Total	10,419,390	10,896,066

It might have been supposed, that if any argument at all was to be founded upon this (so-called) 'religious census,' it would be based upon these figures, and not upon any further conjectural manipulation of or inferences from them. But this is not the case.

Mr. Mann estimated the maximum number of persons who, with reference to the 'sittings' provided in all the different places of worship, might have been able to worship simultaneously 'at one period of the day,' as 10,398,013;[1] something less than the number observed or estimated as worshippers at the aggregate of all the day's services. But he observed that (4,647,482 persons being reckoned as present at the morning services, which were those most largely attended) 'less than half the possible number' attended any one service. He went on to calculate how many individual worshippers might be supposed to be represented by the 10,896,066, the sum total of his Tables, and to make a conjectural distribution of them between the Church of England and the other religious bodies. 'There exist' (he frankly said) 'no *data* for determining how many persons attended twice and how many three times on Sundays;' adding, in a note,[2] that this part of his calculations was

---

[1] *Report*, p. clii. (As to sittings, see pp. xli and clxix *et seq*.) Mr. Mann estimated the number of those who, from various causes, 'would *of necessity* be absent, whenever divine service was celebrated,' at 7,500,000 persons.—Report, p. cxxi.

[2] Mann's *Report*, p. clii.

T

'mainly conjectural.' By '*supposing*' that of those who attended in the afternoon one-half had also been present in the morning, and that of those who attended in the evening two-thirds had been present either in the morning or in the afternoon, he reduced the total of 10,896,066, hypothetically, to 7,261,032 'separate persons:' of whom he assigned to the Church of England 3,773,474, and to other Bodies 3,487,558, thinking it probable 'that a larger proportion of Non-Conformists than of Conformists attended public worship more than once on a Sunday.'

If 7,261,032 are deducted from 10,398,013 (Mr. Mann's estimate of the maximum number of sittings in all the places of worship taken together), the number of those who, according to that test, might have attended, but did not attend, would be 3,136,071. But Mr. Mann, estimating those who might be 'able to attend once at least' at 12,540,326,[1] brought this latter figure up to 5,288,294.

'It must not, however' (he said[2]), 'be supposed that this 5,288,294 represents the number of habitual neglecters of religious services. This number is absent every Sunday: but it is not always composed of the same persons. Some may attend occasionally only; and, if the number of such occasional attendants be considerable, there will always be a considerable number of absentees on any given Sunday. The number of habitual non-attendants cannot be precisely stated from these Tables.'

How Mr. Mann, upon the materials which we have seen, could arrive in his own mind at the conclusion that 'this number' (viz. 5,288,294) was 'absent every Sunday,' I confess myself unable to understand. But his observation as to the inconclusiveness of such figures, even if that were true, is just. Besides the other arbitrary elements which

---

[1] Mann's *Report*, p. clii.   [2] *Ibid.*, p. cliii.

entered into his calculations, there are many causes, depending upon the season of the year, weather, and other accidents, which must necessarily make the attendance at divine service upon any single Sunday a very imperfect measure of the average attendance, at the same church or churches, throughout the year. We have (as has been already observed), in Mr. Mann's Tables, no column for average attendance.

4. *The Argument from Mr. Mann's Figures.*

Mr. Mann's calculations are paraded, with as much confidence as if there were no elements of uncertainty at all in them, in the *Case for Disestablishment;*[1] with the following conclusions :—

'The final result, therefore, stands thus :—

Attendants at other Churches . . .	3,487,558
Absentees (Mr. Mann's estimate) . .	5,288,294
	8,775,852

'These last figures represent the extent of the failure of the Church of England to induce the people to attend the ministrations of the clergy.'

And :[2]—

'It is obvious, therefore, that looked at from any point of view, the Census of 1851 proved that, up to that time, the Church of England had failed to win to itself the great mass of the population. It was established by law as the National Church, but it was not in any proper sense the Church of the nation ; and, had it not been for other denominations, the religious condition of England would have been appalling in the extreme.'

---

[1] *C. D.*, p. 100.   [2] *Ibid.*, p. 101.

I have no wish to decry or disparage any good work which may have been done by other denominations; but I may, without reproach to them, retort those words, and say, that the religious condition of England might assuredly have been, and would be now, 'appalling in the extreme,' but for what the Church of England has done, and is doing still.

The 'figures,' which are thus adduced to show 'the extent of the failure of the Church of England to induce the people to attend the ministrations of the clergy,' represent, as to rather more than three-eighths, worshippers of other denominations; and as to the other five-eighths (or a little less), those who were estimated by Mr. Horace Mann as 'absentees:'—two very different descriptions of persons. As to the separation of the former from the Church of England, I shall have something to say in the next chapter: as to the latter, their absence (if they were absent) from the services of the Church on the 30th of March 1851 proves nothing at all.

To suppose that 5,288,294 of the population for whom there is room in Churches,—even if the sittings provided had been exactly ascertained, and were a true measure of the numbers who might be present at one service or another, where there are two, three, or more services on the Sunday, and often on other days also,—to suppose that all those people were heathens, and beyond the pale and influence of the Church, because they might not have attended public worship on one particular day, is surely the height of unreasonableness: as Mr. Mann himself saw, when he wrote those words of caution against it, which I have quoted from his Report. Nobody can tell how many of them were as good Christians, as any of those who did attend—that a large proportion of them were so is (to say the least) quite as probable as any other supposition.

5. *Judgments of Statesmen.*

After making so much use of this 'census of 1851,' the *Case for Disestablishment* observes,[1] that

'The friends of the Established Church have not unnaturally sought to disparage' it :—but 'it was not until after the disclosures of the census had proved so damaging to the Establishment, that any complaint was made ; and the substantial accuracy of its figures is above suspicion.'

As to '*substantial accuracy*,' the facts speak for themselves. The case is not, in my view, one of 'complaint,' or of 'suspicion' :—Mr. Mann, who could not make bricks without straw, has told us (as well as he could) how his figures were arrived at. Of their value, dispassionate men are likely to form the same judgment, which was publicly expressed in 1860, not only by such 'friends of the Established Church' as Sir John Pakington and Lord Robert Cecil (now Lord Salisbury), but by Sir George Cornewall Lewis and Lord Palmerston ; who, though much too wise statesmen to desire a severance of the existing relations between Church and State, were not so ardent in their Churchmanship, or so antagonistic to Non-Conformity, as to 'seek to disparage' what had been done in 1851, because it was 'damaging to the Establishment.'

Sir George Lewis was Home Secretary in 1860; Sir George Grey, who filled that office in 1851, and had authorised what was then done, was in 1860 a member of the Cabinet. When the Census Bill of 1860 (which con-

[1] *C. D.*, p. 101.

tained a clause for taking a real census, founded on every man's own declaration, of the various forms of religious profession throughout the country), went into Committee,[1] Sir George Lewis, while not pressing that clause against the objections of Non-Conformists, who strongly opposed it, explained his reasons for proposing it, and for not thinking it right to repeat the course taken in 1851. He was following 'the general practice of civilised States in which differences of opinion exist;' and also 'the example of a religious census taken in Ireland under a Royal Commission in 1835.' On the other hand (he said):—

'Upon mature consideration, I decided against recommending a repetition of the plan of 1851, and in favour of the one now before us. . . . It seemed to me that the system adopted on the former occasion was altogether more lax and less accurate than was requisite for statistical purposes. It is obvious that an enumeration of the persons who attend places of worship on a given Sunday, even if quite accurate, must lead to very fallacious results, if relied on as the basis of a religious census. . . . I doubt not the returns were made with perfect honesty, and as far as possible with perfect correctness. But what I object to is the method, which is loose and inaccurate, and necessarily leading to fallacious inferences.'

Lord Palmerston,[2] in the same debate, said :—

'I have said that I concurred with the honourable member for Leeds' [Mr. Baines] 'in thinking that there is value in a periodical enumeration of the different sections of the Christian Church; but I do not agree with him as to the mode of obtaining the information, because nothing could be more entirely fallacious than the mode adopted in 1851. . . . To ask, as was done in 1851, how many people attended on

---

[1] Hansard's *Debates*, vol. clix. (11th July 1860) pp. 1705-1707.
[2] *Ibid.*, p. 1733.

a given Sunday in different places of worship, would procure no information from which any useful conclusion could be drawn.'

Lord Robert Cecil,[1] commenting on the resistance of the Non-Conformists to a real denominational Census, and on the success of that resistance, expressed himself in a way which evinced but an imperfect apprehension of the vitality of exploded fallacies, and their power of reappearance, even under the most unpromising conditions :—

'The victory' (he said) 'of instinctive feeling, which they had witnessed that day, would for ever dispose of Mr. Horace Mann and the Census of 1851.'

6. '*Newspaper Census.*'

Considering the weight of the authorities just cited as to the statistical value of Mr. Horace Mann's Report, the decision (adhered to down to the present time) against any official repetition of what was done in 1851, and the pertinacious and successful resistance of Non-Conformists to a genuine denominational census,—it is difficult for a man to preserve his gravity when reading, that 'in the autumn of 1881 and the beginning of 1882 an independent Newspaper Census of public worship was taken in various parts of the country, and the results were afterwards collected and published by the Liberation Society.' However 'carefully compiled' the 'summary of this newspaper religious census' (which follows, in the pages of the *Case for Disestablishment*[2]) may be, I must be excused for passing it over, and giving my space to matters more deserving of attention.

---

[1] Hansard's *Debates*, vol. clix., p. 1722.
[2] *C. D.*, pp. 101-104.

7. *Objections of Non-Conformists to a Denominational Census.*

What is the reason assigned for the refusal of the Non-Conformists represented by the 'Liberation Society' to allow the question of numbers to be brought, by a real and authentic census, to the conclusive test of the personal declaration of those concerned, to what Church or religious persuasion they belong, or whether they belong to none at all? The reason assigned[1] is this:—

'In the hope of diverting attention from the fact that the overwhelming majority of the people decline the ministrations of the Establishment, they' [*i.e.* Churchmen] 'propose to substitute for an actual enumeration of worshippers a requirement that each householder should state in his census paper to what denomination he is attached. They desire to substitute a nominal for a real census, fiction for fact. To such a proposal the advocates of religious equality cannot give their consent. Any return, save of the actual attendance at public worship, would be worse than useless; for it would mislead and label irreligion and neglect of the ministrations of religion with the name of attachment to some religious denomination.'

The upshot of this rhetoric seems to be, that the people of England are not to be heard upon the question, whether they belong to the Church of England or not; and that, while their mouths are stopped, it is to be assumed as an ascertained fact, that 'an overwhelming majority' of them 'decline her ministrations.' A man's own declaration of his adherence to a particular Church or religious denomination is not to be accepted, is not to go for anything, unless the quality of his religion is investigated by a new test,—not a subscription test or a communicant test, or any other kind of test ever before imagined or heard of, but that of the regularity or irregularity of his attendance at public worship. Far be it from

[1] *C. D.*, pp. 101, 102.

me to say a word in disparagement of the stated public ordinances of religion; but I protest against this sweeping excommunication of all who are not, in that respect, everything which might be desired. There always have been, and there always will be, many degrees in the scale of Christian experience and attainment. Nor is punctuality of attendance at church or chapel (however much to be wished for and commended) any infallible sign of true religion now, more than it would have been in the days of the Pharisee and the Publican. It is not even an infallible sign of the denomination to which a man may belong; for some go about to hear preachers, not always of their own Church.

8. *Imperfect Christians not to be rejected.*

Youth, carelessness, ill-health, infirmity, domestic engagements, fatigue from week-day toil, indolence on the one day when rest is possible, habits (too easily contracted) of letting secular cares or amusements encroach on that day, moral backslidings and failures, which may occur when there is no utter apostasy of mind or heart from religion and goodness—these, all taken together, are causes which go far to account for the irregularity or infrequency of the attendance at church—perhaps at chapel too—of many, whom no Church or denomination would refuse to acknowledge as its members, and whom no man with a spark of Christian humility or charity would regard or treat as heathens and publicans. If Non-Conformist Bodies would disavow and reject all such, it is a happy thing for religion and for the nation that the Church of England does not. Granted that many of them may be weak members of a Christian Church. But are they for that reason to be renounced? Who is he that presumes to call their profession of religious belief or of Church membership merely nominal and not real, a fiction and not a fact, and to identify it with that irreligion, which is certainly no bar to fellowship, when the object is to disestablish the Church of England? The Church does not reject them from her pale, though they may fall short of their profession; they desire to remain in it: who else has a right to reject them? Nor can any one really measure the influence of the Church for good upon such men as these, till the end is seen. The time may come—it does come continually to many of them, in all ranks,—when levity is succeeded by seriousness, when the attractions of the world decline; and then comes also the opportunity of the Church, which did not cast them off when their hearts were farthest from her. At the worst, few men wish their families to be neglectful of religion. The wife or the child is constantly an angel in the house: to the man himself, as well as to his house, the power and consolation of religion generally, in such circumstances, comes home at last. It is for the benefit of these, and of other souls estranged from the ordinances of religion, at least as much as for that of consistent and advanced Christians, that Churches exist. Why should they, because of their great spiritual need, count for nothing in the question, whether the Church to which they profess their adhesion shall or shall not retain her present means of reaching them and doing them good? Preaching is not all in the Church of England: she is sent, like her Divine Master, to call 'not the righteous, but sinners to repentance.'[1] Her mission work and pastoral work outside the sacred building are not less important than her services within it.

[1] Matthew ix. 13.

CHAPTER XVI

DIVISIONS AND CAUSES OF OFFENCE

THERE is a notion, which has influence with some minds, (and where it has influence may perhaps appear to have a bearing upon the question of Disestablishment), that there is, or in idea at least ought to be, some corporate identity between a national Church and the State or Nation.

1. *Theory of the Unity of Church and State.*

This notion had its origin in the fact, that there have been times when the English Church and Nation were outwardly coextensive, or nearly so; and that some of the incidents of 'Establishment,' and some of the endowments of the Church, date from those times. Some persons appear to think, that when the Church was coextensive with the nation, it lost its distinct existence and character. This is a strong example of the tendency of men to substitute theories for facts.

The ecclesiastical unity of Western Christendom, before the Reformation, though consistent (here as elsewhere) with the separate organisation of National Churches, was not merely coextensive with, nor was it limited by, nationality. When, by the Reformation, the Church of England had become separated from the Continental Churches as she was not before, both the ecclesiastical and the civil Powers endeavoured to repress those inevitable tendencies towards further religious division, which manifested themselves during the reigns of Elizabeth and her Stuart successors. Hooker, among other arguments by which he sought to justify such interference of the Civil Power in matters of religion as then took place, formulated the theory (contained in the Eighth Book[1] of his *Ecclesiastical Polity*) of the identity, in some sense, of Church and State, because of the identity of the natural persons constituting them:—an identity even then apparent, rather than real, and soon to disappear; and requiring (as Hooker perceived), exceptions and qualifications, difficult to reconcile with the theory. Dr. Arnold,[2] in the present century, took up the same notion, and carried it farther than Hooker had done. Hooker never lost sight of the independent origin, and the separate provinces, of the ecclesiastical and temporal Powers: he knew that upon that distinction the ultimate hold of any organised system of religion upon the conscience depended; and, although he spoke fancifully and mystically of the union of the two characters in the same body of persons, he had no more idea of merging Church in State, than he had of absorbing the State into the Church. Whatever, in that respect, may have been the views of Dr. Arnold, or of any of his disciples, no idea could be more opposite to that of the advocates of Disestablishment than the merger of Church in State, or the assertion of that kind and degree of State authority in matters of religion for which Hooker, and Arnold also, contended. Nor is it true that, now or at any other time, the

[1] Hooker's *Works* (ed. Keble, 1841), vol. iii. pp. 330-340.
[2] Stanley's *Life of Arnold* (1844), vol. i. p. 206; vol. ii. p. 139.

Church of England has made that theory her own; or that the State of England has ever asserted it. On the contrary (as was shown in a former chapter), both Church and State agreed, by solemn acts which remain to this day among the laws governing their mutual relations, to recognise the substantial distinction between the temporal authority claimed by the State, and acknowledged by the Church, and the spiritual mission claimed by the Church, and disclaimed by the State.

Turning from theory to facts, it is to be observed, that such approximation towards identity of the constituent members of Church and State as may have existed during the middle period of the Church of England (*i.e.* from the general conversion of the people to Christianity until the origin of modern dissent) was not the original, any more than it is the present, condition of things. The kingdoms of the Heptarchy, under which the Church of England was founded and received endowments which it has ever since preserved, comprehended heathens. It was not until Egbert's time, that the State and the Church could be said, with any near approach to truth, to have become practically coextensive; the Danish incursions again broke, for a time, that approximation to unity. There is no ground, legal or historical, for representing any later endowments as given to the Church upon conditions substantially different from the earlier. Whether she might fail to gain, or fail to retain, in a greater or less degree, the adhesion of the whole people, was a question which never entered into the minds of the givers, or into the conditions of the gifts.

Even if it might have been possible for any confusion to arise between the ideas of Church and State, in respect of endowments, if endowments had been given to the Church as one aggregate body when the same individual persons composed both Church and Nation, the fact, that the Church as one aggregate body was never so endowed, but that all her property was given to particular ecclesiastical corporations—Bishoprics, Chapters, and Rectors or Vicars of parishes—made that confusion impossible.

It must be added, that the idea of an absolute personal identity, between the constituent members of the Church and of the Body Politic in England, was never truly realised in fact. Exclusion from each, by its own proper authority, was always possible, and from time to time happened to particular persons, without having for its consequence exclusion from the other. Outlaws lost (temporarily, or permanently) their rights of citizenship; they did not cease to be members of the Church. Excommunicated persons lost the rights of Churchmen; but did not cease to belong to the Body Politic. Some who had never been members of the one, were nevertheless members of the other. I do not mean Jews, who might be regarded as having a separate nationality of their own. But unbaptized persons were not on that account excluded from national citizenship: and baptized aliens resident in England,—of whom there were always many, Flemings, Lombards, Scots, and others—were members of the Church, and entitled to the full rights of Churchmen—they were not so much as disqualified from holding Church preferments. But they were not citizens of the State.

When we come to later times, in which liberty of thought produced ecclesiastical separation, it was certainly not competent for the Separatist, by asserting his own freedom, to innovate upon or derogate from the position and rights of the Body from which he seceded. When and how is it to be supposed that this was done? Was it when those who obeyed Pope Pius the Fifth left the communion of the Church of England under Queen Elizabeth? Was it when the Brownists first met in conventicles of their own? Was it when the spread of Anabaptist or Quaker tenets led to the disuse by many of the practice of infant baptism, and so to the inclusion in the State of a much larger number of unbaptized persons than in former times? Or was it when the law began to extend toleration to Non-Conformists? No man in either Church or State,—no Churchman, no Non-Conformist,—at any of those periods, dreamed of any such consequence. The most ancient schisms were those under the Byzantine Empire, when the previous religious unity of all the subjects of that Imperial State was broken by the secession or exclusion of the Arians, and of the Nestorian, Jacobite, and other considerable Churches which dissented, and to this day continue to dissent, from the doctrinal standards of the 'Orthodox' Greek Church. Nobody then, or in all the ages which followed, imagined that the right of the Church to her possessions, or to anything else, there or anywhere, was dependent upon the condition of universal national Conformity.

2. *Causes of Disunion.*

Nor is it just or consistent with truth to impute either the existence of Non-Conformity, or the numbers of Non-Conformists where they are numerous, to failure or fault of the Church.[1] The authorities both of Church and of State erred in past times, in taking such measures as they did to compel outward Conformity; but those measures

[1] *C. D.*, p. 95.

were not the true causes of division. It is right that there should be religious freedom; and where religious freedom is, there will be more or less diversity. Divisions once begun tend in their own nature to multiplication and further subdivision. How otherwise is it possible to account for the number of Non-Conformist sects and denominations at the present time in England? If we look at the Registrar-General's Report of marriages in 1884,[1] we find there the Wesleyan Methodists subdivided into (1) 'Original Connexion;' (2) 'New Connexion;' (3) 'Primitive Methodists;" (4) 'Bible Christians;' (5) 'United Methodist Free Church;' and (6) 'Other Wesleyan Methodists.' The first of these sub-denominations had 1687, the second 147, the third 675, the fourth 94, the fifth 394, and the 'others' 32, places of worship registered for marriages. The Presbyterians are subdivided into (1) 'Church of Scotland,' with 16 similarly registered places of worship; (2) 'United Presbyterians,' with 25; (3) 'Presbyterian Church of England,' with 194; and (4) 'Presbyterian Church in England,' with 100. The other denominations enumerated by name (besides a number of minor sects not separately named, and the Roman Catholics) are the 'Independents,' with 2227 similarly registered places of worship; 'Baptists,'[2] with 1778; 'Calvinistic Methodists,' with 502; 'Unitarians,' with 139; 'Lady Huntingdon's Connexion,' with 35; 'New Jerusalem,' with 40; and 'Catholic and Apostolic Church,' with 33.

To have been unable to prevent the natural consequences

---

[1] 47th *Report*, p. xlii.

[2] In Mr. Horace Mann's Report of 1851 (p. ix), the Baptists are also subdivided into (1) 'General;' (2) 'Particular;' (3) 'Seventh Day;' (4) 'Scotch;' and (5) 'New Connexion General' Baptists.

of freedom is no reproach to the Church, however much our ancestors may deserve blame for having at any time endeavoured to keep back the free movement, in the field of religious thought and practice, of the human mind. It is far better for the Church, and for the truths which she teaches, and for every object which in her character of a national Church it is her duty to promote, that there should be this state of things, than a forced and unreal conformity, such as existed when the principles of civil and religious liberty were not equally well understood. So far from the actual state of facts being any evidence of failure on her part, that immense power of central attraction which she still exercises everywhere, notwithstanding all these things, over the masses of the people who voluntarily and without constraint adhere to her communion, is the best and strongest proof of her general fidelity to her calling and success in her work. It is no paradox to say, that the existence of so many classes of Separatists makes such a centre of religious unity in the nation, and such a representation of historical Christianity, now more than ever important.

3. *Divisions within the Church.*

Among other arguments in support of the charge of failure, one has been drawn from dissensions within the Church's own pale.[1]

There have always been in all Churches different parties and schools of thought; nor is this a reproach. The human mind is naturally so constituted, that few see all things alike; very few (if any) see all truths and all aspects of the same truth with equal distinctness. Some are carried

[1] *C. D.*, p. 96.

in one direction, some in another, by influences which have been to themselves identified with the reception of truth, or by the greater or less acuteness of their perception of the dangers of particular errors, or tendencies towards error. There are central and necessary truths, as to which substantial difference would be inconsistent with that profession of a common faith, on which every Church and religious society is founded. But those who hold these honestly may, as to many things, differ among themselves. The *Case for Disestablishment* puts this question:[1]—'Do Evangelicals, Broad-Churchmen, and Ritualists really hold "one faith"?' The question is put, not as to any exceptional cases of unsettled minds or insincere professions, but in a broader and more general way. So taking it, I answer without hesitation: 'Yes: They do.' There can be no greater error than to confound articles of faith with matters of mere opinion; nothing would be more dangerous to faith than to insist that there cannot be substantial religious unity where there is any divergence of thought upon religious subjects.

It is an evil, and might easily become a dangerous evil, when divergent views are so exaggerated and carried so far as to produce (as they sometimes do) violent partisanship, and an acrimonious controversial spirit. But the zeal and earnestness, of which strong opinions and warm attachment to them are the necessary products, are indispensable to the life and spiritual power of a Church; and there is always, between the extremes, a very large middle ground of charity and moderation, by means of which a just balance may be, and generally is, upon the whole preserved. Agreement in all things being imposs-

[1] *C. D.*, p. 96.

ible (the Church of England has never required such agreement), it tends to preserve that just balance, when within the range of lawful liberty there are different schools of opinion, complementary each to the rest.

The effervescence of individual piety and earnestness—the habit of pushing doctrines to their extreme consequences, which the pursuit of absolute truth in the highest region of thought is apt to engender,—impatience of restraints and disturbing forces,—produce, unavoidably, some eccentricities and some friction. But these are shadows, which must be present where there is light. Unless there is an approach to predominance, in any direction, of opinions adverse to the true spirit of the Church, it may be safer and wiser to allow considerable latitude, even to those which come near the dividing line, and to rely for their correction upon the power of charity and good sense, rather than to make martyrs for every seeming, or even every real, transgression of the bounds of lawful liberty. It is true of all the parties in the Church of England, that men are from time to time found in them,—sometimes men well affected to the Church, sometimes disaffected,—who will not be restrained within those bounds: who transgress them, to the offence of others, for what may seem very slight causes. For my own part I regret this, whenever and wherever it happens; I do not justify it; I admit that, if carried to certain lengths by a sufficient number of persons, it might raise serious questions, which, in the actual circumstances of the case, do not arise. But it is not, in my judgment, true, that the Church of England has failed to preserve, generally and for needful practical purposes, the substance of that uniformity, which her laws are intended to secure. It is not failure, if she has not been able, in this or in other things,

> 'To wind herself too high [1]
> For sinful man beneath the sky.'

It is not failure, if those relaxations of exact uniformity, to which the law itself has given its sanction after the experience of two centuries, have been occasionally exceeded in matters of form and ceremony; in one place (it may be) through the force of local custom, in another, perhaps, with the general consent of minister and congregation. Such deviations from strict law may become (as I have said) dangerous: but they are not failure. Public opinion, either within or without the Church, is not on the side of those who would treat them as if they were. I do not find fault with men who are sensitive about such things; although I cannot think it wise to exaggerate the importance of anything in its proper nature indifferent, or to blame the rulers of the Church for the mildness of their government, or for the tolerance with which they endure what they regard as less, rather than provoke greater evils. Such evils as these have been the accompaniments of all outbursts of enthusiasm: and there is nothing for which former generations of Churchmen have been more generally (not always justly) stigmatised and censured, than for repelling from the Church that kind of enthusiasm, rather than endure any deviation from her disciplinary laws.

4. *Causes of Offence.*

The existence, therefore, of these diversities of opinion and practice within her pale, is no proof that the Church has failed in her mission. And the same may be said of all such spots and blemishes upon the system of law and ad-

[1] Keble's *Christian Year.*

ministration under which she has now to act, as may need, and are capable of, amendment. Some such there will always be in every system. So far from the Church or her defenders shutting their eyes to such blemishes, or wishing them to continue, the reverse is the case. Whatever difficulty in that respect there may be comes (as most of the mischief itself does) from the side of the State. That the law, for example, should be so amended as to arm the authorities of the Church with more power than they at present possess to reject or remove unfit and unworthy ministers, and to prevent lay patrons from making a traffic of their patronage to the scandal and detriment of the Church (which, after all, not more than a small proportion of their whole number do, or have done), is as much desired by the rulers and members of the Church, as the need of such amendments can be demonstrated by her censors. To exaggerate the extent to which these evils actually prevail, and the mischief they do, is easy; it is done (as might be expected), in the *Case for Disestablishment.*[1] But, on the other hand, I am not disposed to extenuate evils which I desire to see corrected. It is enough to deny (and truth justifies me in denying), that they prevail, even now, to any such extent, or in any such degree, as to be a material make-weight against the proofs of the general faithfulness and success of the Church in her work. It will not be the fault of the Church if they are not removed or cured.

[1] *C. D.*, pp. 84-93.

CHAPTER XVII

INVECTIVE AND QUOTATION

I HAVE dealt with the more substantial accusations brought against the Church of England. The rest are gladiatorial.

1. *Alleged Hindrance to Religion.*

First, under the head of 'the religious argument,' comes 'hindrance, rather than help, to the cause of religion'[1]—which, of course, begs the question. Ancient sins are to be visited on modern times: all the persecutions which have been in the world since the thirteenth century are to be made evidence in support of the present indictment against the Church of England. I suppose, however, that nobody would think the crimes of the Anabaptists of Munster, or the burning of Servetus by Calvin, good cause for taking away the chapels and endowments of the Baptists or Calvinistic Methodists of the present day, or even for imputing to their systems an inherent tendency towards violence or persecution.
But it is said:[2]—

'Wherever an Established Church is found, the principle of persecution is present; leavening the whole lump; and

---

[1] *C. D.*, p. 11.   [2] *Ibid.*, p. 12.

making dissent an offence to be punished, if not by the magistrate, then by individuals in their private capacity, or as members of a social circle.'

For my part, I should say, that Established Churches are now in much more danger of being persecuted, than of persecuting. The Church of England is not actively invading, or threatening to invade, other men's rights, liberties, or privileges; she only desires to keep what is her own; which other people are actively endeavouring to take away from her. Is it *only* 'where an Established Church is found,' that 'the principle of persecution is present'? To Churchmen, the spirit of the *Case for Disestablishment*, — the whole crusade against the Church of England,—the scheme propounded by the 'Liberation' Society,—may all appear to savour of 'the principle of persecution.' Doubtless, the 'Liberationists' do not see it in that light :—but neither do Churchmen see in that light the natural influence of the bonds of religious association. To 'punish,' or attempt to punish, dissent as 'an offence,'—publicly, privately, or socially,—would certainly be wrong :— I hope there are few Churchmen who think, or who act as if they thought, otherwise. But that is a different thing from the preference of religious unity and co-operation to religious discord and opposition, in the family, or in other voluntary relations. That can never cease, as long as the Bible contains the precept,[1] 'As we have opportunity, let us do good unto all men, *especially unto them who are of the household of faith.*' If there are (it can hardly be otherwise) some, who draw the line more narrowly and rigidly than is necessary or wise, that is not an evil which would be removed or mitigated by disestablishing and disendowing the Church :—I

---

[1] Galatians vi. 10.

cannot conceive anything, by which it would be more certainly increased and aggravated.

2. *Restraint on Free Action.*

We are told, also,[1] that Establishment '*fetters the free action of Churches.*' To some extent, this is true; to some extent, it is no disadvantage. Such is, in a greater or less degree, the necessary consequence, not only of all positive relations between Church and State, but of all definite systems of doctrine and discipline. Stability and permanence[2] are characters, which a Church believing herself to hold and to teach the truth must desire to maintain; restlessness and continual innovation are against her principles. I do not say, that a greater freedom of action than she now has, for purposes consistent with faithfulness to her principles, might not be desirable for the Church of England:—but her elasticity, progress, and expansion during the present century show that she is not so far handicapped, even in the race with Non-Conformists (who have also their own 'fetters on free action,' arising out of the systems which they have made for themselves), as to prevent her from performing with ever-increasing efficiency her appointed work. Whatever difficulty there may be in removing impediments to her free action, in any beneficial direction, by reason of the necessity for Parliamentary concurrence in changes of her laws, that difficulty is on the side of the State: and this, as long as the Church can with a clear conscience acquiesce in it, constitutes no reason for disestablishment.

---

[1] *C. D.*, p. 13.   [2] 1 Tim. iii. 15.

3. *Worldliness.*

The next assertion [1] is, that 'it [Establishment] lowers the spiritual tone of the Church,' and 'infuses into it an element of worldliness, which greatly impairs its efficiency and its success.' The proof [2] offered is an extract from an 'Essay on the Union of Church and State,' written forty years ago by the late Mr. Baptist Noel on his quitting the Church; in which he spoke of 'secular cupidity,' 'balls and race-courses,' 'hunting and shooting,' and 'ignorance of the Scriptures.' It is not, generally, even to a good man who changes his party or his Church, and writes under the excitement of that change bitter things against those whom he has left, that persons who wish to form dispassionate judgments will look for evidence on which they can rely. The *Case for Disestablishment* admits,[3] that 'in many respects, a great change for the better has taken place in the general character of the clergy since that work was issued.' I will only, therefore, observe, that, while it is true that a clergyman ought not to have the character of a man too much addicted to secular amusements, there was a tendency in the religious school to which Mr. Baptist Noel belonged to elevate counsels of perfection into laws of bondage, and to make, out of some things in their proper nature innocent or indifferent, artificial sins:—and it may, perhaps, be worth the while of serious persons, in and out of the Church of England, to consider, whether this may not possibly

---

[1] *C. D.*, p. 15.
[2] What is quoted, at pp. 15, 16, from the present Bishop of Carlisle (as to 'some' cases, which he evidently regards and represents as exceptional) is even less to the purpose.
[3] *C. D.*, p. 15.

have had something to do with the aberrations from that school, in various directions, of many who were brought up in it.

The adversary, while admitting some improvement, still contends[1] that 'the evil principle which it' [Mr. Noel's essay] 'condemns is still productive of the most mischievous results.' He has to make out, not that worldliness may be met with in the Church of England,—where is it not?—but that the system of the Church of England has a natural or a practical tendency to produce it. If more is meant than that the prospect of obtaining a living by any calling may be a motive to some minds to embrace it, I deny the fact: if that only is meant, there are other religious bodies besides the Church of England in which such a temptation may operate, and may possibly induce those who yield to it to preach what is popular. America is sometimes appealed to as a model: most of us have heard of popular preachers there (not in communion with the Church of England) who have been said annually to let the sittings in their churches for sums compared with which the emoluments of the best livings in the Church of England are insignificant. My denial is as valid as an assertion incapable of proof. I have no wish to retort such accusations, but is there never any element of worldliness in political agitation? Is it quite an unheard-of thing, even among Non-Conformist ministers? The argument is only confused by representing the common frailties of mankind as if they were peculiar fruits of 'Establishment.'

4. *Exclusiveness.*

Last, under the 'religious' head (of things with which I

[1] *C. D.*, p. 15.

have not dealt before), comes '*exclusiveness*.'[1] Here again the accuser is conscious

> 'That separation of Church and State will not necessarily issue in the union of Christians and Churches. Sacerdotalism, unholy rivalries, sectarian bigotry or animosity, and social antipathies, may, and probably will, keep asunder those who ought to meet as children in the Divine family and servants of the Divine household.'[2]

It is, I am afraid, easy to be effusive about unity and comprehension when the object is not comprehension, but destruction. It has been seen, in a former chapter, how little tendency to union and cohesion, and how much to frequent multiplication of divisions, there has been in some of those voluntary bodies which constitute the strength of the movement for Disestablishment. As to 'unholy rivalries,' 'sectarian animosity,' and 'social antipathies,' the situation would not be improved by the provocation which the success of that movement would give to passions and resentments, from which such feelings might naturally result. Still less would those deeper convictions disappear, which lead religious men to take serious views of the importance of religious differences, and (not always on the side of the Church only) to find some practical difficulty in reconciling fidelity to the truth (as they have received and understand it) with the wish to be on comfortable terms with everybody as far as they lawfully can, even with those who cross their paths daily as opponents and antagonists, and perhaps denounce as no Gospel the faith which they believe and teach. Levity or indifference on such points would be more culpable than over-scrupulousness;—although there is, doubtless, an ideal relation, of perfect personal good-will and

---

[1] *C. D.*, p. 16.   [2] *Ibid.*, p. 17.

friendliness, and willingness to meet on common ground as far as may be possible without compromise of principle, at which good men on all sides may and ought to aim, and which (if not hindered by the movement for Disestablishment) they might have a tendency, under the circumstances of these times, and of the assaults made upon Christianity itself, more frequently and more nearly to realise.

Of the natural effects (either on the better or on the worse side) of the mutual estrangement in matters of religion of men separated in communion and not agreeing in their views of the ministerial commission, the Establishment of the Church is *not* the cause. It is rather, if truth must be spoken, the opposition and antagonism (justifiable, of course, from its own point of view) of Non-Conformity to the Church. That evil, as well as others, would be aggravated, not diminished, by Disestablishment.

5. *Conservatism in Politics.*

There remains a charge, expanded under several heads in the chapter of the *Case for Disestablishment* entitled 'the political argument,'[1] which comes really to one point; the leaning of the clergy towards Conservative politics. The Church ought to be disestablished and disendowed, because the clergy have either opposed or have not taken an active part in promoting political reforms; because their votes at elections are supposed to be generally on the Conservative side. Is it really the opinion of the writers of this book that every influence in the country which is, upon the whole, Conservative, ought for that reason to be proscribed? Is that considered to be a 'Liberal' opinion?

[1] *C. D.*, pp. 20-31.

I cannot follow the assailants of the Church in all their excursions through the history of remote and recent times down to the general elections of 1868, 1874, and 1880—those of 1885 and 1886 would doubtless have been added if they had been foreseen. But (whoever may be quoted for them) I repel, as substantially unjust and untrue, the charges of 'hostility to liberty,'[1] and to 'national righteousness,'[2] and to all reforms,—if made against the general body of the clergy of the Church of England. Neither at the time of the Restoration, nor at that of the Revolution, were they open to such an impeachment. The Bishops were willing, and it was the Commons of 1662 who were unwilling, that toleration clauses, in fulfilment of Charles the Second's promises at Breda, should have found a place in the Act of Uniformity; and the resistance of the Seven Bishops to the illegal measures of James the Second contributed not a little to the success of the constitutional cause in 1688; though five of them preferred the loss of place, power, and possessions, to swearing new oaths, inconsistent (as they deemed) with those which they had already taken. As for later times, I never heard that the clergy generally opposed themselves to such measures as the abolition of the Slave-trade or of slavery, or to such economical reforms as that of the Poor Law, which they could understand. Nor can I admit it to be the fact (whatever Mr. Cobden may have said in a private letter [3] in 1842), that they exerted themselves against the repeal of the Corn-laws, whether they understood the true bearings of that measure or not—much less that they ever wished to keep up a high price of bread. What Mr. Gladstone,[4] or any one else, may have

---

[1] *C. D.*, p. 22.   [2] *Ibid.*, p. 31.   [3] *Ibid.*, p. 25.
[4] Quoted in *Radical Programme* (1885), p. 152. 'The secret' of the

thought they ought to do 'in the rural controversy between capital and labour,' I do not know; I, for one, cannot blame them, if in that controversy some of them may have seen dangers (to poor as well as rich), economical, moral, and social; as there always must be when efforts are made (even under a belief that good may result from them) to produce mutual opposition and antagonism, and accompanying feelings of distrust and ill-will, between classes whose true interests are bound together. It is not the mission of the clergy to arbitrate between capital and labour, any more than it was that of their Divine Master to be a divider of earthly inheritances;[1] nor can they be expected to have the qualifications for doing so with good effect. Nothing will persuade me (even if it could be shown that they formed a wrong judgment as to some economical question) that any considerable number of them has ever had, as to that or any such matter, any other motive or disposition than to promote the welfare of the poor, and the interests (as they understood them) of honest labour on the one hand and fair and just dealing on the other.

That Bishops may have voted in Parliament[2] against large constitutional changes, from which such men as the Duke of Wellington and Sir Robert Peel apprehended dangers to Church or State, may affect the reputation of those who did so for political wisdom and foresight,—neither more, how-

---

bitterness against the clergy of what is in the same page of that publication designated 'the organ of the agricultural labourers' is an open one. The political personage who has been most concerned in the association of which that paper is really the organ, has always combined with his philanthropy a bitter sectarian hostility to the Church. Where that paper is read the labouring man is not generally so foolish as not to know who is his friend.

[1] Luke xii. 13, 14.   [2] *C. D.*, p. 24.

ever, nor less, than it affects the reputation of those other illustrious men, whom the nation nevertheless holds in honour. It cannot do more—it cannot establish against them, much less against the Church or clergy of England, the charge of hostility to liberty, or to national righteousness.

In contending earnestly, as she did, for freedom of religious instruction in voluntary schools, and preferring schools in which such instruction might be freely given, without offence to any man's conscience, to Board schools (where the latter were not necessary), the Church of England was only faithful to her trust, and to the cause of liberty.

Putting aside the misleading influences of party-spirit and prejudice, the truth is this. The Christian religion, in a Christian country (when no disturbing force, such as persecution, civil disability, rivalry of sects, Disestablishment or Disendowment, comes in), is a Conservative principle in the truest and highest sense of that word; which, I need hardly say, is not identical with the party sense. That it should be otherwise—that religion should be a destructive and disorganising, and not a law-abiding, law-supporting, power—would be fatal to the well-being of any State. In the Christian Code, the precepts, 'Fear God,' and 'Honour the King,'[1] stand side by side together. If the Church of England, or any other Church, may sometimes have seemed to 'honour the King' too much, or to give more 'to Cæsar' than was his due, far worse would it have been for the nation if the Church had claimed 'the things which be Cæsar's,' and had inflamed, through her ministers, popular passions against law, public order, or constitutional government.

The natural and legitimate bias of every Church which

[1] 1 Peter ii. 17.

understands and does its duty being thus on the side of public order, as against disturbance and confusion, it follows that in a well-governed[1] State the political leanings of the clergy of an ancient historical Church (when nothing is done to alienate them) may be expected to be, generally, towards that party which represents the principle of stability rather than that of change. If there were no other moral or social forces to be taken into account, or if clerical interference in politics were carried beyond the limits imposed by a just sense of the pastoral relations of the clergy to all their people, it is conceivable that the course of political reforms might be too much retarded. But, ever since the Revolution of 1688,—perhaps I might go farther back,— political progress has been going on in this country, with results all the safer and better for that conflict and balance of opinions, which has educated men of all sorts in the practice of liberty, has taught them forbearance towards each other, and has prepared the way gradually, by forethought and deliberation, for every forward step. Things might have been far less favourable to orderly progress and true liberty, if the clergy of the Church of England had continued (as they were during some reigns after the ejection of the Nonjurors) discontented with the system of government under which they lived, and anxious for change. No wise man will say that the pace of political movement (whether it be now really forward, or in some respects backward, time will show) is not, at present, fast enough.

As a fact, the clergy of the Church of England have seldom taken any part in political agitations. They have left that to others. Were they wrong in doing so? I think not. They have had their party attachments; but,

[1] *I.e.* well-governed, in a comparative, not an absolute sense.

as a rule, they have contented themselves with the quiet and inoffensive exercise of those civil franchises, with which, in common with their fellow-citizens, the law has entrusted them. It has not been their general habit to endeavour to overbear, or intimidate, or control by spiritual influence, the independence of laymen. They may not, as a class, always be wise politicians;—it has been a common saying, from the days of Lord Clarendon or earlier (even of some who understood and appreciated their virtues), that they are not. That (if it be true) may be due to two causes. One is, that men whose minds are very much exercised on questions of absolute duty and absolute truth, and who in their proper sphere speak with such authority as belongs to the accredited ministers of a Divine Religion, do not always perceive how many questions in politics depend upon considerations of practical wisdom, variable with times and circumstances, and not upon immutable principles. The other is, that the fact of their proper duties lying elsewhere, and being adverse to much activity in the field of politics, prevents them from studying some political questions in a practical way, and makes them indisposed towards changes, of which they do not clearly see the necessity or the advantage.

If it is desirable that the clergy of the Church of England should become a greater, a more active, a more coherent and highly organised political power than heretofore, and at the same time less attached to, and less influenced by, the government under which they live, then I admit that Disestablishment and Disendowment may tend to produce that result. But I cannot be persuaded that this would be for the true interest of either the Church or the Nation.

6. *Quotations.*

The *Case for Disestablishment* is an anthology of quotations. Whatever cannot be proved by evidence or argument, is (it seems) to be proved by authority; and for that purpose all is grist which comes to this mill. The author must have kept a common-place book, in which he collected, for future use, everything unpleasant which he met with about the Church of England, and every argument on any subject used by either friends or enemies of the Church which seemed capable of being, at any time, turned against her. Bishops, zealous for the reform of things which they thought amiss;—clergymen of all sorts, some eminent, some obscure,—some 'high,' including one [1] who (unless report did him wrong) was a prominent member, it was even said a self-constituted bishop, of a body called 'The Order of Corporate Reunion,'—some 'low,' including one [2] who, when he wrote, had become a Non-Conformist;—politicians, chiefly of one colour (myself included); historians and men of letters, of very various qualities; anonymous and other writers in *The Times*, the *Church Times*, the *Record*, and other newspapers, periodicals, or pamphlets;—even the 'once famous Black Book' [3] of 1831 (which, according to my recollection, set down every Knight of the Garter, and every Lord Lieutenant of a County, as receiving out of the public purse £10,000 a year):—all are pressed into this service. I cannot acknowledge their authority: as witnesses, I refuse them.

Some few [4] of them are cited to show that a new Church of England was made at the Reformation. On this subject,

---

[1] *C. D.*, p. 41.
[2] *Ibid.*, p. 15.
[3] *Ibid.*, p. 70.
[4] *Ibid.*, pp. 32, 61.

facts are of more value than assertion or invective, from whatever quarter it comes : I have stated the facts. As I myself have been quoted, on another point, in a way which might lead, and has led, those ignorant of the context to mistake my meaning,—so a late Bishop of St. Asaph, Dr. Short, who wrote a *History of the Church of England* (beginning, like other such histories, with Augustin, and proceeding through all later ages), is quoted as if he had said, or meant to say, that the Church of England came into existence in the reign of Henry the Eighth. But what he dated 'from the period of Henry the Eighth's divorce' was only 'the existence of the Church of England *as a distinct body, and her final separation from Rome.*' That is no more than to denote (as I have myself done, by the headings of my two first chapters) the commencement of that new epoch, marked by the Reformation and by the breach with the Papacy and the Roman communion, in the history of the same Church which Augustin founded.

Many Parliamentary speeches and controversial opinions are quoted (chiefly in the Appendix [1]) in support of the proposition, that the State has a right to interfere with Church property in a manner, and to an extent, different from that applicable to private property. I have endeavoured, in former chapters, to state with as much accuracy as I could the principles on which that right (as distinct from mere power) depends, so far as it exists, and the rules of justice which ought to govern its application. None of those opinions or speeches can settle historical facts, or establish principles, not otherwise proved.

Severe judgments of some historians, politicians, men of letters, and newspapers, are quoted, as to the part taken by

[1] *C. D.*; pp. 190-198.

or imputed to the clergy in public affairs, during the Tudor and Stuart reigns;[1] and also in more recent times.[2] In some of those censures there is much exaggeration, and a bitterness and virulence which goes far to answer itself, by the indication which it affords of hostile motive, from whatever cause arising. Such a general answer to those imputations as, with reference to the present time, seems to me sufficient, I have given in the earlier part of this chapter.

On some points urged in support of other charges brought against the clergy and the Church, eloquent reformers within the Church itself have, by their free and strong speaking, appeared to afford materials for attack. They are quoted,[3] as if they had condemned the Church generally as unfaithful to her mission, and unworthy to retain her position of power and trust. This they have not done, or intended to do. It is very much the habit of earnest Reformers to concentrate their energies upon the things which they want to reform: without that method, it is seldom that the needful impulse for practicable reforms can be obtained in this country. But in the body politic, ecclesiastical or civil, as well as the natural, the effort and the ability to correct bad habits and expel morbid humours (an operation which requires patience, and takes time) is healthful and strengthening, not the reverse. When I read (as I sometimes do) strong things of the same sort, said or written by ministers or members of Non-Conformist bodies, about the faults of their own systems, the impression produced upon me is far less unfavourable, either to the body or to the individuals, than if all were self-flattery and mutual applause. Those who have most

---

[1] *C. D.*, pp. 22, 23, 96.   [2] *Ibid.*, pp. 24-31.
[3] *Ibid.*, pp. 14, 16, 18, 89, 90, 98, 105, 116, 136.

good in them (Churches, and men) will be most sensitive to the presence of evil. But I venture, with very great confidence, to affirm, that genuine Reformers within the Church of England (I am not, of course, referring to any who may be reasonably supposed to be in their hearts alienated from her) have no idea of flying from 'the ills they know' to 'others that they know not of;' of going into the net spread for them in their own sight; of seeking for liberty and reform by the road of Disestablishment and Disendowment.

There remains another class of quotations,[1] intended to show how successful the voluntary principle has been in the United States of America, in the British Colonies, and in Ireland since the Disestablishment of the Irish Church. I have no wish to cast doubt upon any testimonies favourable to the state of religion in the United States of America, or to say a word in discouragement of the brave and righteous efforts which Churchmen in our colonies or in Ireland have made and are making to overcome the difficulties which surround them. But as, when failure is spoken of, it is necessary to ascertain what is meant by failure, so, when success is spoken of, it is reasonable to inquire, what is meant by success? The words are not absolute, but relative. Bishop Cleveland Coxe[2] may not have wished for 'Establishment' in his own country: but he did not the less clearly see, and declare his opinion, that Disestablishment would be an evil for the Church of England. Nothing which is quoted for this purpose, nothing that I have ever read or heard, leads me to believe that the extent and degree of the success of the Disestablished Church in Ireland, or of the Anglican Church in any of our colonies, or even of the Protestant Episcopal Church in America, is either greater, relatively

[1] *C. D.*, pp. 143-152.   [2] *Ibid.*, p. 143.

to the circumstances in which each is placed, than that
of the Church of England in this country, or equally great;
whether regard be had to its influence upon the people at
large, to its numerical strength, to its rate of progress and
extension, or to the results of its pastoral and evangelising
work. I know nothing which ought to induce any well-
affected member of the Church of England, free from
Romish or Dissenting proclivities, to wish to see his own
Church in the same situation. The late Bishop Merriman,
of Graham's Town, used (it seems) strong language in
1877,[1] as to his unwillingness 'again to put his neck under
the yoke of the Church as it exists in England.' Unless I
misunderstand his meaning, I should myself have agreed
with him: a yoke of any sort on one side, and nothing at
all in the way of countervailing benefit for the spiritual work
of the Church on the other (which had been the situation
of the Churches in South Africa), is certainly not desirable.
But even from that yoke I am afraid he discovered, before
his death,[2] that his escape had not been so complete as he
supposed: and there has since been some voluntary reaction
of the South African Church in the direction which he de-
precated. Bishop Mitchinson,[3] in 1878, spoke (it seems) of
the diocese of Barbadoes and the Windward Islands as
'suffering from the paralysis of Establishment;' and was more
hopeful in 1881, so far as he could then judge of the effects
of such 'Disestablishment' as those islands had, in the meantime, experienced. But what sort of 'Establishment' was that,
and what sort of 'Disestablishment'? The words may have
the same sound: but the things of which he and of which

---

[1] *C. D.*, p. 147.
[2] See Law Reports, *Appeal Cases*, vol. vii. p. 484 (Merriman *v.* Williams, Privy Council, 1882).   [3] *C. D.*, p. 148.

Bishop Merriman spoke were entirely different from 'Establishment' as it is, and 'Disestablishment' as it would be, in England. The history, the circumstances, the whole conditions, are in every way dissimilar. So it is in every other British colony: so also in the United States of America. Of those differences I need say no more here: I have spoken of them in the Introductory Letter prefixed to this work. There could be no greater fallacy, no self-delusion more transparent, than to reason from examples like these to the case with which we have to do.

CHAPTER XVIII

LIBERTY, EQUALITY, AND THE SCHEME OF DISESTABLISHMENT

1. *Civil and Religious Liberty.*

CIVIL and Religious Liberty is now well understood, and is universally, and without qualification or exception (unless certain forms of oaths still required to be taken are an exception) put in practice among us. It means freedom from civil restraints, and the absence of exclusion from civil rights and franchises, on account of differences of belief or worship; liberty of speech, writing, and association for religious purposes, without distinction of name or creed; and even (as an unavoidable corollary from this) liberty of opposition to all creeds, and to religion itself. If, when the phrase 'religious equality' is used, it is intended only to signify this equality of citizens in the eye of the law, this equal enjoyment of religious liberty, no exception need be taken to it. But in that sense it is irrelevant to the present controversy.

Mr. Disraeli and Mr. Gladstone are quoted on this point in the *Case for Disestablishment*.[1] The former said:—

'I hold that civil equality, that is, equality of all subjects

---

[1] *C. D.*, p. 21.

before the law, and a law which recognises the personal rights of all subjects, is the only foundation of a perfect commonwealth.'

Mr. Gladstone (speaking on the Affirmation Bill in 1883) said :—

'We will take care that full justice, nothing more and nothing less, shall be accorded to every citizen of England. . . . I am convinced that on every religious ground, as well as on every political ground, the true and the wise course is not to deal out religious liberty by halves, quarters, and fractions, but to deal it out entire, and to make no distinction between man and man on the ground of religious difference from one end of the land to the other.'

My own convictions, and also my political action from the first beginning of my public life, have been in accordance with the words of these statesmen. Most assuredly, they were both as far as myself from the opinion, that in the principle either of civil equality, or of religious liberty, there is anything inconsistent with the existence or the maintenance in a nation of an endowed or an Established Church.

In the *Case for Disestablishment* there is a chapter[1] entitled '*Progress of the Movement*,' which enumerates the successive steps by which we have reached that equality of civil and religious liberty which now prevails among us, and which at the beginning of this century was subject to many exceptions. The Repeal of the Test and Corporation Acts; Roman Catholic Emancipation; the Marriage and Registration Acts; the admission of Jews into Parliament; the removal of tests and religious qualifications for civil offices, and for offices or other benefits in schools and Universities; —all these were cases of the admission of particular classes

[1] *C. D.*, pp. 153-164.

to participate in civil franchises or benefits, from which, on account of their religious persuasion, they had been excluded. Each of those measures was a process, not of subtraction, but of addition; not a demolition, but an enlargement of the bounds, of existing institutions. The principle of the Burials Act of 1880 was the same ;—nothing was taken from the Church or from Churchmen; but Non-Conformists were relieved from a condition attaching to a civil right already possessed by them which did not recognise their religious liberty. All these were steps forward, vindicating for Non-Conformists, Roman Catholics, and Jews, positive civil rights, from which they had been before shut out, except under conditions derogatory to their religious liberty. But the movement for Disestablishment and Disendowment, which is now represented as a just consequence from them, and as a measure of further progress in the same direction, differs essentially from them all in principle and in character. It is a measure for 'levelling down'; its object is not to comprehend, or to remove exclusions, but to destroy; not to give to those who have not, but to take away from those who have; not to alter, for better or for worse, the status or the rights (as to property or otherwise) of Non-Conformists, but to depress and despoil the Church of England.

2. *Equality.*

Equality is a rule of distributive justice, applicable when there is something to be distributed, a class among whom the distribution ought to be made, and no good reason for making any difference among the members of that class. In such cases, equality is equity. But it is a truism, so obvious as to make the statement of it superfluous, that equality of all men in all things is no law of nature; it is not a law either of natural or of political society. If, in any country, the ideas of Socialism or Communism should ever so far prevail as to lead to an attempt to establish such a system of levelling equality, it would be a revolt against nature, on which nature would infallibly revenge herself. Much wrong might be inflicted upon one generation of men, and much suffering, confusion, and disorder might follow for more than one generation; but it could not be very long before there would be a return to that unequal distribution of temporal advantages which always has been, and always must be, the inevitable consequence of inequality of bodily and intellectual gifts and moral habits.

In the case with which we have to deal there is no distributable fund, and no class among whom distribution is to be made. On one side there are lawful titles and lawful possession, guaranteed for ages by law; on the other, there is no competing claim.

The argument from *equality* as a reason for Disendowment, under such circumstances, will not bear a moment's examination. It is well treated in a tract[1] now before me —so well, that I cannot do better than adopt that author's words :—

'If religious equality means, that the wealth of the various communities should be equalised, and that, therefore, the Church of England, as being the richest of them all, should be deprived of a large part of her resources and revenues,—we are at a complete loss how to answer so astonishing a proposal. Is it honest? Is it Christian? Is it justifiable on any ground whatever? Would the law of England support the same

---

[1] Entitled '*Down with it, a Mistaken Cry: Think Twice,*' by Mr. Sowter, of Shirley, Southampton.

morality if put into practice between man and man? Are A, B, and C justified in robbing D, because D happens to have more money than either A, B, or C? Where would such morality lead us to?'

What sort of 'equality' the Scheme for Disestablishment and Disendowment put forth by the 'Liberation Society' would produce, we shall presently see. Nobody, that I am aware of, proposes to apply any such principle to Non-Conformist chapels or endowments; to inquire whether Wesleyans have more than Baptists, or Baptists than Independents; or to take all that any of them may have into the hands of the State, with a view to let out their chapels and distribute their funds equally among all denominations, or for the general purposes of the nation. Nor am I aware that any one expects that sort of equality to be a result of Disestablishment and Disendowment. As is again well said, in the same tract from which I just now quoted,

'Religious equality in this sense is an impossibility. If all religious communities were set upon an equal footing to-morrow, that one would surely force its way to the front, both in wealth and the number of adherents, which provided the fullest spiritual nourishment for the people.'

If the Church of England were disendowed, and were yet to maintain her present hold over her present members, and if by their bounty she were again provided with large and valuable endowments, so as still to have, in that respect, a decided preponderance and advantage, ought she to be disendowed again and again in the name of equality? If not, why is she to be disendowed on that pretence now, because, in past ages of her history, this has been already done for her?

How is this matter put by the adversaries of the Church? In the *Case for Disestablishment?*[1] Thus:—

[1] *C. D.*, pp. 20-22.

'The removal of the civil disabilities of Dissenters merely diminished the injustice of the establishment system ; it did not put an end to it. Nor, again, does that injustice consist in the circumstances that the Churches established are the Churches of only a minority of the population, and that they are largely supported by public property. Those facts greatly aggravate the injustice of establishment, but they do not constitute the essence of that injustice. It is establishment itself, apart from these accidents, which is incompatible with the principles of justice. The State is the organ and representative of the whole community, and it acts justly, only when it deals on equal terms, and with strict impartiality, with every subject of the realm.' [Here the quotations from Mr. Disraeli and Mr. Gladstone come in.] 'Now the establishment of a Church, whatever may be the form that establishment takes, is the conferring of some favour upon the Church in question by the authority of the State, that is, by public law ; and for law to confer favour upon one part of the community, is to violate the fundamental principle of equality, and to be guilty of injustice in respect to every other part.'

To this passage may be added another, from the *Radical Programme*:[1]—

'It is in the nature of things impossible, that, so long as the Establishment exists, there should be anything like complete religious liberty. What Radicals dislike and condemn on principle is the arbitrary selection by the State of a single religious community, and the investiture of its officers with exceptional dignity and emoluments. The Church of England was made by Parliament, and, in the opinion of many thinking men who are not Radicals, scarcely even Liberals, the time has come when Parliament may reasonably be asked to unmake it.'

Now, I need not repeat that the Church of England was *not* made by Parliament, and Parliament cannot unmake it. The State did *not* 'arbitrarily select a single religious community' for privilege or favour; there was no selection at

[1] *Radical Programme*, pp. 43, 44.

all; there was no other or competing religious community when those relations between the Church and the State which constitute establishment were contracted; all the religious communities which are now in that position came long afterwards into existence, because those who formed them, dissenting from one part or another of the doctrine or discipline of the Church, preferred to separate themselves from her. So naturally did those relations betwen Church and State at first arise, that no man can point to any definite act of the State which created them. The particular terms of those relations which are embodied in Acts of Parliament of Henry the Eighth's, or any other time, were (as has been shown) restraints and securities imposed or taken by the State in its own interest, and not favours or privileges conferred upon the Church. Those Statutes neither 'made' the Church, nor 'invested its officers with exceptional dignity and emoluments.' Of the emoluments we know the history. The Church has only been permitted to retain what she had before lawfully acquired; she has received from public law no greater protection than that which has always been extended to all other property lawfully acquired by religious or other corporations, or upon religious or other perpetual trusts. If some of the rights of the Church had their origin in customs, which afterwards acquired the force of law, there are other rights of corporations and private persons (for instance, of the whole class of copyholders), which had a similar origin. As for 'dignity,' whatever may be properly described by that word—that which the Church possesses is only her historical inheritance, from a time when it came to her, not as an exceptional privilege, but because the State wanted her counsels and her learning; it is balanced (more than equally balanced) by disabilities to which Non-Conformists and their ministers are not subject. Matters of that sort may be discussed on their proper merits—wise men will, in each such case, judge with what object and purpose. But they have no real bearing upon the present question.

The propositions of the *Case for Disestablishment* are more transcendental. They depend less on historical assumptions; they do, indeed, represent the Church as 'largely supported with public property;' but they treat that as a secondary consideration, matter of aggravation, but not 'the essence of the injustice.' What do they mean? Nothing less, as it seems to me, than Jacobinism, in its wildest and most absolute form. They conduct us, at one bound, to universal suffrage; to the abolition, not only of the House of Lords and all titles of honour and distinctions of rank, but of all Royal Charters, all Municipal Corporations (unless every town and village is to be incorporated also); of all Universities with powers to grant degrees; of all compulsory and other special powers granted to Railway or other Companies; of all Banks of issue; of all licensed or privileged trades and professions; all rights of markets, fairs, and other special franchises; all exemptions of dissenting and other places of worship from taxes and local rates, and of particular classes of persons from liability to serve on juries; to the abolition of the exception of persons with less income than £100 a year from income-tax; and much more besides. There are, I believe, persons who object on like grounds to the protection of any man by law in the possession of property which is coveted by his neighbour. This principle of the *Case for Disestablishment*, if pursued to its logical results, would subvert the whole order of the civilised world.

3. *The Scheme of Disestablishment.*

It is time now to examine the scheme presented, in the name of this principle of 'equality,' by the 'Liberation Society,' by the *Case for Disestablishment*, and by the *Radical Programme*,—for in this they all agree.

The terms on which the Irish Church was disestablished are declared to have been too liberal[1] to be equitable. What were those terms?

The operation of Disestablishment was effected in Ireland[2] by dissolving all the Ecclesiastical Corporations, abolishing all the ecclesiastical jurisdictions, and repealing all the ecclesiastical laws, considered as parts of the general law of the realm. But it was mitigated, by provisions which had for their object the preservation and recognition of the continuity, as a religious body, of the disestablished with the established Church. Power was given for the Bishops, clergy, and laity to meet synodically, and make and alter laws for the future government of their Church: and in the meantime (proceeding upon the true principle, that the existing body of Churchmen was actually united together upon those terms of Church membership which were contained in the creeds, articles, formularies, and disciplinary laws of the Church), all the old ecclesiastical law as to doctrine, worship, and discipline was to remain in force for ecclesiastical purposes, as the starting-point of voluntary association among the members of the Church. And, for the better security and enjoyment of such property as would be left to the Church after Disestablishment, or might afterwards be acquired by it, the assembled Synod was enabled to constitute, and the Crown to incorporate, a 'Representative

---

[1] *C. D.*, pp. 55, 56.   [2] 33 and 34 Vict., cap. 42.

Church Body':—in other words, a Board of administration and management, in which all such Church property might be vested.[1]

These provisions worked, on the whole, smoothly and well; and together with those exceptions from Disendowment, to which I shall presently refer, they enabled the disestablished Church of Ireland to face the difficulties of its new position in a manner which (in the *Case for Disestablishment*) is appealed to[2] as proof of the success of that measure.

But all these provisions are odious to the 'Liberation Society' and its friends. 'It is suggested that this method should be *reversed* in the case of England.'[3] 'The chief precedent in the Irish Act to be most avoided is the re-creation and re-endowment of that Church which was supposed to have been dissolved into its original and constituent atoms.'[4] Whatever Parliament can do to humiliate, to break up, and as far as possible to efface and extinguish the Church of England, not as a State-Establishment merely, but as a Church, ought to be done.

With that view 'the principle' is laid down, 'that, in the payment of compensation for loss of income, offices, or vested rights, the State *should deal only with the individuals concerned*,[5] and not with any Body acting on behalf of the members of the disestablished Church, or with any ecclesiastical corporation which has been dissolved by the Act of Parliament;' and, 'releasing them from obligation to discharge their present duties,' should (instead of preserving their vested life-interests), pay them off 'in the same way as other public

---

[1] The same thing (as has elsewhere been noted) was done for the Irish Presbyterians by the Act of 1871.
[2] *C. D.*, pp. 149-151.
[3] *Ibid.*, p. 175.
[4] *Radical Programme*, p. 158.
[5] *C. D.*, p. 175.

officials whose services are no longer required by the State.'[1] The Bishops and parochial clergy of the Church of England are to be dealt with as so many discharged servants; as disbanded soldiers, or sailors whose ships can no longer go to sea. Their compensation is to be cut down, according to each man's age, and so forth. If, on the one hand, the men 'will have been deprived of offices held by a secure tenure,' on the other, 'they will be free to contract any obligations, in connection with an Episcopal or any other Church organised by voluntary arrangements; there will be freedom on all sides, without the embarrassment which must be occasioned by compulsory connection with a new system of men habituated to one which has been abolished.'[2] An old man, say past seventy, may be permitted to receive his whole income; but (in consideration of the option which he will thus have to take his share of the spoil of the Church of England with him into any other religious communion, Roman Catholic or Protestant, or into any secular profession or business), 'if thirty-five, or less, he might receive one-half; and, if between thirty-five and seventy, a proportionate amount.'[3]

Another consequence of the principle is, that the Church of England, as an aggregate religious body, is to be ignored (because it is not, as such, a legal corporation [4]), even in dealing with those exceptions, of churches recently built, and recent private endowments, which it may be proposed to make from the general operation of disendowment. The

[1] *C. D.*, pp. 175, 176.   [2] *Ibid.*, p. 176.   [3] *Ibid.*
[4] *Ibid.*, pp. 172, 173 :—'Though an Episcopal Church may afterwards be organised, on a different basis, when Disestablishment is determined on, there will be no body having a legal existence capable of either claiming or receiving compensation.' And see *Radical Programme*, pp. 158, 159.

existing corporations are all to be dissolved : and yet the fact of its not having been incorporated is to be a reason for ignoring *the Church.* The 'congregations' are not 'bodies having a legal existence':—nevertheless, part of what now belongs to the Church is to be given, by this scheme, to them. If a sole founder or donor happens to be living (in that case only, and those cases would be so few, that they need not be taken into account), he is to be permitted to take back the property which he gave. In all other cases the excepted churches and endowments are to be transferred, under a brand new trust or title to be created by the Act of Disestablishment, as 'the property of *the existing congregation* '[1]—which, to Congregationalists, may be intelligible ; to Churchmen, is not. The objection, that 'the proposal recognises only the existence and interests of congregations, and ignores the Church,' is met by the avowal, that such is the intention ; and that the disintegration of the Church, as well as its disestablishment, is a main object in view.

'Who' (it is answered[2]) 'are most concerned in the matter, —the persons who have been accustomed to worship in the churches, and have had the benefit of the endowments hitherto, or a vague intangible body, designated "the Church"? . . . The greatest possible disservice might be done to them, by handing over the property to an institution to which they might not wish to belong, or to some of the regulations of which they might strongly object. . . . The legislature has no right to assume, that all Episcopalians will, throughout all time, constitute but one Church ; neither ought it, either by bribes or by legal compulsion, to bind the Church of England together as it now does by the still more cohesive forces of an Establishment. It will be seen that these suggestions, while they would leave a considerable amount of Church property in the hands

---

[1] *C. D.*, p. 179. And see *Radical Programme*, p. 166.
[2] *C. D.*, pp. 180, 181.

of Episcopalians, recognise the right of congregations, and of the inhabitants of particular localities, to determine for themselves their future ecclesiastical relationships.'

The author of the *Radical Programme*, understanding and sympathising with the object, has nevertheless doubts [1] as to the sufficiency and efficacy of the method thus proposed.

'The weak point of the project will not escape those in whom all other views of disestablishment are overpowered by their dread and suspicion of a great ecclesiastical corporation, endowed with vast revenues, animated by a rigorous spirit of discipline, and uncontrolled by the moderating hand of neutral authority. The project assumes, that the Disestablished Church will divide itself into an indefinite number of groups. We must, however, remember, that the Church will still be episcopal, and not congregational, and that episcopacy, especially where it has such deep traditional roots and so ancient an organisation as in England, is essentially a system of centralisation.'

He consoles himself with the hope, that there will be, in all probability, 'at least two of these great associations;' that 'the High Churchman and the Low Churchman will not receive their liberty for nothing;' that 'it is even possible, that their struggles may ultimately lead to the best solution of the difficulties of disendowment.' What he considers to be that 'best solution,' he makes abundantly clear, by referring to the example of Canada; where, after a season of discontent among competing religious bodies,

'There arose up a political party of a Radical persuasion, who were called Clear-Grits; and the Clear-Grits declared for the secularisation of the Clergy Reserves, as the best and shortest way out of the confusion. The cry caught the growing sentiment of the time; it carried all before it; and the Reserves were at length duly and legally secularised.' [2]

I turn to Disendowment—a subject in part anticipated.

[1] *Radical Programme*, p. 169. [2] *Ibid.*, pp. 169, 170.

From the general operation of Disendowment, there were excepted, by the Irish Church Act, all churches (Cathedrals included), which were then actually in use for the religious services of the Church of Ireland, with their plate and furniture, etc.; and also such school-houses as were used in connection with them. All these, if claimed within a certain time, were to remain, as before, for the use and as the property of the Disestablished Church, under the new conditions resulting from the Act. An option was also given to the Representative Church Body to retain such residence-houses and gardens attached to them as they might wish, on payment of ten times the estimated value of the sites, as land, without taking buildings into account; and to purchase limited quantities of glebe lands on favourable terms.

The life interests of all the existing incumbents of Bishoprics and parochial and other benefices, and also of a class of curates regarded as permanent, in their whole emoluments (subject to the performance of the same duties as before, if required of them by the authorities of the Disestablished Church), were preserved intact. To other curates, and to some Church officers holding office by more precarious tenures, gratuities were given. Facilities were offered for the commutation of the life interests so preserved, under arrangements to be made with the consent of the Representative Church Body, for capital funds to be vested in that Body. Those funds were to be charged with such annuities as might be agreed to be paid to the commuting clergymen; and any ultimate surplus, which might be left of them, was to be in aid of a Sustentation fund for the permanent benefit of the Church. If, in any diocese, three-fourths of the incumbents of benefices whose life-interests were preserved should commute, a bonus of twelve per cent, for the benefit of the diocesan Sustentation fund, was to be added to the commutation money.[1]

Besides these provisions, the Bill, as introduced, contained a clause reserving to the Disestablished Church all private endowments of later date than 1660. During the progress of the measure through Parliament it was (with the concurrence of the authorities of the Church) considered preferable to fix a capital sum, to be paid to the Representative Church Body, as the equivalent, and in lieu, of all those private endowments. The sum so fixed was £500,000, which was paid accordingly.[2]

I have now to compare with these provisions of the Irish measure the proposals, as to England, of the 'Liberation Society' and its allies. Their views are not dissembled. Those provisions, it seems,[3]—

'Have brought the Irish Church Act into disrepute, and have created in many minds the feeling, that it would be better not to disestablish the Church of England at all than to do so on the terms of the Irish Act.' . . . 'The mischief done in Ireland may be small; but it is felt that it would not be so in England, where the property held by the Church is so vast, and its re-endowment on a large scale—in the guise of compensation to the members of the disestablished Church—would prove a source of serious and lasting evil.'[4]

---

[1] Arrangements for commutation, on similar terms, were also extended (as has been seen, *ante*, pp. 215, 216) to the annuities given to the Presbyterian Clergy, in lieu of the Regium Donum in Ireland.

[2] Irish Church Act, 1869, sect. 29, and Auditor-General's Report, 27th January 1886, p. 15 (*Parl. Paper*, H. C., 24th February 1886, No. 53).

[3] *C. D.*, pp. 174, 175; and see p. 66 :—' It would, for many reasons, be something more than a blunder to adopt a similar course in the disestablishment of the English Church.'

[4] *C. D.*, pp. 167, 168. And see *Radical Programme*, p. 156 :—' If disendowment were to be conducted on the same rules of equity and

The principle which they lay down [1] is, that—

'Both ancient and modern buildings, as well as all endowments, now appropriated to the use of the national Church, must be regarded as national property, at the disposal of the State.'

If any exceptions are proposed, it is not as required by the principle; it is only because 'it would not be consonant with public feeling to act strictly on this principle, however logically defensible.' [2] The scheme propounded is therefore not 'mercilessly logical;' on the contrary, it takes credit to itself for 'dealing generously, as well as justly, with vested interests of every kind.' [3] 'Some' (it is said) 'will think that these concessions are pushed too far.' [3] Whether the author of the *Radical Programme* is of that opinion, is not quite clear. In one place he says: [4]—

'If there was a living donor he might fairly claim that any property with which he had presented the Church should revert to him. But failing this, and without saying anything of the manner in which the property was for the most part derived by its original possessors, to whom else can it go but to the State? If all existing interests were compensated, and endowments given within a certain limit of time were to be exempted from the operation of the Act, no injustice would be done.'

In another: [5]—

'It is the property of the nation as a whole; and the State is perfectly within its rights, if the Legislature shall think fit,

---

liberality as were adopted in the case of the Irish Church, Mr. Gladstone has made out (16th May 1873) that "between life incomes, private endowments, and the value of fabrics and advowsons, something like £90,000,000 sterling would have to be given, in the process of disestablishment, to the ministers, members, and patrons of the Church of England." That would indeed be a sovereign triumph of injustice, and a political catastrophe of unmeasured magnitude.'

[1] *Radical Programme*, p. 178. [2] *C. D.*, p. 178.
[3] *Ibid.*, p. 168. [4] *Radical Programme*, p. 45. [5] *Ibid.*, p. 162.

in diverting every shilling of Church property to secular uses, from the lands with which Edward the Confessor endowed the Abbey of St. Peter's at Westminster, *down to the last sovereign subscribed to build a church in a destitute district.* The church that was built yesterday by the pious munificence of a man still alive, is *in law* (!!) 'as much a piece of national property as St. Paul's Cathedral or the Tower; and Parliament *is not bound to pay any respect whatever* to the wishes of the founder, whose voluntary generosity has placed his hopes and his design *at the mercy*[1] of the State. But, though there is no difference in principle, in logic, or in legality, between ancient fabrics and endowments and modern, it would seriously jar upon right feeling to treat them in an identical manner.'

Why should it '*jar upon right feeling*,' if the principle is sound, if the State would be 'perfectly within its rights,' if the thing is just?

Let us now see what these 'just' and 'generous' terms are; what is this sacrifice of strict logic to 'right feeling.' I will state the main points in the 'Liberation Society's' proposals;[2] omitting secondary details.—

1. All 'the Cathedrals, Abbeys, and other monumental buildings should be under national control, and be maintained for such uses as Parliament may from time to time determine'—without regard to any amount of money which Churchmen may have spent upon them.

2. All Churches 'existing at the date of the passing of the first of the Church Building Acts, 1818'—(a reason for drawing such a line, not more relevant than the death of Queen Charlotte in the same year),—including all such of them as have since that time been rebuilt or restored with the monies of Churchmen,—are to be taken away from the Church and Churchmen altogether, and 'vested in a

---

[1] The italics in this extract are mine.
[2] *C. D.*, pp. 178-180.

parochial board, to be elected by the ratepayers, which board should have power to deal with them for the general benefit of the parishioners in such ways as it may determine;' with 'power of sale, at a fair valuation, and under proper regulations.'

3. Churches built after 1818, at the sole expense of any donor 'living at the date of disestablishment,' may, on his application, be vested in him, or in such persons as he may appoint. If the sole donor is dead, they are (I suppose) to go, like old Churches, to parochial boards.[1]

4. Churches built after 1818, by means of voluntary subscriptions *exclusively*, and also such as might be, but are not, claimed by a sole donor still living, are to 'become the property of the existing congregation, and to be held in trust for their use,' if accepted on their behalf within a limited time. If not so accepted, they are to vest, like old Churches, in parochial boards.

5. Churches built after 1818, partly by voluntary subscription and partly from Parliamentary grants 'and other public sources,' are to be 'in like manner offered to the congregations;' charged, however, with the repayment to the State of 'the amount so derived from public sources.'

6. Existing incumbents are to be allowed, 'on payment of rent, according to the valuation adopted in settling their claims for compensation'—(about £750,000 a year, I suppose, if Mr. Frederick Martin's valuation[2] is to be assumed as correct),—to retain, during their lives, the use and occupation of their residence-houses; without obligation to do any duties. Of the way in which it is proposed to pension them off, by way of 'compensation' for the life-

---

[1] This case is not expressly provided for; but see *Radical Programme*, p. 45.   [2] *C. D.*, p. 63.

interests in their emoluments, of which they are to be deprived, I have already spoken.

7. All endowments of earlier date than 1818 are to be confiscated. Those of later date are to be dealt with in the same manner as churches.

These are the results of the new ideas of justice and religious equality. From the Church, as a Church, everything, down to the last stone and the last shilling, is proposed to be taken away; while Roman Catholics, and all Non-Conformist Bodies of every denomination, are to be left in possession of all that they now have, without any disturbance whatever of their existing titles. The number of Churches belonging to the Church of England, built before 1818, is (we are told) about 11,700;[1] they are all to be absolutely taken away; they are to be used for whatever purposes parochial boards of ratepayers may please; they may be sold, if those boards please, to Roman Catholics or Non-Conformists; they may be turned (as may also the Cathedrals) to any secular use. If the clergy and lay-people of the Church of England are allowed the use of them at all for the services of their religion, and if the buildings themselves and their accessories are maintained in such a state as to enable them to be so used, it is to be only on terms of payment;— what those terms of payment might be, may be inferred from their valuation, in the *Case for Disestablishment*,[2] at £2,000,000 a year. As to all churches and chapels of ease built after 1818 (disregarding that infinitesimal number, of which persons 'living at the date of disestablishment' may be sole donors), they also are to be taken away from the Church of England as a Church;—new Parliamentary

---

[1] *C. D.*, p. 65; and see Mr. Horace Mann's Report of 1851, p. 40.
[2] *C. D.*, p. 65.

titles to them are to be created after the model of Congregational Independency. Whatever the State has in any way contributed towards their cost, is to be repaid to the last shilling; while, for the expenditure of Churchmen on what the State takes away from them, not one farthing is to be allowed.

So much for one side of this picture. Now let us turn to the other.

The Roman Catholics and Non-Conformists, all taken together, had (as we have seen[1]), at the end of 1884, 9377 Churches and Chapels, certified and registered for the solemnisation of marriages,—the equivalents on their side of the 15,709[2] parish Churches and Chapels of Ease of the Church of England. (I do not here include the Channel Islands, and I take no account, on either side, of places of worship which may be private property or of a temporary character.) All these 9377 Churches and Chapels they are to retain for the religious purposes of their several denominations, according to the organic constitution of each, without interference by any 'parochial' or other public board, and without any payment to the State, exactly as before; while all the 15,709 Churches and Chapels of the Church of England are to be alienated from the religious purposes of the Church according to her organic constitution; and ·11,700 of them are to be taken away both from the Church herself and from her congregations, and from all religious uses of Churchmen, except on terms of payment; and even on those terms their use is not to be of right. And all this in the name of religious equality!

---

[1] 47th *Report of the Registrar-General*, pp. viii, xlii.
[2] According to the Returns made by the Archdeacons at my request (see *ante*, p. 112).

What might become of the churches, or of their sacred vessels, etc., under these circumstances, can only be matter of speculation. For the benefit of those to whom such speculations may be interesting, I extract a passage from the *Radical Programme*.[1]

'In many cases the parish churches would be let at a nominal or other rent to Episcopalians; in some, if not in many, they would be used by one sect at one hour and by another at another hour. It is possible that, under certain circumstances, the board would sell the fabric out and out to the Episcopalian or other religious body. It is also conceivable that it might be used for secular purposes of a public kind, as meeting-houses now are, and churches have been before now; and some people have cried out that this would be a shocking desecration. We need only say that such desecration could not take place without the consent of the parishioners; and if they should be willing to consent, then this shocking act of desecration would have taken place in their minds and consciences, and the real part of the mischief at which establishmentarians profess alarm would already have been wrought.'

As to all the other endowments, of which the Church is to be despoiled, the ideas of the authors of the project are these:[2]—

'The surplus may be devoted to education, to the maintenance of the poor, to effecting great sanitary improvements, to the reduction of the national debt, or to other objects of a secular character which would be beneficial to the whole nation. It may, however, be suggested that, inasmuch as a large portion of the property now devoted to ecclesiastical purposes belongs to the parishes, such portions of it as Parliament may from time to time determine should be applied to local objects, and be administered by municipal and other local authorities.'

There are some things which speak most forcibly for

[1] *Radical Programme*, p. 163.   [2] *C. D.*, p. 184.

themselves when left without comment. This practical exposition of the new doctrine of equality is one of them. It has been for about ten years before the 'Liberation Society' and the public: I am not aware that its authors have retracted or abandoned any part of it. They may, of course, do so now, if they find it convenient for their main objects. But for some purposes it is incapable of being retracted. It must remain for ever an imperishable record, worthy to be engraved on tablets of brass wherever true liberality and distributive justice are held in any regard, of the idea of those things, entertained by the persons and the party whose war-cry is the Disestablishment and Disendowment of the Church of England.

CHAPTER XIX

THE ATTEMPT TO SEPARATE WALES

THE objects of those, who propose to break up the Church of England by piecemeal, and to begin in Wales, can hardly be misunderstood by Churchmen, or by any serious politicians.

1. *The Separatist Argument.*

With this view, language is addressed to the Welsh people, tending to a disintegration of the United Kingdom in this, as in other directions. From the time of Alfred, if not earlier, the Princes of Wales acknowledged the Kings of England as lords paramount; and, by the wars of Henry the Second and Edward the First, the direct government of the English Crown was established, first in South Wales, and afterwards throughout the Principality. Two hundred years later, Wales gave to England a dynasty descended from her own Princes, the most masterful which ever ruled over us. Under that dynasty the Reformation took place:—the existing division of Wales into counties was made; Monmouthshire became an English county; and Wales was, by statute,[1] united with England, and admitted to a full and equal participa-

[1] 27 Hen. VIII., cap. 26.

tion in English laws and liberties. Descendants of that dynasty have ever since occupied, and still occupy, the throne. The union has been a very happy and prosperous one, both to England and to Wales. To denounce the Church in Wales as 'the Church of the alien,'[1]—to urge disestablishment on such grounds, as that the Celtic population of Wales 'is still divided from the Anglo-Saxon race by a seemingly insurmountable diversity of tastes and habits,'[2]—does not, I venture to think, become a liberal Englishman, or a patriotic Welshman.

2. *The Ancient Welsh Church.*

The Church in Wales has a peculiar historical interest. Its Episcopate is a connecting link between the Church founded among the Anglo-Saxons by Augustin, and the original British Church of Roman times. The remnants of that Church, not exterminated by the heathen invaders whose dominion succeeded that of Rome, found refuge in the mountainous parts of the island, and survived, with a complete ecclesiastical organisation, in Wales only. Of that earliest British Church, the present four Welsh Bishoprics are monuments.

Those who study the learned work[3] of the late Mr. Haddan and Bishop Stubbs will find in the materials there collected (from which alone it is possible to obtain any knowledge of the ancient Welsh Church) nothing to justify the statement,[4] that the disappearance of differences, or the

---

[1] *C. D.*, p. 109.
[2] Mr. Osborne Morgan, *Nineteenth Century*, November 1885, p. 764.
[3] *Councils and Ecclesiastical Documents*, etc., vol. i. (Oxford, 1869).
[4] *C. D.*, p. 108.

establishment of practical unity, between the Church of England and that of the Principality, was the result of Norman wars or conquests, or of the interference of Norman Kings, Barons, or Bishops. The differences[1] were of a trivial kind, quite unworthy to divide Churches; they disappeared (as much under native Welsh as under Saxon influence), during the Anglo-Saxon period, about the end of the eighth century.[2] Full intercommunion, and close ecclesiastical relations between the Churches, followed: during the reign of Edward the Confessor, the English diocese of Hereford was, for several years, administered by one of the Welsh Bishops.[3] It was, no doubt, after the Conquest, that the Welsh Bishops first acknowledged the Metropolitan jurisdiction of the See of Canterbury, and began to be summoned to, and to attend, Synods and Legatine Councils,[4] as Bishops of that province. It is true, also, that the power and influence, which the Norman Kings and their Barons acquired in Wales, extended, there as in England, to ecclesiastical as well as temporal matters: and that Normans were promoted to Welsh Bishoprics. But this did not interrupt, in Wales more than England, the continuity or identity of the Church:—and we are, happily, now remote from the time, when the words 'alien,' or 'stranger,' might have been appropriate, in any part of Great Britain, to describe, relatively to each other, men of Norman, or Saxon, or Celtic blood.

---

[1] Haddan and Stubbs, vol. i. p. 152.   [2] *Ibid.*, p. 203.
[3] *Ibid.*, p. 291.
[4] Eadmer, *Hist. Nov.*, lib. iii. p. 67; Spelman, *Conc.*, vol. ii. p. 33; Wilkins, *Conc.*, vol. i. p. 408.

3. *Dissent in Wales.*

It was not till the preaching of Whitefield and Wesley, and their followers, in the last century, that there was any considerable amount of Non-Conformity in Wales. Among their followers were some Welshmen of remarkable gifts and ardent zeal, who, preaching to the Welsh people in their own language, obtained great ascendency over them. I do not wish to detract from their praises: it is beyond all question that they did much good. The natural consequence was, that Dissent became a power in Wales, relatively greater than it is in England: and so it is now. So much as this must be admitted: but I believe it to be equally true, that the Church has since recovered in Wales much of her lost ground, and promises to recover more, if fair scope is left to her. To ascertain the true numerical ratio of Churchmen to Non-Conformists in Wales is not possible, unless those means were taken, which the general body of Non-Conformists in England has hitherto resisted. It is easy, under these circumstances, for political or religious partisans to magnify the disproportion much beyond the truth. The so-called religious census of 1851, and other unauthorised and still less trustworthy attempts to substitute for a real census computations of comparative attendances at church or chapel, made by private and not impartial persons, are of no greater value for Wales, than they are for England.

4. *Position and Work of the Present Welsh Church.*

Some facts there are, which I am content either to take as I find them in authentic sources of information, or to accept as they are stated by those with whom I am in controversy.

The number of parishes in the four Welsh dioceses (not all of them in Wales) is 998.[1] The total amount of the whole revenues of the Welsh parochial clergy, as represented in the *Clergy List* (on which I will not repeat the observations made in a former chapter), is, as I have reckoned it up, £226,962: less than an average of £227 for each benefice. As to places of worship and marriages, the following table (which does not include those of Roman Catholics or Jews), is as correct as the materials at my command can make it :—

Church of England (consecrated churches and chapels) [2]	1263
Non-Conformist places of worship, certified for marriages [3]	1417
Non-Conformist majority . .	154
Other places of worship, Church of England [4]	357
Ditto, Non-Conformist [5] . . .	2101
Non-Conformist majority . .	1744
Marriages solemnised in Churches (1884) [6] .	4404
Ditto in Non-Conformist places of worship [7]	3209
Church majority . .	1195
Marriages solemnised in Registrars' Offices [8]	4214

Conclusions drawn from the relative numbers of places

---

[1] *Clergy List*, 1884, pp. 372-374, 380-382, 397, 398.
[2] From the Archdeacons' Returns, made at my request.
[3] 47th *Report of Registrar-General*, pp. viii, xlii.
[4] *Official Year-Book*, 1886, p. 518.
[5] Residue, after deducting 1417, of the numbers stated by Sir R. Cunliffe at a meeting of 'Liberation Society,' May 1885 (quoted in *Nineteenth Century* for November 1885, p. 766).
[6] 47th *Report of Registrar-General*, 'Abstracts,' p. 4.
[7] *Ibid.* [8] *Ibid.*

of worship must be uncertain without knowledge of their relative capacity, and of the use practically made of them. As to marriages, if those celebrated in Non-Conformist places of worship, and those without any religious ceremony, were put together, the Church would be outnumbered in about the ratio of 37 to 22. But, if marriages with religious rites only are regarded (even with the addition of Roman Catholic and Jewish marriages, 399 in number), the Church more than holds her own.

As to burials, I do not know how far the example of Ruabon may be taken; but it is a town with about 15,000 inhabitants, and I find[1] that during the five years after the commencement of the operation of the Burials Act of 1880 (to December 1885), there were no more than 39 burials there in the unconsecrated, and only two under the Act in the consecrated, portion of the cemetery; one of which was without any religious service.

The 'untiring zeal and energy'[2] of the Welsh clergy, generally, at the present time, is admitted by the more candid of their opponents. It has long been a necessary qualification for institution to a benefice in any place where the Welsh language is spoken, that the clergyman presented should speak that language: and in the choice of Bishops for Wales, connection, by birth or otherwise, with the Principality, and knowledge of its language, has been also, of late years, greatly regarded.

Of the Church work which has been and is going on (in

[1] Letter of Rev. E. W. Edwards, Vicar of Ruabon, to *Liverpool Courier*, 1st December 1885.

[2] Mr. Osborne Morgan, *Nineteenth Century*, November 1885, p. 768. He adds (p. 769) that he believes them 'to be as earnest, as hard-working, and as self-sacrificing a priesthood as any to be found in the realm.'

South Wales especially), evidence will be found in the *Official Year-Book* for 1886.[1] In North Wales, I have no reason to suppose that what has been done in Ruabon[2] during the last fifty years is an exceptional case. Fifty years ago—

'Ruabon, with its one clergyman, was the only church for the whole parish. There are now eight clergy, four parish churches, one iron church, a private chapel, and a mission-room; and four national schools, still maintained as voluntary schools, in which the new electors and their children were educated before rate-aided schools were heard of.'

Since 1840, large sums, amounting to £114,219, have been spent upon the restoration of the four Welsh Cathedrals.[3] Lord Hampton's returns show a total expenditure, from 1840 to 1875, by means of voluntary gifts and contributions, of £1,187,753,[4] on the building, rebuilding, and restoration of parish churches and chapels of ease in the four Welsh dioceses: all unconsecrated buildings, and everything which cost less than £500, being excluded. During the ten years from 1875 to 1884, the number of new churches built, or old rebuilt, has been 68, and 134 have been restored or enlarged.[5] In one year only, 1884, £107,094[6] was given by Welsh Churchmen, for churches, parsonage-houses, burial-grounds, and endowments.

A zealous reformer, the late Dean of Bangor, has been quoted[7] as saying:—'The Church has made material progress of late; churches, parsonages, and schools have been

---

[1] *O. Y. B.*, 1886, pp. 22, 23.

[2] Letter of Vicar of Ruabon to *Liverpool Courier*, 1st December 1885.

[3] *Official Year-Book*, 1886, pp. 500, 512.

[4] *Parl. Paper* (H. L., 13th August 1875, No. 291), pp. 3, 4, 33-35, 63-67.

[5] *O. Y. B.*, 1886, pp. 514, 515.   [6] *Ibid.*, p. 511.

[7] *Nineteenth Century*, November 1885, p. 768. *C. D.*, p. 116.

built; but how many of the churches are empty?' On this, his brother, the Vicar of Ruabon,[1] observes :—

'My poor brother's words are quoted in a sense that all who knew him would see at once that he never meant. It is one thing to exhort church-builders not to rest contented with the mere material building, and empty churches; but quite another thing to say that the churches, old and new, are empty!'

Doubtless, the fabric of brick or stone, if it is really empty, proves neither life nor progress. But, nevertheless, there is as much meaning in such material indications of life and progress, and as much propriety in reasoning from them, on the side of the Church, as on that of Non-Conformity. The same authority, the late Dean of Bangor, is appealed to,[2] as against some 'statistical apologists,' who 'hinted that,' of the great numbers of Welsh Non-Conformists spoken of, many 'existed only on paper.' 'Paper adherents' (said the Dean) 'do not give money; and the Welsh Non-Conformists give far more than £300,000 a year.' Whether those figures are correct, I have no means of knowing: but the answer was sound in principle; and it is as good for the Church as for dissenters.

Mr. Osborne Morgan—(I name unwillingly, in this context, a distinguished man, whom I reckon among my friends, —but it would not be respectful to pass over without notice his public advocacy of the cause which I oppose)—Mr. Osborne Morgan has said:[3]—

'A traveller has only to leave the fashionable watering-places on the coast, which are really English colonies, or the beaten track where, in summer and autumn at least, the tourists or

---

[1] Letter to *Liverpool Courier*, 1st December 1885.
[2] Sir R. Cunliffe, at meeting of Liberation Society, May 1885 (*Nineteenth Century*, November 1885, p. 766).
[3] *Nineteenth Century*, November 1885, p. 766.

those who cater for their pleasure almost outnumber the inhabitants, and strike across country for himself to see how the land lies. He will find the solitary parish-church, if not actually deserted, comparatively empty, while the numerous Non-Conformist chapels are crowded to suffocation.'

It is easy to invite 'a traveller' who has no political purpose to do this, but he is not likely to do it; and I do not know why Mr. Osborne Morgan should be a better witness on that point than the Vicar of Ruabon. A clergyman of the Church, however upright, may have a bias; but so also, I think, may a candidate for a Welsh county, pledged to Disestablishment, on the eve of a general election, at which he thinks the question 'will exercise a very decisive influence at the polling-booths.'[1] Granted that both are equally incapable of saying that, of the truth of which they have not become persuaded; but I prefer to the politician the man who speaks from the observation and experience of a life, spent in the discharge of the highest duties. The Vicar of Ruabon has no unkindly feeling at all towards Non-Conformists; part of his testimony is, that the Welsh Non-Conformists, when not stirred up by party politicians, are by no means generally hostile to the Church. 'The Welsh people,' he thinks, ' do *not* love dissent for its own sake: the Independents make no progress in Wales. The Welsh dissenters are Methodists,' chiefly 'because they are the followers of their fathers and grandfathers.'

'Even now, in many country parishes in Wales, many of their followers avail themselves habitually of the ministrations of the Church; and even their ministers and elders have their sons not unfrequently brought up to the ministry of the Established Church.'[2]

---

[1] *Nineteenth Century*, November 1885, p. 763.
[2] Letter to *Liverpool Courier*.

He adds, at the end of a published letter, from which I am quoting :—

'I shall never forget the true sympathy and Christian charity shown by those thousands of Welsh Non-Conformists, and that procession of more than a hundred Non-Conformist ministers, who followed the remains of the Dean of Bangor to the grave, all joining in our beautiful service.'

The Vicar of Ruabon challenges Mr. Osborne Morgan's facts; and believes,[1] that, 'if he would think it necessary to bring forward particular proofs,' he would be himself constrained to acknowledge their incorrectness. He states his own experience, and that of members of his family who, during a long series of years, have served in the ministry of the Welsh Church, not in sea-side or other 'watering-places,' or places frequented by tourists. He gives facts and names as to not a few parishes, in Merionethshire, Cardiganshire, Flintshire, Montgomeryshire, Anglesey, and Denbighshire, in which the churches were for years not only well attended, but often and in many places crowded. Nor were these specially selected places : they were those which fell within the range of his personal knowledge.

'What is wanted' (he says) 'to be known are facts. If the clergy would give their parochial experience in the same way, it would probably be found that the inference to be drawn from the several particulars would be the very reverse of Mr. Osborne Morgan's general statement. . . . In fact, there can be very little doubt that a religious census, honestly taken, would prove that the present accepted estimate of the comparative attendance at Sunday services is greatly over-stated in favour of Welsh Non-Conformity.'[2]

I am aware that there are some Welsh (as there are some English) clergymen, who favour the views and designs of

[1] Letter to *Liverpool Courier*.   [2] *Ibid.*

the 'Liberation Society.' Mr. Osborne Morgan says [1] that 'the theology of the Welsh Celt is Puritanical, his ideas of Church government essentially democratic,' and that he is 'by nature predisposed to be a Non-Conformist.' The 'Liberation Society' has circulated a letter [2] from the Rector of a very large and important town parish in Wales, written to be read at a meeting in favour of Disestablishment in July 1883; it contains passages, which I read with pain, and abstain from criticising. He appears to have persuaded himself that Disestablishment would bring the mass of Non-Conformists in Wales over to the Church. He thinks there is a 'terrible leaning to Popery in vogue among the Welsh clergy;' nothing else 'so much strengthens him in his views of Disestablishment;' and he 'confesses he can see no other way of stopping it in Wales than through Disestablishment;' adding, 'once give us that, we will soon clear the country of Ritualism, and make a clean sweep of them all.' It is curious, but I believe there are some strong partisans of what is called 'Ritualism' in England, who, from exactly the opposite point of view, and (I suppose) with opposite expectations, have also allied themselves with the party of Disestablishment. I believe that such expectations, on both sides, would be disappointed. Men would be compelled, then as now, to endure some considerable divergence of opinions within the limits prescribed by the formal standards and historical principles of their Church; and there would be, then as now, men who—using their own liberty in the direction which they prefer—would identify with views and doctrines alien to those of the Church almost all who used their

---

[1] *Nineteenth Century*, November 1885, p. 768.
[2] Entitled 'The Rector of Merthyr on Disestablishment in Wales.'

liberty on the opposite side. I cannot, for my part, accept this charge of 'Popery' or 'Ritualism,' against the general body of the Welsh clergy. And, although nothing can be farther from my purpose than to found conclusions upon theological premisses, I must be permitted to doubt, whether the absolute and unchecked predominance of Calvinism in Wales, or anywhere else, would be likely, in the long-run, to answer the sanguine hopes of its adherents, or to promote (as I am sure they desire) the true interests of religion. In Scotland it can hardly be said to have entirely maintained,—in Geneva it has entirely lost,—its ground.

5. *The Practical Question.*

I have said so much as to the special circumstances of the Church in Wales; not that I think the practical question depends, or ought to depend, upon any numerical or statistical comparison between the Church and Dissent in the Principality; but because that question ought not to suffer prejudice from exaggerated representations, or unproved assumptions. Even if the case were not one of particular dioceses belonging to a larger Church, it could not with truth be said, that the purposes for which the Church is endowed in Wales have failed, or that its endowments are excessive with reference to the work done. But the case is one, not of a distinct Church, but of particular dioceses :—dioceses, too, not simply co-extensive with Wales;—there are parts of England comprehended within Welsh dioceses, and parts of Wales comprehended within at least one English diocese. Monmouthshire, an English county, of which Mr. Osborne Morgan says, that it is, 'ethnographically at least, as Welsh as most parts of the Principality,' is included in the diocese of Llandaff:—Oswestry, and ten other parishes, with parts of three more,—all in the English county of Salop,—are included in the diocese of St. Asaph. Part of another parish in that diocese is in Cheshire. Montgomery, and four other Welsh parishes in Montgomeryshire, and a sixth partly in that county, are in the English diocese of Hereford. The endowments of all the Welsh Bishoprics and Capitular bodies are largely (most of them mainly) supplied, not from Welsh, but from English funds, under the administration of the Ecclesiastical Commissioners. The unreasonableness and impracticability of the proposal to deal separately with Wales receives illustration from these facts; though no such illustration was necessary to prove it. Is England to be taken district by district, diocese by diocese, county by county, parish by parish? Is it to be determined, by counting heads in every separate place, whether the Church of England is still to be established and endowed there, or not? No sane man would ever think of thus resolving a great organisation into its elements, and calling upon every part to justify its existence in the same way as if it were the whole, unless he had determined beforehand to destroy it, or were at least supremely indifferent to its preservation. Even if, in some provinces of England, the Church were considerably outnumbered by Non-Conformists, no man, who had not prejudged the whole question of disestablishment, would entertain the idea of disestablishing the Church there:—no man, in whom the faculty of foresight was not absolutely wanting, could fail to see, that the rest was intended to follow. The Church of Wales is part of the Church, as Wales itself is of the realm, of England: what would be true of an operation of this kind anywhere else in England, is true of it also in Wales, in

Monmouthshire, in Shropshire, in the dioceses of Llandaff, St. David's, Bangor, St. Asaph, and Hereford.

In Wales, as in other parts of the United Kingdom in which the strain of Celtic blood is strong, the people are naturally warm-hearted, generous, enthusiastic, and impulsive. It is only too possible for political agitators to take advantage of such qualities, and of the zeal for sect or party, which is often closely allied with them. But I think too well of my Welsh fellow-countrymen to believe that they will sully the purity of their religious fervour by lending themselves permanently to such destructive designs. It is not quite forty years since they saved from suppression one of their ancient Bishoprics: the association of those Bishoprics with the earliest organisation of Christianity in this island can hardly be so soon forgotten by a people proud of their antiquity and their history, as to make them now really desire the suppression of them all. It is part of my own experience, that there is no portion of the country in which, when benefices in public patronage fall vacant, a keener or more energetic interest is manifested, by Non-Conformists as much as by Churchmen, in the choice of fit persons to fill them, than in Wales. The Welsh are not only a generous, they are also an intelligent people. There are, no doubt, some Welsh as well as some English Non-Conformists, who will say of the Church of England, 'Down with it, down with it, even to the ground.'[1] There are even some who, having had their attention recently directed to Irish models, and setting aside the Ten Commandments as well as the law of the land (when poor clergymen are concerned), take the abrogation of other men's rights of property into their own hands: and there are politicians, calling themselves Liberal, to whom such

[1] Psalm cxxxvii. 7.

forms of political activity seem not to be odious. But men who do not share those feelings and principles are not likely to be long, even if some of them may be for a time, carried away by the idea of a separate disestablishment, limited to Wales.

CONCLUSION

THE task which I had imposed upon myself is now done—imperfectly, but to the best of my power. It has been done, I trust, without the use of any weapons unworthy of a righteous cause. If anything which I have written may have the effect of strengthening the hands or encouraging the hearts of loyal Churchmen, of confirming any who are doubtful or irresolute, of helping honest politicians to see that the designs which I have opposed are not politic nor for the common good and general interest of the nation, just men to see that they are not just, liberal men to see that they are not liberal, and religious men (Non-Conformists especially) to see that they are not religious,—I shall be rewarded.

We are told, with loud voices,[1] that the Church of England is doomed, that the accomplishment of these designs is coming inevitably upon us. I do not believe in any such doom; I acknowledge no such necessity. If God has appointed that, for the faults of this Church and nation, that judgment is to fall on us, then come it will; not otherwise, if we, who believe that it would be disastrous for our country, acquit ourselves like men, and 'are strong.'[2]

If we fail, it will not be through the power of our

[1] *C. D.*, p. 164; *Radical Programme*, p. 126.
[2] 1 Corinthians xvi. 13.

adversaries, but through our own faults. Let us take warning from their reproaches. Neglect, in one place, of ministerial duties; in another, political narrowness, driving friends into the ranks of foes; in a third, faction or intolerance, impatience of the restraints of law, exaggeration of private tastes or party notions at the expense of edification,—these things, wherever they are found, are against us, these may be real dangers. Good men and wise men should, now more than ever, discourage and avoid them. The issues are in higher hands: but much may depend upon the way in which each man does his own particular duty.

Meanwhile, since the contest is forced upon us, let us put our armour on, and gird ourselves up with a good courage, in defence of what we hold most dear: finding encouragement in those promises, in which, though not made to particular or national Churches, every Church (in the degree in which it is faithful), and every Christian man, has a share.

'God is our hope and strength: a very present help in trouble. Therefore will we not fear, though the earth be moved: and though the hills be carried into the midst of the sea. Though the waters thereof rage and swell: and though the mountains shake at the tempest of the same. The rivers of the flood thereof shall make glad the city of God: the holy place of the tabernacle of the most Highest.'[1]

[1] Psalm xlvi. 1-4.

APPENDIX

WHILE these sheets were passing through the press, I received, from a friend on the other side of the Atlantic, the following extract from a Sermon lately preached on a public occasion in the principal Methodist Church at Toronto, by a clergyman of eminence in the Methodist persuasion there. It illustrates some passages[1] of the foregoing work in a manner sufficiently interesting to induce me to add it as an Appendix :—

'I think that Presbyterianism and Independency were necessary to the creation of the laurel of liberty with which our mother-land has crowned all her sons. The review of all the facts seems also to indicate that these two bodies taught the English people sterner ideas of morality and duty to God and man than perhaps would have been learned without their decisive and instructive ministry. To me also they appear to have given to the people a more spiritual interpretation of Christianity than they otherwise would have had. But on the other hand, standing within walls where no one would expect any fulsome laudation of England's Established Church, I think it must be said that that Establishment has contributed many of the noblest elements to the national character. Take for one illustration the fact that the Englishman is a reverent man. It seems to be natural to him, and it is only after he has come under the educating influence of extreme democratic

---

[1] See particularly, pp. 72-74, 247-251, 289, 309-311, *ante*.

ideas that he with difficulty throws off this characteristic quality, and then, as sometimes appears, he runs to the opposite extreme.

'A traveller from this side the sea cannot but be impressed with the formal recognition of the Deity in England, in ways which here would not be considered at least in good taste. Over the door of the Bank of England[1] you may read the words: "The earth is the Lord's, and the fulness thereof." In a certain city an old house is pointed out to the visitor with much gratification because it bears the inscription "God's Providence is mine inheritance." This, I may be told, is a relic of Puritanism; but in St. George's Hall, Liverpool,—a structure of quite recent origin,—in the mosaic of the floor, as I sat there to rest, I read in Latin the testimony: "From God have we received all this wealth and greatness." Now this is all characteristic of the English character, but on this side the sea it would be condemned as ostentatious piety, and therefore unworthy display. A devout man, whom I hold in the highest esteem, built a fine block in Winnipeg, and in the topstone he engraved the words: "The earth is the Lord's, and the fulness thereof," and his fellow-citizens criticised him severely for his offensive religious display. But in England the most refined taste of truly educated people is not offended by anything of this kind. It is quite in harmony with the feeling of reverence which constitutes a chief part of the national character.

'And this lesson of reverence, once fairly engrained into the national character, appears everywhere. The well-educated and refined Englishman carries with him a higher regard for authority, a more tender respect and esteem for the parental relation, and he is more impressed with whatever is grand and inspiring in nature and art, than one who has been educated in a different school.

'Now I give the Church of England very largely the credit of educating the people into this national quality. I wish not to be understood as meaning that the other two great religious bodies exerted any opposing influence to this direction of the national character; but in their earnest pursuit of other aims, the liberty of every man—a rigid morality, and a purely

---

[1] An error, for the Royal Exchange.

spiritual interpretation of religion—they naturally would not instil the highest feelings of reverence for all that was venerable and sacred by age, and when hard pressed in pursuit of their laudable aims, they perhaps did not always inculcate the highest reverence even for what was sacred by consecration. But these points have always been studiously guarded by the Established Church. Then in addition to this, it seems to me very clear that the belief in the existence of God takes a much stronger hold upon the nation, and wields a much more powerful influence over the individual, than would be the case were it not for the constant influence of the State Church. So also does the belief in the Holy Scriptures hold the heart of the masses more firmly to truth and righteousness and duty for the same cause. And this same influence has caused the English Sabbath to differ by the whole breadth of the heavens from the Sabbath of the nations of Continental Europe, for there the true idea of the Sabbath is scarcely preserved at all.'—(*Extract from Sermon preached before the St. George's Society of Toronto, in the Methodist Metropolitan Church, by the Rev. E. A. Stafford.*)

INDEX

AELFRIC, the Monk, 151, 154
Alien Priories, suppression of, 241
America, United States of, xix, xx, xxi, 310, 311 ; Southern and Central, xxv
Anti-Christian tendencies, xxvi, xxvii
Appeals to Pope, 13-17, 41 ; to King, 15, 41-43, 76
Appropriations of Churches, 96, 139, 144, 145, 155
Archbishops—Abbot, 54, 55 ; Aelfric, 151 ; Aldred of York, 121 ; Anselm, 15, 20, 37, 117, 137 ; Bancroft, 55, 58 ; Becket, 9, 14, 16 ; Boniface of Canterbury, 10, 12 ; Boniface of Mentz, 129 ; Cuthbert, 129 ; Dunstan, 36 ; Egbert of York, 150 ; Honorius, 138 ; Juxon, 172 note ; Lanfranc, 37 note ; Sancroft, 172 note ; Sheldon, 172 note ; Stratford, 145, 154, 155 ; Theodore, 14, 138, 151 ; Wake, 51 note, 60, 61 ; Walter, 135, 144 ; Warham, 31, 38 ; Whitgift, 65 note ; Wilfrid of York, 14, 121 ; Winchelsey, 9, 144 ; Wulfred, 139
Archdeacons, 96, 97, 112 note
Arches, Court of, 205, 206
Argentine Confederation, xxv
Arnold, Arthur, 104, 105, 112 ; Dr. Thomas, 284
Articles of Religion, Thirty-nine, 34, 35, 49, 88 ; Forty-two, of 1552-53, 58-61
Augustin, founder of Anglo-Saxon Church, 4, 129

Austria-Hungary, xxxi, xxxii

BATH AND WELLS, comparative aspect of Church work in the diocese of, 255
Bangor, See of, preserved from suppression, 175, 347
Barrow, Dr. Isaac, 172 note
Bede, Venerable, 129, 138, 139
Belgium, xxxiv
Bishops, Henry de Blois, 16 ; Berkeley, 90 ; Bonner, 29, 56 note ; Browne, 138 note, 244-246 ; Bull, 90 ; Burnet, 161 ; Butler, 90 ; Gardiner, 29 ; Gibson, 117 ; Gunning, 172 note ; Kennett, 147 note, 149 note ; Merriman, 310, 311 ; Mitchinson, 311 ; Morley, 172 note ; Poore, 113 ; Short, 307 ; Stillingfleet, 137 note, 150 note ; Stubbs, 149 note, 158 ; Taylor, Jeremy, 90 ; Tunstall, 32 ; Warner, 172 note ; Waynflete, 21 ; Wulfin, 151 ; seats of Bishops in Parliament, 24-26, 45
Bishoprics, donative before King John's time, 18-20 ; afterwards elective, with consent of Crown, 20, 21 ; claim of Chapters to elect, 19 ; Papal encroachments as to, 21-24 ; legislation of Henry VIII., 43, 44, 76, 77 ; numbers of, at different times, 17, 18, 44, 95, 117-122 ; tenure of endowments by barony, 18, 24, 25 ; lands belonging to, 111, 117-119 ; translations

after Conquest, 118; Welsh, 120, 335, 336; Norman foundations, 119, 120; Henry VIII.'s foundations, 120, 121; foundations of the present century, 121, 122, 174; Bangor, preserved from suppression, 175, 347; Bristol, to be restored, 95, 175, 176; Wakefield, in course of foundation, 95, 174
Blackstone, Sir William, 133, 142, 149
Bona, Cardinal, 49 note
Bracton, 12
Brazil, xxv
Brewer, J. S., 149 note, 172 note
Bristol, union with, and proposed severance from, See of Gloucester, 95, 175, 176
Burials Act of 1880, 188, 189, 314
Burke, Edmund, 178, 226

CAMPBELL, Lord, 170, 197
Canada, Clergy Reserves, xxi, xxii; Roman Catholic Church in Lower Canada, xxii, xxiii
Canon Law, Roman, 8, 13, 35
Canons of Anselm, 37, 117, 137; of Boniface, 12; of Lanfranc, 37 note; of Stratford, 139, 154; of Winchelsey, 144; of Wulfred, 139; of A.D. 1604, 65; what Canons had force in England, 12, 13, 39, 40
Capitulars of Charlemagne and his successors, 127, 147, 150
Case for Disestablishment, publication entitled, xvii, xxiii, 45, 52, 70, 71, 73, 77, 78, 79, 98, 99, 100, 102, 104, 105, 106, 146, 162, 167, 168, 169, 177, 188, 189, 196, 198, 200, 204, 205, 211, 212, 214, 233, 250, 251, 252, 253, 256, 259, 262, 263, 267, 272, 275, 277, 279, 280, 287, 289, 290, 293, 294, 296, 297, 298, 299, 300, 301, 302, 306, 307, 308, 309, 310, 312, 313, 316, 320, 321, 322, 323, 326, 327, 328, 329, 330, 332, 335, 348
Catechism of Edward VI., 59, 60; of Pope Pius V., 89
Cathedrals, 44, 95, 113, 114, 328

Cecil, Lord Robert (now Lord Salisbury), 279
Census, 'Religious,' of 1851, 267-279; 'Newspaper,' 281; objections of Non-Conformists to denominational, 280-282
Chalchyth, Councils of, 130, 139
Channel Islands, 96, 112
Chantries, suppression of, 241
Chapters, 28, 44, 95
Charters, their general use came in with Normans, 115, 116
Chili, xxv
Church corporations, 18, 108, 109; property, 108-110; rates, 153, 158, 170
Churches, collegiate, 28, 95, 121, 122; parish, 106, 111, 112, 113-116; Parliamentary grants for building, 116, 167
Clarendon, Constitutions of, 14, 16, 24, 42
Clergy, their relations to Convocation and Parliament, 13, 25, 26; marriage of, 36, 37; Cathedral and Collegiate, 95; their numbers, 107; their work, 245-249; their character, 249-253; 339
Coal-duties granted for church building after Fire of London, 116, 166
Coke, Sir Edward, 17 note, 18, 133, 134, 141 note
Colonies, British, xxiii, xxiv, 310, 311
Common Prayer, Book of, 50-67; revisions of, 52, 57, 61, 63, 65, 66, 88
Communion in both kinds, 48, 49, 88
Conferences, Diocesan, 265
Congresses, Church, 265
Conservatism, charged as a fault against the clergy, 300-305
Constance, Council of, 49, 50
Continuity of Church of England, 4, 28-31
Convocation, 13, 17, 25, 26, 29, 31, 34, 37, 38, 39, 41, 42, 46, 49, 51, 52-61, 65, 66, 265
Cottenham, Lord, 223

INDEX

Councils, General—Constance, 49, 50; Lateran, 50, 133-135; Trent, 49, 88-90
Courts, Ecclesiastical, 10, 11, 12, 28, 37, 38, 39, 83, 205, 206; Temporal, 11, 12, 199, 203, 207, 208
Creed of Pope Pius IV., 89
Cunliffe, Sir Robert, M.P., 338 note, 341 note
Cy-pres, doctrine of Equity, 190

DECRETALS, forged, of Isidore, 7, 8, 15, 153, 154
Dee, river, tithes of fisheries in, 141
Degge, Sir Simon, his *Parson's Counsellor*, 153-155, 157
Delegates, Courts of, 42
Denmark, xxxiv
Devonshire, petition from, in 1549, 56
Diocesan Synods and Conferences, 265
Disendowment in Europe, xxvi, xxix, xxxv; scheme of, for England, 321-323, 326-333; what would be its effect, 242-246
Disestablishment, scheme of, xvi, 320-333; by piecemeal, xv, 346, 347.
Dissenters, State legislation as to, 198, 199, 217; authority of State Courts in their ecclesiastical controversies, 199-208; their chapels and endowments, 209, 210; State grants to them, 211-217; Dissenters' Chapels Act of 1844, 218-225; their position relatively to the Church of England, 196, 197, 236-239, 253, 283-289; their many sub-divisions, 288, 299
Disraeli, Right Hon. B., 312, 313
Divisions in the Church of England, 289-292
Doctrine, legislation concerning, 26, 46-48, 83
Döllinger, Right Rev. Dr., his conversation with Canon Liddon in 1885, xxvii, xxviii, 81
Drawbacks of duties on building materials, 168, 169; on paper of Prayer Books, 169
Dugdale, Sir William, 115, 118

ECCLESIASTICAL COMMISSIONERS, 100, 101, 102, 120, 163-166, 189-192
Education, comparative statistics of, 259-262
Edwards, Very Rev. H. T., late Dean of Bangor, 340, 341
Edwards, Rev. E. W., Vicar of Ruabon, 339, 340, 341, 342, 343
'Egbert's Excerpts,' 150
Endowments, royal and private, of the Church, 114, 115, 118, 119, 120, 121-124, 162, 165, 167, 171-176, 182-185, 211, 212, 318; of Dissenters, 209-227
Episcopate, increase of Indian and Colonial, 265
Equality, 314-319, 330, 331, 333
Equity, xvi-xviii, 314
Established Churches abroad, xxv, xxxi, xxxii
Establishment of Church of England, 10, 68-84, 317, 318
Ethelred the 'Unready,' laws ascribed to him, 152
European nations, xxv-xxxiv
Exclusiveness, 298-300
Excommunication, Papal, resisted by Edward I., 17; of Henry VIII. by Pope Paul III., 29, 85, 86; of Queen Elizabeth by Pope Pius V., 29, 87; of the Patriarch Michael Cerularius, by Pope Leo IX., 85, 86

FAILURE, charge of, against the Church, 251-266
Fasting and Thanksgiving, days of public, 66, 67
Fees, 98, 99, 112
First-fruits, 160, 161
Foxley, Rev. Joseph, 210 note
France, xxviii-xxx
Free Chapels, 43
Freedom, restraints on ecclesiastical, 72, 74-77, 296

INDEX

Freeman, Professor E. A., 4, 27, 28, 108, 125, 149 note, 152 note, 178, 183, 224, 230, 231, 232, 235
Froude, Richard Hurrell, 89, 90
Fuller, Thomas, 53, 61; Tract on alleged tripartite division of tithes by Rev. Morris, 149 note, 151 note

GENEVA, xxx, xxxi
Germany, xxxiii, xxxiv
Gladstone, Right Hon. W. E., xi, xii, xiv, xvi, xviii, xix, 68, 69, 72, 177, 211, 222, 234, 244, 254, 266, 301, 302, 313, 327 note
Glebe lands, 103, 104, 111, 117
Greece, xxxiv
Griffiths, Rev. J., Rector of Merthyr Tydvil, 344

HALE, Chief Justice Sir M., 13, 16, 43; Ven. Archdeacon, 149 note, 150 note
Hampton, Lord, his Parliamentary returns of expenditure on Church building, 1840-1874, 172, 340
Herbert, George, 90
Heresy, 26, 41, 83, 85
Heylyn, Peter, 52 note, 53, 57, 61
High Commission Court, 40, 41, 83
Hobart, Chief Justice Sir H., 133 note
Holland, xxxiv
Homilies, First Book of, 48
Hook, Very Rev. W. F., Dean of Chichester, 85
Hooker, 90, 284
Hospital Sunday Collections, 264, 265
Hugh Lupas, Earl of Chester, 121, 136, 141

INCOME of Bishops, Chapters, and Archdeacons, 97, 107, 164; of parochial clergy, 98-104, 338; extravagant estimates, 104-106; deductions, 106, 109; proportion of, to work, 106-108

Ingulphus, 19
Injunctions of Queen Elizabeth, 33, 34
Institution of a Christian Man, (Bishops' book) of 1537, 33
Invective against the Church and Clergy, 294-305
Investiture, 20
Irish Church, 232-236, 239-241, 320, 321, 325, 326
Isidore, forger of decretals, 7
Italy, xxxii, xxxiii

JOHNSON, John, 142, 152 note
Judicial Committee of Privy Council, 42, 201, 202, 205
Jurisdiction of Church Courts, 10-13, 37, 38

KEBLE, John, 90, 292
Kings of Heptarchy—Aelfwald of Northumberland, 129; Bertulph of Mercia, 139; Ethelred of Mercia, 120; Kenulph of Wessex, 130; Offa of Mercia, 130, 131; Penda of Mercia, 120; Wihtred of Kent, 19; Wulfhere of Mercia, 120; others, 118
Kings of England, Anglo-Saxon and Danish—Athelstan, 131; Canute, 132, 142, 153; Edgar, 10, 121, 131, 142; Edmund, 121, 131; Edward the Confessor, 19, 132; Egbert, 118; Ethelred the Unready, 132, 149; Ethelwolf, 131
Kings and Queens of England since the Conquest—William I., 10, 15, 19, 118, 132; William II., 9, 15; Henry I., 16, 20, 120, 132; Stephen, 16, 41; Henry II., 9, 16, 136; John, 9, 16, 20, 25, 44; Henry III., 9, 12, 21 note; Edward I., 9, 12, 17, 21, 25; Edward II., 12, 13, 25; Edward III., 10, 12, 17, 18, 20, 21, 122; Richard II., 22, 26 note, 145 note; Henry IV., 26 note, 145 note; Henry V., 26 note, 122; Henry VI., 25; Edward IV., 122; Henry VII., 36; Henry

INDEX

VIII., 27, 28, 29, 30, 39, 40, 44, 45, 46, 47, 141, 145; Edward VI., 37, 43, 44, 55, 122; Mary, 33, 44, 55, 62; Elizabeth, 28, 29, 33, 34, 35, 40, 44, 52, 62, 63; James I., 52, 65; Charles I., 40, 52 note; Charles II., 65, 301; James II., 301; William III., 70, 161; Anne, 160, 161
Kings, gifts to the Church by, 114, 115, 118, 119, 121-124, 184

LARGE TOWNS, Church work in, 256-258
Lavergne, M. de, xxx
Lay agencies, 257, 266
Legal decisions, Attorney-General v. Gould, 203
    Attorney-General v. Shore, 221
    Baker v. Lee, 170, 196
    Gorham v. Bishop of Exeter, 202, 203
    Heath v. Burder, 201, 202
    Magdalen College v. Attorney-General, 181
    Manchester New College, 188
    Merriman v. Williams, 311
    Prior of Worcester's Case, 141
Lewis, Right Hon. Sir G. C., as to religious census, 268, 277, 278
Lewis, Thomas, *The Reformation Settlement*, 31 note, 49 note
Liberality, 262, 264
Liberation Society, xvii, 77, 81, 99, 100, 131 note, 147, 211, 212, 218, 279, 295, 333, 338 note, 344; its scheme of Disestablishment, xvi, 320-333
Liberties of Church of England, 8-13, 35-41
Liberty, Civil and Religious, 312-314
Liddon, Rev. Canon, his conversation in 1885 with Dr. Döllinger, xxvii, 81
Litany, alteration of, in A.D. 1559, 63, 64
Lollards, Statutes against, 26, 46, 47, 83
London, house tithe, 141; Fire, 51, 57

Lords, Statute for placing, 45, 46
Lyndhurst, Lord, 223

MACAULAY, T. B., afterwards Lord, 223, 224.
Magna Charta, 9
Man, Isle of, 44, 45, 95, 96, 112, 164
Mann, Horace, his testimony to the Church, 256, 268; his Census Report of 1851, 255, 267-277, 330 note; opinions of statesmen as to the value of his 'Religious Census,' 268, 277-279
Marriage of Clergy, 36, 37, 88
Marriages in England and Wales, 258, 338
Martin, Frederick, his valuation of Church revenue, 99, 100, 105, 329
Maynooth College, 186, 215, 217
Membership of Church, 195-198
Mexico, xxv
Michael Cerularius, the Patriarch, 85, 86
Ministries of public worship in Europe, xxxii
Missionary work of Church of England, 265
Monasteries, suppression of, xxxii, 241, 242, 251
Monasticon, Sir W. Dugdale's, 118
Monmouthshire, 333, 345, 347
Morgan, Right Hon. G. O., 339 note, 341, 342, 343, 344

NATIONAL CONSENT, xii-xvi; property, 177-192
Nationality of the Church of England, 5, 6, 9, 68, 69, 72-75, 179, 283-287
Necessary Doctrine or Erudition of a Christian Man (King's book), of 1543, 33, 47
New South Wales, xxiii, xxiv
'Newspaper Census,' 279
Noel, Hon. and Rev. Baptist, 297
Non-Conformists in England, State law as to, 198-208; their historical and practical relations to the Church, 236-239

Non-residence of parochial clergy, laws against, 153, 155-157; earlier complaints of, 157
Nowell, Rev. Dr., not allowed to sit in House of Commons, 26 note
Numbers, argument from, 254; materials for comparison, 254-265; Denominational Census opposed by Non-Conformists, 254, 255, 280, 281, 337

OFFENCE, causes of, within the Church, 292, 293
Offerings, voluntary, 112
Official Year-Book of Church of England, 1886, 107 note, 162 note, 165 note, 167 note, 172 note, 173 note, 174 note, 257, 260, 261, 264, 265, 338, 340
Organisation of Church of England, 95-97
'Ornaments Rubric,' 64, 65
'Orthodox' Greek Church, xxxi, xxxiv, 85, 86, 287

PALMERSTON, LORD, on Mr. Mann's 'Religious Census,' 278
Papal bulls, 35, 36; encroachments, 7, 8, 15, 35, 36, 86; excommunications, 17, 29, 85-87; jurisdiction, 8, 9, 14, 15, 16, 17, 41, 42
Papists in England after Reformation, 29, 30
Paraguay, xxv
Parishes, 96, 138, 140, 142-144
Parliament, seats of Bishops in, 24-26, 45; exclusion of other clergy from, 25, 26, 319
Parliamentary grants to the Church, 116, 161, 166, 167, 186; to Non-Conformists, 212-218
Parnynge, Chief Justice, 134, 135
Parochial system, 247-251
Parsonage-houses, 99, 100, 111, 117, 329
Patronage of parish Churches, 97, 111, 115, 122-124, 293
Persecution, 26, 46, 47, 60, 83, 294-296

Peru, xxv
Pew-rents, 98, 99, 104
Political Church services, 66, 67
Poor, their interest in Church endowments, 158, 159, 244, 245, 246, 249
Poor Laws, 157, 158
Popes—Adrian I., 129; Agatho, 14; Alexander II., 15; Alexander III., 134, 143, 144; Alexander VI., 8; Benedict XII., 17; Clement VII., 27, 121; Gregory I., 129; Gregory VII., 8, 36; Innocent II., 36; Innocent III., 16, 134, 135, 144; Innocent VIII., 36; John VI., 14; Leo IX., 85; Pascal II., 16, 37; Paul III., 29, 85, 86; Pius IV., 89; Pius V., 29, 85, 87, 89; Stephen III., 8; Sylvester, 153, 154; Urban II., 15; Urban VI., 16 note; Popes of Renaissance period, 8
Popish recusants, Acts against, 80
Portugal, xxxii
Præmunire, 17, 24
Presbyterians, English, their change to Unitarianism, 220, 221; Irish, State legislation concerning them and their endowments, 215-217
Prideaux, Dean, 130 note, 131 note, 136, 137
Priories, alien, their suppression, 241
Private gifts for Church building and endowment, 115, 117, 119, 120, 121-124, 162, 165, 167, 171-176, 182-184, 340
Proclamations, Statute of Henry VIII. concerning, 47, 48, 83.
Prohibition, writ of, 12-14
Prussia, xxxiii
Public property, 179-181; public regulation, 186-192, 307

QUEEN ANNE'S Bounty, 100-104, 160-163, 167
Quotations in *Case for Disestablishment*, 306-311

Radical Programme, publication entitled, xvi, xvii, xviii, xix, 301, 317, 320, 321, 322 note, 323 note, 324, 326, 327, 329 note, 332, 348
Rectories, 96
Redistribution of surplus revenues from endowments, 189-192
Reformation in England, 27, 84-90
Reformers, habit of exaggeration, 308, 309
'Regium Donum' in England, 212-214; in Ireland, 214-217
Regulation, power of public, 186-192, 307
'Religious argument' of Liberation Society, 77-81
Repair of churches, 153, 158, 170, 171
Rome, Church of, 5-8; mediæval changes in, 7, 8; temporal power, 8; interference in England, 35, 36
Rural Dean, office of, 265

SACRILEGE, 230, 231
Schoolrooms, etc., 111
Scotland, Church of, xiv-xvi
Selborne, Lord, 66 note, 73, 188
Selden, John, 126, 127, 128, 135, 137, 139, 142, 143, 144, 150
Short, Bishop T. V., *History of Church of England*, 307
Six Articles, Act of Henry VIII., 46, 47, 83
Soames, History of Anglo-Saxon Church, 149 note, 150 note, 151 note, 152
Sodor and Man, Bishopric of, 44, 45, 95, 164
Southey, *Book of the Church*, 147
Sowter, A., 315, 316
Spain, xxxii
Stafford, Rev. E. A., 351
Stanhope parish, tithe of lead ore in, 141
Stanley, Arthur, Dean of Westminster, 52, 56, 196
State Law as to Non-Conformists, 198-208
Statham, Rev. W. M., 195 note

Statutes—13 Edw., I. and 24 Edw. I., Ecclesiastical Law, 12 note
35 Edw. I., Papal encroachments, 21, 123
9 Edw. II. and 17 Edw. II., Ecclesiastical Law, 12
18 Edw. III., Ecclesiastical Law, 12 note
25 Edw. III. and 27 Edw. III., Provisors; Præmunire; 17, 18, 21, 70, 125
2 Rich. II., Pope Urban VI., 16 note
5 Rich. II., Lollards, 26
15 Rich. II., Appropriations, 145, 155
16 Rich. II., Provisors, 21-24
2 Hen. IV., c. 4 and c. 15, Lollards; Vicarages; 26, 145
4 Hen. IV., Exemptions from Tithe, 145
2 Hen. V., Lollards, 26
21 Hen. VIII., Non-residence of Clergy, 155-157
23 Hen. VIII., c. 9 and c. 20, Citations; First-fruits; 30, 37
24 Hen. VIII., Restraint of Appeals, 31, 38, 41, 124
25 Hen. VIII., c. 14, 19, 20, 21, Heresy; Submission of Clergy; Bishoprics; Peterpence; 30, 39; 38, 42; 43; 46
26 Hen. VIII., c. 1 and c. 3, Supreme Headship; First-fruits; 32, 40 note
27 Hen. VIII., c. 20, 21, 26, Tithes; London Tithe; Wales; 38; 141; 334
31 Hen. VIII., c. 8, 10, 14, Proclamations; Placing Lords; Six Articles; 45; 46; 47, 48
32 Hen. VIII., Lay Tithes, 145
34 and 35 Hen. VIII., c. 1 and c. 23, Advancement of Religion; Proclamations; 47, 48
37 Hen. VIII., c. 12 and c. 17, London Tithes; Ecclesiastical Judges; 141, 206

Statutes—1 Edw. vi. c. 2 and c. 12, Bishoprics; Repeal of Proclamation and other Acts; 43; 47, 48
2 and 3 Edw. VI., c. 1 and c. 21, Uniformity; Marriage of Clergy; 37, 50
5 and 6 Edw. VI., Uniformity, 51, 58, 70
1 Mary, Public Worship, 62
1 and 2 Phil. and Mary, Reconciliation with Rome, 63
1 Eliz., c. 1 and c. 2, Supremacy; Uniformity; 40, 91, 70; 64
5 Eliz., c. 1 and c. 3, Oath of Supremacy; Poor Law; 34, 157
13 Eliz., c. 12 and c. 20, Thirty-nine Articles; Non-residence of Clergy; 35; 155, 156
18 Eliz., c. 3 and c. 11, Poor Law; Non-residence of Clergy; 156-158
14 Car. II., Uniformity, 65, 70
1 Will. and Mary, c. 6 and c. 18, Coronation Oath; Toleration; 70; 195, 197
19 Geo. III., Dissenters' Subscription, 198
31 Geo. III., Canada Clergy Reserves, xxi
59 Geo. III., Drawbacks on materials for Churches under Church building Acts, 168
6 Geo. IV., Canada Clergy Reserves, xxi
2 and 3 Will. IV., Ecclesiastical Appeals, 42
3 and 4 Will. IV., c. 30 and 42, Exemption of Places of Worship from Rates, etc.; Judicial Committee; 42, 210
6 and 7 Will. IV., Tithe Commutation, 146
3 and 4 Vict., Canada Clergy Reserves, xxi
7 and 8 Vict., Dissenters' Chapels, 218
13 and 14 Vict., Simplification of Titles to Chapels, etc., 210

Statutes—16 and 17 Vict., Canada Clergy Reserves, xxii
26 and 27 Vict., Lord Chancellor's Augmentation, 115
31 and 32 Vict., Church Rates, 170
32 and 33 Vict., Irish Church, 215, 320, 321, 325, 326
34 Vict., Universities, 197
34 and 35 Vict., Irish Presbyterian Church, 215, 217
37 and 38 Vict., Court of Arches, 206
Strype, 53, 61
Supremacy, Royal, 13, 31-35, 41-43, 75, 76, 81-83, 198, 199, 205, 206
Supreme Headship, 32, 33, 46
Sweden, xxxiv
Switzerland, xxx, xxxi

Tenths, 160, 161
Theodore, Archbishop, spurious canons of, 151
Thomas, Rev. Urijah, 195 note
Thorndike, Rev. Dr., 172 note
Thorpe, *Ancient Laws*, 132 note, 152
Time, effect of, in confirming titles, 183
Tithes, abolition of, in France, xxx; value of tithe rent-charge, 102, 103; lands, etc., granted in lieu of tithes, 111; early history of tithes, 125-128; continental customs as to, 127, 128; Anglo-Saxon canons and laws as to, 129-132; special grants and appropriations of tithe, 133-137; endowment of parish churches with tithes, 138-144; great and small tithes, 144, 145; lay tithes, 145, 146; tithe-free lands, 146; general commutation, *ibid.*; tithes and the poor, 146-159; opinions and documents as to quadripartite or tripartite division in ancient times; 148-154
Trent, Council of, 49, 88, 89, 90
Trinity Church, New York, xxi

INDEX

UNCONSECRATED buildings used for Church services, 111
Uniformity, Acts of, 51, 55, 56, 58, 62, 63, 65, 66, 291, 292
Union, Act of, between England and Scotland, xv, 68, 71
United States of America, xix, xx, xxi, 310, 311
Uruguay, xxv

VAN ESPEN, 7 note, 154 note
Venezuela, xxv
Vicarages, 96, 144, 145
Vicars Apostolic, 29

WALES, ancient princes of, 18, 334; their subordination to the Crown of England, 334; incorporation of Wales with England, *ibid.;* division of, into counties, *ibid.;* gave England Tudor dynasty, *ibid.;* Dissent in, 337; parts of Wales in Hereford diocese, 345; proposal to separate, 334-347
Welsh Bishoprics, 18; representative of ancient British Church, 335, 336, 347; include parts of England, 338, 345, 346; endowed chiefly with English funds, 120, 346
Welsh Church, ancient relations to English, 335, 336; present state of, 337-345
Welshmen, their character, 347
Wolsey, Cardinal, 121
Wordsworth, William, 88, 91
Worldliness, accusation of, against clergy, 297, 298
Wurtemberg, xxxiii, xxxiv

YORK, contest of, with Canterbury for precedence, 15

ZURICH, xxxi

THE END

Printed by R. & R. CLARK, *Edinburgh.*

www.ingramcontent.com/pod-product-compliance
Lightning Source LLC
Chambersburg PA
CBHW030426300426
44112CB00009B/876